Camper's Guide to OREGON ™

Parks, Lakes, Forests, and Beaches

Where to Go and How to Get There

Facts About Oregon

State Capital:	Salem
State Nickname:	The Beaver State
Statehood:	February 14, 1859 (33rd)
Area:	97,073 square miles
Population:	2,847,000 (1990)
Largest City:	Portland (population 440,000; metropolitan area 1.47 million)
Major Industries:	Timber Products, Agriculture, Tourism, Metals, Fisheries
Elevations:	Sea Level, Pacific Ocean to 11,237 feet, Mt. Hood
State Animal:	Beaver
State Bird:	Western Meadowlark
State Fish:	Chinook Salmon
State Flower:	Oregon Grape
State Gem:	Sunstone
State Motto:	"The Union"
State Rock:	Thunderegg
State Song:	Oregon, My Oregon
State Tree:	Douglas Fir
Time Zone:	Pacific

Camper's Guide to ™
OREGON

Parks, Lakes, Forests, and Beaches
Where to Go and How to Get There

Lillian B. Morava

Gulf Publishing Company

While every effort has been made to ensure the accuracy of the information in this guide, neither the author nor the publisher assume liability arising from the use of this material. Park facilities and policies are subject to change. Users should verify the accuracy of important details before beginning a trip. Good camping!

Lillian B . Morava

Gulf Publishing Company
Book Division
P.O. Box 2608, Houston, Texas 77252-2608

10 9 8 7 6 5 4 3 2 1

This title and graphic design are a trademark of
Gulf Publishing Company.

Library of Congress Cataloging-in-Publication Data

Morava, Lillian B.
    Camper's guide to Oregon parks, lakes, forests, and
beaches : where to go and how to get there / Lillian B. Morava.
        p.   cm.
    Includes index.
    ISBN 0-87201-212-3
    1. Camping—Oregon—Guidebooks. 2. Camp sites, facilities,
etc.—Oregon—Directories. 3. Oregon—Guidebooks. I. Title.
GV191.42.07M67   1994
796.54′09795—dc20   94-12526
                                                      CIP

Also look for these popular *Camper's Guides* at your favorite book store or camping/backpacking supplier:

Camper's Guide to British Columbia, Volumes 1 and 2

Camper's Guide to California, Volumes 1 and 2

Camper's Guide to Colorado

Camper's Guide to Florida

Camper's Guide to Indiana and Ohio

Camper's Guide to Michigan

Camper's Guide to Minnesota

Camper's Guide to Outdoor Cooking

Camper's Guide to Texas, Third Edition

Camper's Guide to Washington

Contents

Acknowledgments

I am grateful to the following agencies and individuals for their cooperation in providing information through maps, photographs, brochures, telephone conversations, and personal interviews. Thank you for helping make this guide possible for others to enjoy. (Page numbers indicate photo contributions.)

Kip Anderson, pages 76, 148, 154, 169, 182, 195
B.C. Parks, Canada, pages 112, 210 (top right)
Bureau of Land Management, U.S. Department of Interior
Forest Service, U.S. Department of Agriculture, page 111
Larry Halverson, page 185 (top right)
Fred Harnisch, USFS, page 183
Mickey Little, pages 11 (top left), 69, 70, 92, 93, 137, 159–161, 174–178, 185 (bottom), 204–206
Ministry of Tourism, B.C., Canada, page 7 (right)
Minnesota Department of Natural Resources, pages 96 (top left), 153

National Park Service, U.S. Department of Interior
National Recreation Reservation System
Northwest Interpretive Association
Oregon State Parks and Recreation Department, pages 8, 55 (bottom left), 66, 75, 80, 81, 93 (bottom right), 96 (bottom right), 97, 101, 114, 157, 162, 163, 181
Oregon Tourism Division, pages 86, 119, 121, 186 (bottom), 212
Portland General Electric, page 20
Recreation Department, Portland General Electric
Tacoma-Pierce County Visitor's Convention Bureau, pages 28, 180
Monte Turner
TW Recreational Services, Inc., pages 107, 156
Umatilla National Forest, USFS, page 207
U.S. Army Corps of Engineers
U.S. Fish and Wildlife Service, U.S. Department of Interior, page 207
U.S. Geological Survey

Welcome to the wide open outdoors of Oregon!

Introduction

Oregon has all the ingredients of a camper's paradise! Magnificent landscapes and diverse recreational opportunities fill the state's 97,073 square miles. Campers will find 400 miles of open public coastline, 30 million acres of forest land, 15 million acres of BLM (Bureau of Land Management) lands, 62,000 miles of streams, 1,500 campgrounds, 110 recreation areas, 33 fish hatcheries, plus lakes, reservoirs, pristine wilderness areas, wildlife refuges, historical sites, and lofty mountain peaks that will take your breath away.

The purpose of this *Camper's Guide* is twofold in helping you find the best Oregon has to offer: (1) it concisely describes key features, facilities, and activities of campgrounds in Oregon's parks, forests, and recreation sites, and (2) it provides maps that show how to best access these elements. The *Guide* covers more than 50 state parks, 13 national forests, 35 wilderness areas, 1 national park, 1 national volcanic monument, and 2 national recreation areas. It also provides information about little known public camping and recreation opportunities provided by the Bureau of Land Management, Oregon Department of Forestry, U.S. Army Corps of Engineers, U.S. Fish and Wildlife Service, and even power companies.

Every part of Oregon offers exciting outdoor pursuits in beautiful settings—from its majestic coastline to its snow-capped peaks and high desert plateaus. The following brief descriptions of its major geographic regions only hint of Oregon's fascinating attractions.

Oregon's Coast features wave-sculpted cliffs, long stretches of beach and forested headlands. There are spots for bird-watching, sites for surf and river fishing, and promontories for viewing whales and other marine animals. Oregon Dunes National Recreation Area, near the center of Oregon's spectacular coastline, has some of the continent's highest sand dunes. Hiking trails, wildlife, colorful spring flowers, historic sites, lighthouses, rugged seascapes, and picturesque bays make the coast a haven for campers.

The Columbia Gorge and Mt. Hood offer lakes, rivers, waterfalls, and wooded refuges within a short distance of major cities and highways. The

Beautiful seascapes stretch for 360 miles along Oregon's coast. The least populated and rugged south coast gives way to picturesque bays along the central coast. The northern coast features a scenic shoreline of dense forests and broad beaches.

Columbia River Gorge National Scenic Area preserves a wonderland of water, vegetation, and rocky outcroppings. The winds of the Gorge attract windsurfers from around the world. Hiking trails lead to spectacular waterfalls and vistas of the Columbia River's natural wealth. Scenic byways take campers from the gorge to one of Oregon's most awesome natural features—Mt. Hood. Towering to a height of 11,235 feet, it is the highest peak in the Oregon Cascades. In the midst of this spectacular volcanic giant, opportunities for camping, hiking, fishing, and winter sports abound.

The Willamette Valley was once the destination of pioneers on the famous Oregon Trail. Today it has most of the state's largest and oldest communities. Lying just south of Portland, the valley's green fields and hills are rich with fresh produce; its covered bridges and historic sites provide a perfect destination for backroad adventures.

Central Oregon's diverse landscapes stretch from the Cascade mountain peaks to the high desert plateau. This is Oregon's year-round recreation hot-spot. Alpine lakes, whitewater rivers, canyon reservoirs and geological wonders dot the region. Lake Billy Chinook, Ochoco Lake, and Prineville Reservoir are sun- and water-worshipper favorites. Near Bend, reservoirs with placid, sun-warmed water draw boaters, water-skiers, and anglers. Newberry National Volcanic Monument offers a remarkable showcase of volcanism. The Deschutes River, paralleling the eastern slopes of the Cascade range for nearly 200 miles, is revered by anglers, river rafters, and conservationists. In winter, a new season opens for recreationists who love to play in the snow. This is Oregon's largest ski area.

Eastern Oregon's wide open spaces are filled with amazing rock formations, geological surprises, deep canyons, pine-forested mountains, and a semi-arid high desert. The northeastern corner of Oregon is bisected by I-84 that follows portions of the historic Oregon Trail. Wallowa Lake, lined by forest, is a scenic base for water recreation and wilderness adventures in the Wallowa Mountains of northeast Oregon. Hell's Canyon (the continent's deepest gorge), its National Recreation Area, and the Snake River form an inspiring recreation mecca along Oregon's eastern border with Idaho. To the west, the John Day Fossil Beds National Monument protects fossils that are over 30 million years old. Traveling to the southeastern corner of Oregon, Lake Owyhee stretches 53 miles between steep,

rainbow-colored desert canyon walls. The impressive towers of nearby Succor Creek Canyon rise above prime rockhounding grounds. South of Burns, travelers cross a table-flat desert and the world-famous Malheur National Wildlife Refuge to reach the Steens Mountain. The 30-mile-long, 9,670-foot-high mountain is one of the world's largest fault blocks. As with the entire state, this region's wildlife and recreational opportunities are astounding.

Southern Oregon features the nation's deepest lake, Crater Lake, and one of the West's great rivers, the Rogue. Crater Lake, at the crest of the Cascade mountains, is the centerpiece to this incredible national park. A hike or drive to the crater's rim yields spectacular vistas. Encompassing thousands of acres of national forest and wilderness areas, the region contains one of the country's most treasured fishing waterways as the Rogue and North Umpqua rivers wind from the Cascades to the Pacific. World-renowned for its whitewater trips, the Rogue runs like a blue ribbon through the magnificent green of a wild territory mostly accessible only by boat or foot. Above ground or under, there are breathtaking surprises here. Just southwest of Grants Pass, cave explorers can quench their sense of adventure in Oregon Caves National Monument, better known as the "Marble Halls of Oregon."

Nestled between the scenic wonders of Oregon, there are parks, campgrounds, resorts, and towns to accommodate your every need. Hundreds of natural wonders and many more adventures await you. See Oregon's indescribable beauty, go camping!

Oregon's parks offer plenty of adventure for everybody!

How To Use The Camper's Guide

This *Camper's Guide* covers campgrounds or camping areas in more than 50 state parks, 13 national forests, 1 national park, 1 national volcanic monument, 2 national recreation areas, 35 wilderness areas, and lesser-known public recreation areas operated by the Bureau of Land Management, U.S. Army Corps of Engineers, U.S. Fish and Wildlife Service, and even power companies. The names of the parks, forests, and recreation areas are arranged alphabetically within 3 geographic regions of Oregon and cross-listed by name and city in the index. The first page of each region locates the camping area on the regional map and gives the page number(s) where you can find more detailed information and maps of that specific park, forest, or recreation area.

Camping information provided in this *Guide* is basic—it tells you the location of camping areas, how to get there, cites points of interest, and lists the facilities and recreational activities available. Mailing addresses and telephone numbers of the campground's operating agency are given in case you want additional information prior to a trip. For some camping areas, it is wise to confirm weather and road conditions before traveling. Keep in mind that during the off-season, usually during winter, some camping areas may be closed or facility use may be limited.

Maps of each park, forest, or recreation area show road or trail accesses and location of facilities to help you plan a trip. However, these maps do not show details of roads, trails, and/or terrain features. Maps with greater detail are available to you from the park's headquarters. Visitors who wish to camp off-the-beaten-path should consult with that park's operating agency and purchase topographic or official maps of areas. For example, when camping in a national forest or wilderness area, it is best to contact the ranger district for detailed maps and current information. Although most camping areas are easily found with the help of a good road map, vicinity maps have been included in some instances to clarify accesses. Signs along the roadways can also help you once you have reached the general vicinity of a park, forest, or recreation area.

All information in this *Camper's Guide* has been provided by the respective operating agency, either through literature distributed by them, through verbal communication, or through secondary sources deemed reliable. The facilities available at a campground often change, but a change in status usually means the addition of a service rather than a discontinuation. In other words, a camper often finds better and more facilities than those listed in the latest brochure. When there is a question, particularly for parks with accesses or activities affected by weather, it is best to call the park directly for current conditions. May this *Camper's Guide* serve you well, whether you are a beginner or a seasoned camper. Take time to camp and enjoy the splendor of life in the outdoors. What better way to become truly acquainted with nature . . . and with yourself and your family. Enjoy!

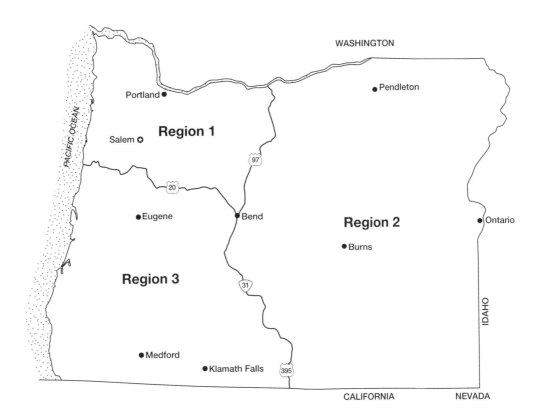

Reservation Systems

Campsite reservations are necessary for popular campgrounds in Oregon usually between Memorial Day and Labor Day. Although campgrounds normally operate on a first-come, first-served basis, it is best to check with the operating agency of a campground to assure campsites are available. Remember the list of campgrounds requiring reservations and their reservation season may change from year to year. Even the agency handling the reservations can change. Perhaps the best procedure for a campground user is, each year, obtain an up-to-date brochure describing the reservation procedure with the reservation application. The brochure also serves as a valuable source of information on current fees and facilities available. Remember that the reservation systems differ for state parks, national parks, and national forests.

State Parks

Campsites may be reserved at 13 state parks from Memorial Day weekend through Labor Day weekend. During the remainder of the year, campsites are available on a first-come, first-served basis. Reservation applications postmarked *no earlier than January 1* are accepted for the current year's reservation season.

Reservations cannot be made by telephone. Mail or deliver requests directly to the park where a reservation is desired. An advance deposit (includes non-refundable reservation fee) needs to accompany each campsite request. Beginning in March, call the Information Center (numbers following) to check on campsite availability before mailing requests.

Reservation applications are available from state parks, state police, most motor vehicles division offices, and many chamber of commerce visitor information centers.

Reservations are recommended during the peak camping months of July and August. Unreserved campsites are assigned on a first-come, first-served basis.

Oregon's tallest mountain, Mt. Hood, is the picture-perfect background to the region's playground.

The following parks are on the campground reservations system (all telephone numbers are area code 503):

Fort Stevens, Hammond, OR 97121 (861-1671)

Cape Lookout, 13000 Whiskey Creek Road W., Tillamook, OR 97141 (842-4981)

Devil's Lake, 1452 N.E. 6th, Lincoln City, OR 97367 (994-2002)

Beverly Beach, 198 N.E. 123rd Street, Newport, OR 97365 (265-9278)

South Beach, 5580 S. Coast Hwy., South Beach, OR 97366 (867-4715)

Beachside, P.O. Box 693, Waldport, OR 97394, (563-3220)

Jessie M. Honeyman, 84505 Hwy. 101 South, Florence, OR 97439 (997-3641)

Sunset Bay, 10965 Cape Arago Hwy., Coos Bay, OR 97420 (888-4902)

Harris Beach, 1655 Hwy. 101, Brookings, OR 97415 (469-2021)

Detroit Lake, P.O. Box 549, Detroit, OR 97342 (854-3346)

Prineville Reservoir, 916777 Parkland Drive, Prineville, OR 97754, (447-4363)

The Cove Palisades, Rt. 1, Box 60 CP, Culver, OR 97734, (546-3412)

Wallowa Lake, 72214 Marina Lane, Joseph, OR 97846 (432-4185)

Current information on campsite availability at all state parks may be obtained from the:

Oregon State Park Campsite Information Center 1-800-452-5687 (Oregon except Portland and vicinity) (503) 238-7488 (out-of-state and Portland and vicinity)

The center operates from the first Monday in March to Labor Day weekend. Staff members are on duty to inform callers about campsite vacancies and recreational information from 8 a.m. to 4:30 p.m., Monday through Friday. *Callers cannot make reservations through the center, but reservation cancellations are accepted.*

National Forests

The Forest Service now provides a nationwide reservations system for campsites in many popular recreation areas. Now you may call one central toll-free number to reserve a campsite in any campground on the system. Most campgrounds on the system have about 50% of the campsites available for reservations.

A list of national forest campgrounds on the reservation system can be obtained from the forest supervisor of any national forest in Oregon. Due to the popularity of campgrounds, this list changes periodically.

Reservations are advised for popular campgrounds during the peak season, which usually runs between Memorial Day and Labor Day. Other campgrounds still operate entirely on a first-come, first-served basis. Weather permitting, most ranger districts keep some sites open after Labor Day.

It is important to note that reservations for some campsites, family and group, are handled directly through ranger districts or concessionaires within a national forest. For campsite reservation information, call the appropriate Forest Service office.

Campgrounds on the National Recreation Reservation System (NRRS) are noted in ranger district descriptions in this *Camper's Guide*. The National Recreation Reservation System offers customer payment through Visa, Discover, Mastercard and personal checks/money orders. Telephone reservations are available as follows:

January–September
Monday–Friday, 9:00 a.m.–9:00 p.m. Eastern Standard Time
Saturday–Sunday, 11:00 a.m.–7:00 p.m. E.S.T.

October–December
Monday–Friday, 11:00 a.m.–7:00 p.m. Eastern Standard Time
Saturday–Sunday, closed

Reservations from NRRS for group sites can be taken up to 1 year in advance; family site reservations are taken up to 120 days in advance. Wilderness permits may also be offered through the reservation system. For details, reservations, procedures, restrictions, and cancellation charges, write or call:

National Recreation Reservation System
P.O. Box 900
Cumberland, MD 21502
1-800-280-CAMP or 2267
TDD number for hearing impaired:
1-800-879-4496
FAX: (301) 722-9802

State Parks

Oregon's natural beauty and excellent state park system are among things that make the state a camper's haven. Quality experiences await visitors at more than 200 state parks, which include 50 exceptional camping parks. The following general information will help make your stay a pleasant one.

▲ **Boater's Pass:** The lower 100 miles of the Deschutes River Scenic Waterway requires boater passes. The fees are used to provide facilities and

Parks provide exceptional facilities for enjoying the state's natural beauty . . .

protect and enhance this unique recreation area. Passes are available from sporting goods stores, and state park regional and Salem offices.

▲ **Camping Facilities:** In addition to the 3,100 campsites at reservation parks, 2,600 are maintained at 37 other state park campgrounds on a first-come, first-served basis. Campsites available may include full utility hookups (sewer, water, and electrical), electrical hookups (electricity and water at the site) or tent (water nearby). All types have paved parking areas, picnic tables, and campstoves or fire rings. Most are near restrooms with flush toilets and showers. Some parks have primitive sites with limited facilities. These sites normally have a table and fire ring, with water and restrooms nearby.

▲ **Camping Season:** All 50 state park campgrounds are open from mid-April to late October and several are open year-round. May through September are the most popular camping months in Oregon. Temperatures are generally moderate and rainfall is less likely to interrupt outdoor activities. Most parks with year-round camping are on the coast where mild winter temperatures normally prevail.

▲ **Campsite Information Center:** Current information on campsite availability at all state parks

may be obtained from the Oregon State Park Campsite Information Center by calling 1-800-452-5687 in all areas of Oregon except Portland and vicinity. Out-of-state residents and people in the Portland area should call (503) 238-7488. The center operates from the first Monday in March to Labor Day weekend. Staff members are on duty to inform callers about campsite vacancies and recreational information from 8 a.m. to 4:30 p.m., Monday through Friday.

▲ **Day-Use Parks:** Nearly all of Oregon's 90,000 acres of state park land are undeveloped ranging from ancient forests in the west to sparsely vegetated high desert country in the east. Day visitors will find facilities that complement each park's natural attractions, including trails, viewpoints, and picnic sites. Most parks also have access to the ocean shore or to lakes, rivers, and streams for anglers and boaters. Some feature significant historic landmarks. At many locations, large grassy areas allow opportunities for group gatherings.

▲ **Facility Accessibility:** State parks with facilities accessible to the physically challenged are noted in the "Facilities and Activities" chart under each park description. Oregon State Parks is continually improving the accessibility of its

. . . and accessibility is made easy for everyone.

Bicyclists and hikers will find special camp-sites available at many campgrounds.

facilities. Please note that all restrooms and other facilities are not equally accessible. Contact a park office for a brochure entitled "Accessibility in Oregon State Parks."

▲ **Group Camping:** Special tent camping areas designed to accommodate 25 people are available at many state parks campgrounds. These areas are popular with church outings, school groups, and family reunions. Groups may also reserve individual campsites in the same area at one of the 13 reservation parks between Memorial Day and Labor Day weekends. Group use at locations not identified in the detailed park listing may also be possible through a special request to the park manager. See the "Facilities and Activities" chart for group camping information.

▲ **Hiker/Biker Camps:** Special campsites designed for hikers and bicyclists are available at many campgrounds. Most sites include a picnic table and fire ring with water nearby; many are in a common area shared by other hikers and bikers. Although hiker/biker areas are normally separated from the main campground, all park facilities such as restrooms and showers are available. Look under the "Facilities and Activities" chart of each park for Hiker/ Biker campsites.

▲ **Horse Camps:** Campsites accommodating horseback riders are provided at Silver Falls in the Willamette Valley and in three coastal parks. These less developed sites enable users to camp adjacent to corrals and/or hitching rails. Detailed information and reservation forms are available from local park staff. Also see the "Facilities and Activities" chart for availability of a horse camp at each park.

▲ **Historic Inns:** Travelers in Oregon find meals and lodging at two establishments refurbished and operated as frontier inns. Originally opened in the 1880s on the Oregon-to-California stagecoach road, Wolf Creek Tavern is one of the state's oldest hostelries. The southwestern Oregon inn is 20 miles north of Grants Pass, just west of I-5. Across the state in southeastern Oregon, the Frenchglen Hotel has a turn-of-the-century decor reminiscent of cowboy frontier days. The eight-room hotel, open from March until mid-November, is near the Malheur National Wildlife Refuge and the Steens Mountain Recreation Area, 60 miles south of Burns.

▲ **Lakes and Rivers:** A variety of water-related facilities and services are available in state parks in every area of Oregon. Boat dock and ramp facilities are included in more than 35 state parks.

State parks throughout Oregon provide excellent facilities and services for those who enjoy being on, in, and under the water!

Oregon is known for its waterfalls. This 177-foot beauty can be found just 26 miles east of Salem in the largest state park, Silver Falls. See page 57 for map and description of park.

Full-service marinas serve boaters and anglers at several locations. Access for windsurfers is available at many state parks along the Columbia River and ocean shoreline. A "Willamette River Recreation Guide," available from state park offices, provides information about access to boat ramps and rivers along Oregon's most popular waterway. Oregon's state parks department manages the Oregon Scenic Waterway Program to protect the natural, scenic, and recreational qualities of 19 rivers and one lake.

▲ **Military Remnants:** Fort Stevens State Park, near Astoria, occupies the grounds of a military outpost that guarded the mouth of the Columbia River from the Civil War through World War II. Summer tours take visitors through many old buildings and fortifications. Oregon coast explorers can also visit inactive lighthouses preserved in 3 state parks and enjoy excellent views of other sentinels still in use at 5 state parks.

▲ **Ocean Shores:** Visitors to the Oregon coast are never more than a few miles away from one of nearly 80 state parks adjacent to the shoreline. Many provide overlooks with views of spectacular seascapes, sand dunes, and miles of coastline. Almost all have picnic areas and trails leading to the beach.

▲ **Outstanding Natural Attractions:** Cascading waterfalls are the centerpiece of many state parks. No less than 10 falls attract hikers to Silver Falls in the Willamette Valley, and Latourell Falls, the second highest in the Columbia River Gorge which drops 249 feet in Talbot State Park. Natural and constructed gardens color state park landscapes in all areas of Oregon. Old-growth forests can be explored in parks along the north and south coasts and Cascade foothills. The oceanside floral garden at Shore Acres is one of Oregon's most impressive formal horticultural displays. Two other coastal parks, Saddle Mountain, site of rare species pushed south during the Ice Age, and Darlingtonia, with its carnivorous plants, draw special attention from botanists.

▲ **Park Rules:** Pets must be kept on a leash not more than six feet long. Rules of courtesy, such as cleaning up messes, and generally keeping pets under control, must be observed at all times. Campers need to be especially observant of the quiet hours between 10 p.m. and 7 a.m. Park users are advised to avoid parking in remote areas or locations hidden from view. Visitors who cannot avoid bringing valuables to a park should keep the items with them at all times. Remember to always be careful with fires.

▲ **Pioneer Heritage:** Adventures and major events from Oregon's past remain alive in state parks throughout Oregon. Information shelters in state parks and highway safety rest areas on I-84 tell the experiences of thousands of pioneer travelers who arrived in covered wagons on the Oregon Trail. Special places of interest to history buffs include Vista House on Crown Point in the Columbia River Gorge, Champoeg State Park, Willamette Mission, Emigrant Springs State Park, and Collier State Park.

▲ **Recreation Trails:** State park trails invite exploration by hikers, bicyclists, and horseback riders in some of the most scenic areas of Oregon. Hiking trails vary in length from multi-mile networks through the canyons of Silver Falls and Tryon Creek State Parks, to short nature walks. Tryon Creek trails include the Trillium Trail, an all-abilities loop designed to be accessible to everyone.

▲ **The Oregon Coast Trail:** Maintained as part of the Oregon Parks System, this trail extends the western length of the state between the mouth of the Columbia River and the Oregon-California border. The 360-mile trail includes both beach and inland stretches. The trail is open only to hikers, many of whom stay in special hiker/biker camps located along the entire coast. Oregon Coast Trail guide maps are available from state park offices.

▲ **Trails for Bikes and Horses:** Several parks have major trail systems designed especially for bicycle and horseback riding. For more information on statewide connector trails, contact the Oregon State Parks Trails Coordinator in the Salem headquarters office.

▲ **Volunteers:** Volunteers are key members of the Oregon State Parks team. They staff visitor centers, assist with special events and help with maintenance chores. Park hosts greet visitors, dispense firewood and help with other park tasks. For more information, request a brochure on "Volunteering In State Parks."

▲ **Wildlife Viewing:** Outstanding opportunities to see whales, sea lions, seals, elk, deer, falcons, eagles, and many other species of wildlife exist in certain state parks. The "Oregon Wildlife Viewing Guide" is available for sale at the State Parks office in Salem and at regional offices.

Many noteworthy trails wind through Oregon's spectacular backcountry. Campers can hike across the entire state along the Cascades from north to south on the Pacific Crest National Scenic Trail.

National Parks, Monuments, and Recreation Areas

Oregon's inspiring national treasures dot the state. Parks that allow camping include: Crater Lake National Park—North America's deepest lake; Hells Canyon National Recreation Area—North America's deepest gorge; Newberry National Volcanic Monument—North America's most diverse display of volcanism; and Oregon Dunes National Recreation Area—some of North America's highest sand dunes. Add to this amazing diversity the incomparable Columbia River Gorge National Scenic Area and visitors will sample only a small tidbit of Oregon's spectacular offerings.

To fully enjoy the abundant opportunities to recreate in these national parks, general information is cited here rather than repeated for each park in the *Camper's Guide.* For detailed information on a specific park, refer to sections "For Information," "Facilities and Activities," or "General Information" within each park description. For information on non-camping national parks, see brief descriptions below.

▲ **Backcountry Camping:** Backcountry use may be restricted in many areas or a quota system may be in effect. A quota program typically requires free permits for backcountry use, but limits the number of people permitted in the backcountry at one time. Contact the appropriate park for backcountry permits and specific restrictions.

▲ **Bicycling and Campsites:** Generally limited to paved and secondary roads, bicycling in some parks is allowed on some trails or backcountry areas. Check with park officials for restrictions. The "General Information" section on parks will allude to bicycling options. Campsites are designated in many parks and are typically described in the "General Information" section for bicyclists.

▲ **Camping Facilities:** Facilities will vary at campgrounds, but usually include a parking space, tent or RV space, drinking water, picnic table, grill, garbage pick-up and basic sanitary facilities to walk-in and primitive tent camping. The "Facilities and Activities" and/or "General Information" sections will clarify campsite features.

▲ **Campsites for Groups:** Offered at many parks, group campsites vary in size and fees charged. Details for group camping are provided for each park under "General Information."

▲ **Fees:** Entrance and recreation use fees are collected at many parks. Entrance fees are not

The Columbia River Gorge National Scenic Area offers a 30-mile vista from Crown Point, a circular stone memorial dating back to 1916.

Awesome geological formations dot the state—from wonderous rock pillars jutting from the Pacific and 500-foot-high sand dunes along the coast . . .

tion about the park's services, features, and history. Interpretive programs are usually provided, and many activities are designed specifically for children such as the "Junior Ranger Program."

▲ **Length of Stay:** Parks may vary from one to fourteen nights in length of stay. See the "General Information" section under each park for details.

▲ **Physically Challenged Visitors:** Questions about accessible facilities and campgrounds should be directed to park headquarters if they are not identified in the "General Information" section of each park.

▲ **Primitive Camping:** Most parks will allow primitive camping in many of the remote, roadless areas of the parks, but occasionally, backcountry use is prohibited due to emergency conditions such as high fire danger or severe weather conditions. Check with rangers at park headquarters to determine current conditions and to secure camping and/or fire permits, if needed.

▲ **RVs:** RV restrictions will vary. The "General Information" or "Facilities Chart" under each park will specify length limits, hook-up availability, and sanitary dump information.

▲ **Wood Gathering:** Campfire wood is either limited to dead material found on the ground or pro-

charged visitors under age 13 or over 61. See "Federal Recreation Passport Program" on page 24 and "General Information" under each park for details. Recreation use fees are collected for campsite users, sometimes only seasonally, at campgrounds that have certain minimum facilities and services. They are charged in addition to any park entrance fee. See "General Information" under each park for such information. Concession-operated facilities charge separate fees from those charged by the managing park agency. These fees are not subject to discounts offered through the Golden Eagle, Golden Access or Golden Age Passports.

▲ **Fires:** Campfires are restricted in most parks to grills provided or campstoves. Backcountry campfires are typically regulated either by permits or limited to campstoves only. Open campfires are often banned due to fire danger or the stripping of firewood that needs to be recycled into the environment.

▲ **Information/Visitor Centers:** Your first stop should be to get brochures, maps, and a schedule of activities readily available at information or visitor centers. Many parks publish a newspaper outlining activities and other pertinent informa-

. . . to volcanoes, lava beds, and North America's deepest gorge in eastern Oregon.

hibited completely. Restrictions often permit only charcoal or wood brought in by campers to be burned. Campers are encouraged to use liquid-fuel campstoves or charcoal for cooking. Check with individual parks for details to properly prepare.

▲ **Water:** Supplies may be limited in parks, particularly in the backcountry. Often, available water has to be treated to prevent illnesses. Check with park rangers about water sources before venturing through parks and be prepared to properly treat water supplies.

▲ **Objects Within Parks:** Artifacts, wildflowers, trees, and rocks are protected by federal law. It is prohibited to disturb, deface, damage, or remove objects from parks. Violators are prosecuted. Please help maintain the integrity and beauty of parks by respecting park laws and regulations that protect these rich resources.

▲ **Pets:** If they are kept on a leash or under physical restraint at all times, pets are allowed in parks and campgrounds. They are generally prohibited in buildings, the backcountry, and on trails.

▲ **Feeding Wild Animals**: Feeding is strictly prohibited for the protection of the animals as well as visitors. Many animals carry diseases or can become dangerous. Food supplies should be locked up or hung out of reach; such measures are required at some parks.

▲ **Fishing:** Fishing is regulated and typically requires a permit and/or a state fishing license. Check for details within each park.

▲ **Hunting:** Hunting is prohibited in national parks and monuments. The use of campgrounds in these areas as base camps for hunting outside park boundaries is also prohibited. Hunting may be authorized in or from other park areas, but in accordance with state laws during season. Check for details with appropriate state departments that regulate hunting and fishing.

▲ **Saddle or Pack Animals:** Use of pack animals is allowed in recreation sites only where authorized by posted instructions. Restrictions on numbers, campsites, type of feed, and trails vary. Check with appropriate park officials for permits and regulations. The "General Information" section will assist in providing basic information.

▲ **Religious Services:** Details on religious services are usually posted at information centers or are available by contacting the park.

▲ **Other National Parks:** Oregon also offers the following National Parks and Monuments *without* camping facilities:

Fort Clatsop National Memorial—The park near Astoria commemorates the Lewis and Clark Expedition, which camped here in the winter of 1805–06. Interpretive exhibits, slide programs, guided tours, and living history demonstrations are provided. (505) 861-2471

John Day Fossil Beds National Monument— Picturesque formations of the John Day River Valley contain a 40-million-year record of the Golden Age of Mammals. Exhibits, interpretive talks, self-guiding trails, and a visitor center are available. (505) 575-0721

Oregon Caves National Monument— Located in the southwest corner of Oregon near Cave Junction, Oregon Caves displays underground passages and intricate flowstone shapes formed by groundwater dissolving marble bedrock. Guided cave tours are available all year. (503) 592-2100

Oregon National Historical Trail—The 2,170-mile-long Oregon Trail was the westward migration route for over 300,000 settlers, gold seekers, fur traders, and missionaries. Contact local chambers of commerce for visitor information.

National Forests

The national forests are truly America's great outdoors! With 156 national forests in 43 states, more people recreate in national forests than anywhere else, yet few forests have reached their full recreational potential. Oregon has 13 national forests that cover approximately 30 million acres. Administered by the Pacific Northwest Region of the U.S. Department of Agriculture, U.S. Forest Service, each national forest is directed by a forest supervisor and ranger districts. Each ranger district is responsible for the management of the forest under a multiple-use program to sustain yield of renewable resources such as water, forage, wildlife, timber, and recreation.

Oregon's national forests have spectacular contrasts and great recreational opportunities. Outdoor recreationists can choose from a float trip on the Snake River in North America's deepest gorge; enjoy a scenic drive around snow-capped Mount Hood; explore a rain forest of spruce and fir growing beside glacier-fed rivers; or visit the surf-splashed coastline. Forest campsites offer a range of options from secluded spots to high density recreation areas. Many campgrounds are open year-round, but some only operate during peak season from Memorial Day to Labor Day.

Because recreation management is becoming more dependent upon visitor self-service and volunteer assistance, it is important for recreationists to understand how to best use national forest resources. The following information will help you enjoy the great outdoors and help keep it beautiful for future generations. Individual national forest descriptions, maps, and addresses are given in this *Campers' Guide* within appropriate regions of the state. For general information about Oregon's national forest contact:

Recreation Information
U. S. Forest Service
333 S.W. First Street
Portland, OR 97204
(503) 326-2877

or

U.S. Forest Service
Pacific Northwest Regional Office
319 SW Pine St.
P.O. Box 3623
Portland, OR 97208
(503) 326-2877

National Parks, Monuments, Recreation Areas, and National Forests

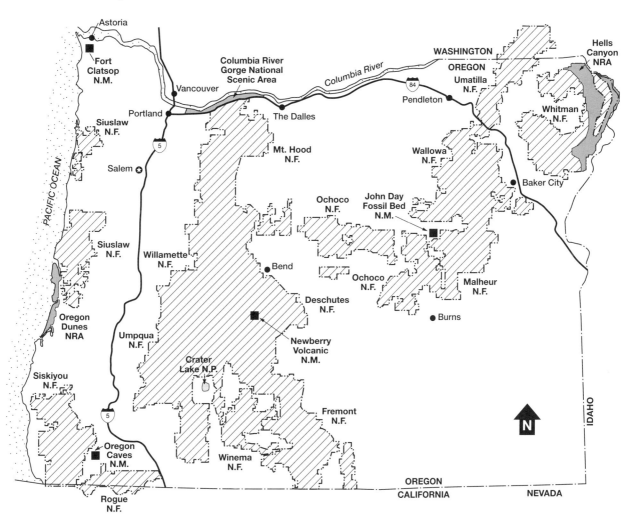

Ranger districts are the best source of specific local information within a national forest. Each district distributes its own maps and materials on campgrounds, trails, recreational activities, road conditions, weather, and wildlife. It is best to first visit either the office of the national forest supervisor or the individual ranger district to obtain the most current information. Not only are specific national forest maps available to show backroads and terrain features unavailable on any other map, but rangers can help in planning trips and pointing out unique features of the area. Information on individual national forests are arranged in this *Camper's Guide* by ranger districts. For specific information on campground locations and facilities, refer to the appropriate national forest.

Information that is basic to all national forests is given here rather than repeated for each forest.

▲ **Barrier-free accesses:** Accesses are noted in the "Facilities and Activities" chart. Typical accesses accommodate wheelchairs to some or all of developed campground's facilities.

▲ **Camping Season:** The peak season generally runs from Memorial Day weekend to Labor Day weekend. After Labor Day many campgrounds remain open, but water systems are turned off and visitors are asked to pack their own trash out. Weather, road or site repair, agency finances, fires, and other factors can alter these dates and cause closures. Check with nearby national forest offices for definite dates and conditions.

▲ **Campsites:** Typical campsites include a parking space for one vehicle, a table, and a fire pit or fireplace. They are available on a first-come, first-served basis. Some campgrounds offer reservations. See "Reservations" below for details.

▲ **Closures due to forest fires:** Campgrounds, roads or forest areas may close or change from season to season due to forest fires. Always check with rangers about closures and changes.

▲ **Fees:** Camping fees are charged for many of the recreation sites. Fees and reservations are required for group sites. Information about fees is available at ranger stations and is posted at recreation sites.

▲ **Fees by Concessionaires**: Private parties often operate some fee sites under special-use authorizations. Operated and maintained as a government-owned facility to provide public services, concessions are awarded on a competitive basis. Fees charged by concessionaires are sep-

arate from fees of the U.S. Forest Service. Permits are required and concessions are monitored and regulated by the Forest Service.

▲ **Fishing and Hunting:** Compliance with state laws are required to fish and/or hunt in national forests. Possession of a valid license is required. Check with the individual national forests for details.

▲ **Fires:** Campfires must be attended at all times and completely extinguished before leaving. Bring a portable stove to use in case open fires are prohibited or firewood is scarce. Only dead wood lying on the ground may be gathered for campfires. Cutting of timber, bushes, or vegetation is prohibited unless a permit allows such gathering.

▲ **Food, Gas, and Lodging:** Available in some national forests along major routes traversing national forest lands; such amenities are seldom found along forest roads.

▲ **Golden Age/Golden Access Passports:** Passports are honored at all concession campgrounds. Persons older than 62 and those who are handicapped may receive lifetime Golden Access/ Golden Age Passports, which provide a 50% discount on campground use fees. Applicants must apply in person and provide proof of handicap or age. There is a one-time $10 fee for the Golden Age Passport. Passports are available at Forest Service offices, national parks and monuments, and federal information centers.

▲ **Horses, Saddle or Pack Animals:** Animals can be ridden or packed into national forest lands with restrictions. Contact the local ranger station for maps, trail information, and forage availability. No-trace techniques are requested to help keep the backcountry pristine. Special brochures for equestrian use are available and recommended.

▲ **Interpretive Programs:** Programs and pamphlets are available to better understand and enjoy the forest. Such programs are available at visitor centers (forest headquarters/ranger district offices), as well as numerous other developed sites.

▲ **Maps:** National forest maps are invaluable in planning enjoyable travel. Maps are sold both at Forest Service offices and through the mail. Detailed maps in ½" per mile for forests and 1" per mile of wildernesses are available for a minimal cost.

▲ **Off-Road-Vehicles:** ORVs, ATVs, or OHVs all refer to recreational vehicles that can be used off-the-road. These may include 3- or 4- wheelers, dune buggies, jeeps, 4x4s, and motorcycles. The state of Oregon offers a wide range of trails and special-use areas for riding in the national forests. The use of these vehicles on public lands is regulated by laws. Check with the appropriate forest service offices for details and permits.

▲ **Pets:** Permitted in national forests, pets must be restrained or on a leash while in developed recreation sites, along designated trails, and within wilderness areas. Pets (except guide dogs) are not allowed in swimming areas.

▲ **Reservations:** Reservations are available at popular campgrounds for both families and groups. For details and reservations call the National Recreation Reservation System (NRRS). Operators have access to information on each campground on the reservation system. The NRRS will be able to help select a campground and a campsite of interest without the camper knowing the area. See "Reservation Systems, National Forests" for details and telephone numbers on page 5.

▲ **Roads:** Many national forest roads are low-standard, one-lane roads with turnouts for meeting oncoming traffic. Many roads on the east side of the Cascade Mountains are not graveled. Most roads are not maintained or snowplowed in winter weather. Encounters with logging trucks are likely, even on weekends. Driving rules used on state highways apply to national forest roads.

▲ **Road Markers:** Markers identify two types of national forest roads maintained for automobile travel. These markers are posted at the entrance of primary and secondary routes. Primary routes usually offer the better choice for the traveler. Secondary routes may not be maintained as well.

Primary Route

Secondary Route

These signs use white numbers on a brown background and are clearly posted at road entrances and intersections.

▲ **RVs, Trailers, and Campers:** Campers should stay posted as to road condition warnings and maximum length recommendations. RV camp-sites usually accommodate a 22-foot trailer. Smaller limits are noted in the "Campground Chart" under each ranger district.

▲ **RV Hookups:** Normally, hookups are not available in campgrounds. A few campgrounds, particularly those operated by concessionaires, provide hookups. See the "Facilities and Activities" chart under each ranger district for hookup information.

▲ **Sanitary Disposal Stations:** Dump stations and central water hydrants are provided to serve some campgrounds as indicated in the "Facilities and Activities" chart under each ranger district.

▲ **Special Permits:** Information and requirements are available from Forest Service offices on special permit requirements for wilderness areas or stretches of river managed as Wild and Scenic. Permits may also be required to operate certain off-road recreational vehicles.

▲ **Users:** Recreationists have significant responsibility for personal safety during any activity pursued in national forests. It is the users responsibility to know the hazards involved in activities and to use the proper safety procedures and equipment to minimize the inherent risks and hazards.

▲ **Volunteers:** People interested in becoming involved in the conservation work of the forests may join the "Volunteers in the National Forest" program. Campground Host and Wilderness Information Specialist are just two of the job titles for volunteers. Whether interested in maintenance, administration, information, or education, anyone interested can contact one of the ranger stations or Forest Service offices for details.

▲ **Water:** Water is not always available at campsites. Check the "Facilities and Activities" chart for details. Water from developed systems at recreation sites is safe to drink. Open water sources are easily contaminated by human or animal wastes. Water from springs, lakes, ponds, and streams should always be treated. Recommended method is to boil water for a minimum of five minutes.

▲ **Winter Recreation:** All ski areas are in whole or in part on National Forest administered lands. Although ski lift facilities are operated by concessionaires, they are regulated by the Forest Service. Hundreds of miles of marked trails are also available for cross-country skiers and snowmobilers. Check with specific national forest headquarters or see "Important Contacts" in the Introduction of this *Guide* for details.

Wilderness Areas

Oregon's 39 wilderness areas encompass over 2,116,800 acres of inspiring scenery. Dedicated to preserving a part of our national heritage in its natural state, there are no roads, motorized travel, logging, resorts, or other commercial developments allowed. Trails traverse these great natural treasures for those who are willing to hike, ride a horse, pack an animal, or ski.

These wilderness areas are managed by the U.S. Forest Service and are described under their managing national forest within this *Camper's Guide*.

Topographic quad maps are available either through camping suppliers or directly from the U.S. Geological Survey. For information or a free index map to select the quad map(s) needed for a wilderness trip contact:

U.S. Geological Survey
Denver Federal Center
P.O. Box 25046
Mail Stop 504
Denver, CO 80225
(303) 236-5829

or

Western Mapping Center-NCIC
U.S. Geological Survey
345 Middlefield Road
Menlo Park, CA 94025
(415) 323-8111

Wildernesses are unique and vital resources. Their pristine character can remain dominant and enduring with the wise use of such lands. Outdoor enthusiasts who act with a sense of land stewardship and responsibility will help protect the lands for all to enjoy in the future.

Wilderness Area	National Forest(s)	Acreage
1. Badger Creek	Mt. Hood	24,000
2. Black Canyon	Ochoco	13,400
3. Boulder Creek	Umpqua	19,100
4. Bridge Creek	Ochoco	5,400
5. Bull of the Woods	Mt. Hood, Willamette	34,900
6. Columbia	Mt. Hood	39,000
7. Cummins Creek	Siuslaw	9,300
8. Deschutes Canyon (Steelhead Falls)	Ochoco	10,200
9. Diamond Peak	Deschutes, Willamette	52,300
10. Drift Creek	Siuslaw	5,800
11. Eagle Cap	Wallowa-Whitman	358,500
12. Gearhart Mountain	Fremont	22,800
13. Grassy Knob	Siskiyou	17,200
14. Homestead	Wallowa-Whitman	7,700
15. Hells Canyon	Wallowa-Whitman	130,100
16. Kalmiopsis	Siskiyou	179,700
17. Menagerie	Willamette	4,800
18. Middle Santiam	Willamette	7,500
19. Mill Creek	Ochoco, Willamette	24,900
20. Monument Rock	Malheur, Whitman	19,700
21. Mountain Lakes	Winema	23,100
22. Mt. Hood	Mt. Hood	46,500
23. Mt. Jefferson	Deschutes, Mt. Hood, Willamette	107,100
24. Mt. Thielsen	Deschutes, Umpqua, Winema	55,100
25. Mt. Washington	Deschutes, Willamette	52,500
26. North Fork John Day	Umatilla, Whitman	121,400
27. North Fork Umatilla	Umatilla	20,200
28. Olallie	Mt. Hood	8,700
29. Pine Creek	Malheur	5,300
30. Red Buttes	Rogue River, Siskiyou	3,800
31. Rock Creek	Siskiyou	7,500
32. Rogue-Umpqua Divide	Rogue River, Umpqua	33,200
33. Salmon-Huckleberry	Mt. Hood	44,600
34. Sky Lakes	Rogue River, Winema	116,300
35. Strawberry Mountain	Malheur	68,700
36. Three sisters	Deschutes, Willamette	285,200
37. Waldo Lake	Willamette	39,200
38. Wenaha-Tucannon	Umatilla	66,400
39. Wild Rogue	Siskiyou	25,700

Noteworthy Trails

1. High Desert Recreation Trail

Hikers on this National Recreation Trail will eventually be able to hike the arid lands east of the Sierra and Cascade Mountains from Mexico to Canada. Currently, about 240 miles of trail have been established with field guides for seven separate sections written by and available from the Desert Trail Association. Planners purposely did not construct an actual trail so that visible scars on the delicate desert landscape could be minimized. Instead, rock cairns have been constructed as guide points along the trail to help hikers choose their own paths within a general trail corridor. For more information contact:

Bureau of Land Management
Burns District
HC-74, 12533 Highway 20 West
Hines, Oregon 97738
(503) 573-5241

2. Oregon Coast Trail

The Oregon Coast Trail, maintained as part of the Oregon Parks System, extends the western length of the state between the mouth of the Columbia River and the Oregon-California border. The 360-mile trail includes both beach and inland stretches. The trail is open only to hikers, many of whom stay in special hiker/biker camps located along the entire coast. Oregon Coast Trail guide maps are available from state park offices. For more information contact:

State Parks and Recreation Department
525 Trade Street S.E.
Salem, OR 97310
(503) 378-6305

3. Oregon National Historic Trail (for vehicles)

The Oregon National Historic Trail combines the overland routes that nearly 350,000 emigrants followed to the West. Beginning in the 1840s, and for nearly thirty years afterward, west-bound emigrants followed the many different overland trails from Independence, Missouri, west to destinations in California, Utah, Washington, and Oregon. More than 50,000 followed the Trail across the Snake River to settle in Oregon's Willamette Valley. There are some 40 historic and scenic points of interest along the 547 miles of historic trail from Oregon's eastern border to Oregon City; National Historic Oregon Trail Interpretive Center is located near Baker City. Step from your vehicle and walk along the wagon ruts. Someone, just like you, took those same steps a century ago. Imagine and sense the story of a growing nation, heartache and hardship, and the search for opportunity in a new homeland. For more information contact:

Oregon Tourism Division
775 Summer Street N.E.
Salem, OR 97310
1-800-547-7842

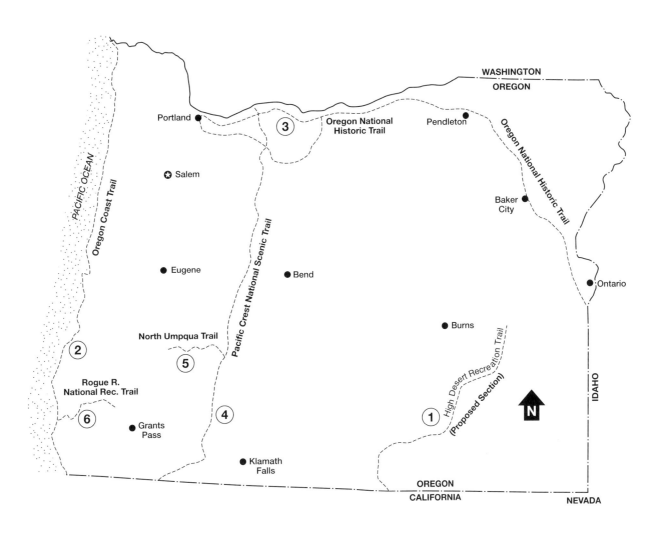

4. Pacific Crest National Scenic Trail ————

The Pacific Crest National Scenic Trail extends 2,638 miles from Manning Provincial Park in Canada to east of San Diego at the U.S.-Mexico border. It was one of the first two National Scenic Trails designated by the National Trails Act in 1968. Today, eight National Scenic Trails are officially recognized in the U.S. The Pacific Crest is the longest of them all in existing mileage.

In Oregon the Pacific Crest offers many challenges and outstanding vistas of backcountry. Markers identify the route, which is mostly at high elevations along north-south mountain ranges. Vehicles of any kind, including bicycles, are prohibited.

To test endurance and tenacity or re-invigorate the spirit, the Pacific Crest National Scenic Trail is a national treasure of incomparable magnitude. For more information contact:

Pacific Crest Trail
P.O. Box 2514
Lynnwood, WA 98036-2514

5. North Umpqua Trail ————

The North Umpqua Trail follows the North Umpqua River for about 77 miles on lands administered by the Umpqua National Forest, Bureau of Land Management, and Douglas County. The trail provides a variety of outstanding recreation opportunities for anglers, photographers, backpackers, equestrians, mountain bicyclists, and those who simply want to enjoy the natural attractions of scenery and wildlife. The North Umpqua Trail crosses the Oregon Cascades Recreation Area east of the Kelsay Valley Trailhead and ties in with the Pacific Crest Trail high in the Cascades near Maidu

Lake, the source of the North Umpqua River. For more information contact:

Umpqua National Forest
P.O. Box 1008
Roseburg, OR 97470
(503) 672-6601

or

Bureau of Land Management
Roseburg District
777 N.W. Garden Valley Blvd.
Roseburg, OR 97470
(503) 440-4930

6. Rogue River National Recreation Trail ————

The trail provides hikers with access into the "wild" section of the Rogue National Wild and Scenic River. Whisky Creek Cabin and the Rogue River Ranch, on the National Register of Historic—places, can both be reached by river or the Rogue River National Recreation Trail. For more information contact:

Siskiyou National Forest
200 N.E. Greenfield Road
P.O. Box 440
Grants Pass, OR 97526
(503) 471-6516

or

Bureau of Land Management
Medford District
3040 Biddle Road
Medford, OR 97501
(503) 770-2200

Other Recreation Sites and Public Campgrounds ——

Bureau of Land Management (BLM) Recreation Areas ————

The Bureau of Land Management (BLM) manages 15.7 million acres of public land in Oregon together with about 36 million acres of federal minerals.

Approximately 2.8 million acres lie on the moist, heavily forested western side of the Cascades and 12.9 million acres of high desert to rolling sagebrush plains and pine-covered mountains lie east of the Cascades.

Outdoor recreation opportunities are unlimited and virtually undiscovered on much of the acreage managed by BLM. These lands contain a wide range

of unique and interesting places with breathtaking beauty, solitude, and recreation opportunities.

While the number of formal BLM campgrounds is small, campers will be able to find a special place "to get away from it all" on the public lands—places where you can follow the paths of native Americans, fur trappers, pioneers, and buckaroos who created the legends and lore that make up the Spirit of the Old West.

Maps of BLM recreation areas and charts of available facilities are provided within each of the three regional sections of this *Camper's Guide*. See Bureau of Land Management Recreation Areas on the first page of each region; it will refer to the specific page that provides the BLM sites' map and facilities chart.

Fees are charged at many BLM's developed sites, but in general there are no fees. **Reservations** are required at some of the group picnic and camp sites, and on certain float-boating rivers. Check with district offices for more information on these sites. Use of other developed sites is on a first-come, first-served basis. The Golden Age and Golden Access Passports entitle the holders to use BLM recreation facilities for half the usual fee.

National Back Country Byways designated and administered by the BLM provide an added bonus for campers. These byways are located in government-owned lands and cover some 774 miles in Oregon. Kiosks along the way provide information on cultural history, area plants and animals, and road conditions. There are nine BLM district offices located throughout Oregon to assist visitors. For detailed information and maps contact the headquarters:

Bureau of Land Management
P.O. Box 2965
Portland, Oregon 97208
(503) 280-7001

Pacific Power Recreation Sites

Pacific Power has been serving the Northwest with electrical energy since 1910. Part of Pacific's effort to serve communities has been the development and maintenance of recreational sites adjacent to many of its power facilities. Today, Pacific has 42 recreational sites providing almost 300 camping spaces and 400 picnic facilities in five of six states it serves.

Facilities on the Oregon portion of the Klamath River include Keno Camp with both camping and picnicking sites, and Pioneer Park, equipped for day-use only. Both sites offer swimming and boat ramps. Located just northwest of Keno, Keno Camp provides water, flush toilets, showers, and a trailer dump station. A small fee per night is charged. The campground typically operates between May and October.

Three more campgrounds are located just south in California where the Klamath River becomes more rugged, rushing through deep gorges and narrow canyons. The river slows as it reaches Copco Lake behind Copco Dam and again behind Iron Gate Dam forming Iron Gate Reservoir. Rimrock country surrounds Iron Gate Reservoir.

Noteworthy day-use areas in Oregon include Pacific Park on the Wallowa River (sits amid America's answer to Switzerland in the northeastern corner of the state near Enterprise), the North Umpqua River recreation area (six sites that include spectacular Toketee Falls), and the Rogue River (located in the heart of Hellgate Canyon along the National Wild and Scenic River).

For more information contact:

Recreation Department
Pacific Power
920 S.W. 6th Avenue
Portland, Oregon 97204
(503) 464-5035

Portland General Electric Recreation Areas

Portland General Electric has endeavored to preserve and make available for public use recreation resources associated with company generation projects. As a result, there are nine recreation areas for the public to enjoy; three provide camping facilities. Five areas, three with camping facilities, are located on the Clackamas River system, two on the Deschutes River in Central Oregon, and one near the Bull Run River east of Portland.

Fees are charged for all campsites, group picnic shelters, and at Roslyn Lake and Trojan for auto entrance. See map for location and availability of facilities.

Campground Locations/Activities

1. **Faraday Lake:** One mi. SE of Estacada. Signs on the river side of S.R. 224 show the point for pedestrian access to the lake. *Activities:* Fishing only.
2. **Lake Harriet:** At head of lake; about 7 mi. N of S.R. 224 bridge over the Oak Grove fork of the Clackamas River. *Activities:* Boating (ramp) and fishing.
3. **Pelton Park:** N of Madras on Deschutes River, travel W on Belmont Lane and follow directional signs. *Activities:* Picnicking and boating (ramp and dock).
4. **Promontory Park:** Travel 7 mi. E of Estacada on the Clackamas River Road, S.R. 224. *Activities:* Playground equipment, picnicking, group picnicking, fishing, boating (launch/motor and boat rentals), mooring and docking, and hiking trails; concession store available with fishing tackle.
5. **River Mill:** On the Clackamas River, 20 mi. SE of Portland. Travel S.R. 224 to signed junction 1 mi. W of Estacada. Follow directional signs to park access road. *Activities:* Playground equipment, hiking trail, boating (launch), and fishing.
6. **Roslyn Lake:** 3.5 mi. N of Sandy. From Portland travel E on U.S. 26 to Sandy, then travel N on Ten Eyck Road. *Activities:* Picnicking, group pic-

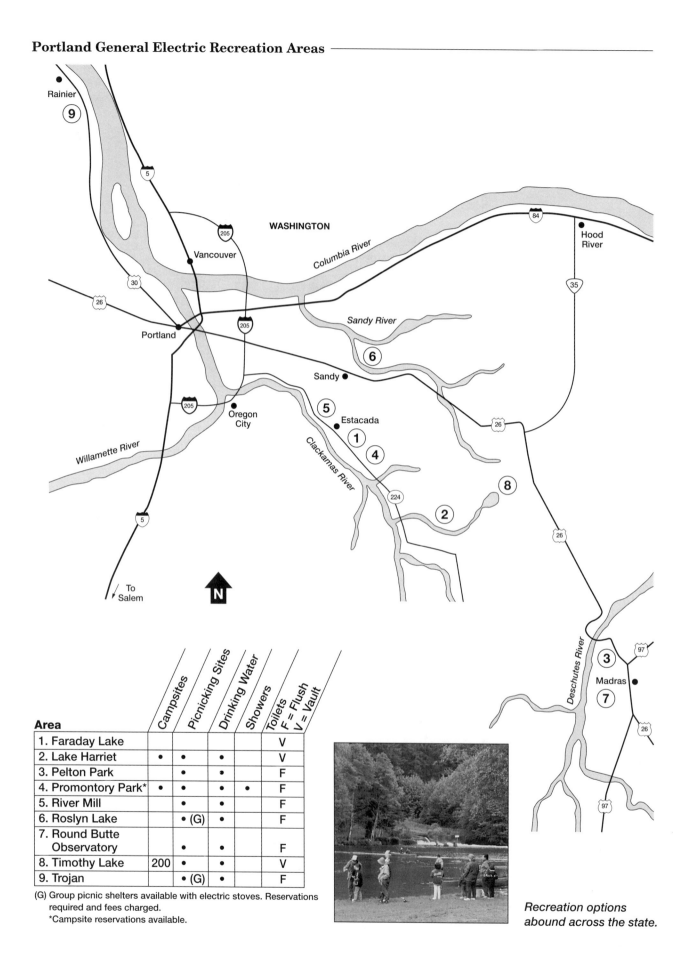

Area	Campsites	Picnicking Sites	Drinking Water	Showers	Toilets F = Flush V = Vault
1. Faraday Lake					V
2. Lake Harriet	•	•	•		V
3. Pelton Park		•	•		F
4. Promontory Park*	•	•	•	•	F
5. River Mill		•	•		F
6. Roslyn Lake		• (G)	•		F
7. Round Butte Observatory		•	•		F
8. Timothy Lake	200	•	•		V
9. Trojan		• (G)	•		F

(G) Group picnic shelters available with electric stoves. Reservations required and fees charged.
*Campsite reservations available.

Recreation options abound across the state.

nicking, playfield, horseshoe courts, boating (ramp), fishing, swimming; concession for food supplies available.

7. **Round Butte Observatory:** From Madras, travel W on Belmont Lane and follow directional signs to observatory. *Activities:* Picnicking and exhibits.

8. **Timothy Lake:** Two routes from Portland (see local maps for details): By Estacada, S.R. 224 and Forest Service Roads for a total of 74 mi.; or U.S. 26 and a skyline road about 79 mi. from Portland. *Activities:* Picnicking, hiking, horseback riding, windsurfing, boating, and fishing.

9. **Trojan:** 42 mi. N and W of Portland on the Oregon shore of the Columbia River; adjacent to Trojan Nuclear Power Plant. *Activities:* Picnicking, group picnicking, non-motorized boating, fishing, playfield, playground equipment, hiking trails, and wildlife viewing shelter/exhibits.

For more information contact:

Portland General Electric
121 S.W. Salmon Street
Portland, OR 97204
(503) 464-8515

Tillamook State Forest Campgrounds

Nestled in the northern Oregon Coast Range, Tillamook State Forest was called the "Tillamook Burn" by generations of Oregonians. It was named for the devastating fires that left the land bare and charred in 1933, 1939, 1945, and 1951. Today the area has been reforested and is covered with young trees. There are twenty-five miles of trails for non-motorized use that wind through the forest's lush hillsides and river canyons. The varied trails are suitable for horseback riding, others are set aside for walking or mountain biking, and still others, on steep and fragile sites should be used only by hikers and backpackers. Numerous other trails and old roads exist for motorcycles and other off-road vehicles, especially in the Browns Camp area. Note: No off-road riding is allowed on the north side of Highway 6 between Gales Creek and Lees Camp.

There are four semi-developed campgrounds located along the trails. All sites have drinking water, vault toilets, picnic tables, and fireplaces. No fees are collected and there are no hookups. Following is a list of camps, number of campsites, and locations. See the map for locations.

Campground Locations/Activities

1. **Browns Camp** (15 campsites): Located 45 miles west of Portland, go about a mile south of the Wilson River Highway (S.R. 6). *Activities:* It is a motorcycle park staging area and provides a starting point for trails to Rogers Camp and University Falls.

2. **Elk Creek** (15 walk-in campsites): Lies 48 miles west of Portland, just north of the Wilson River

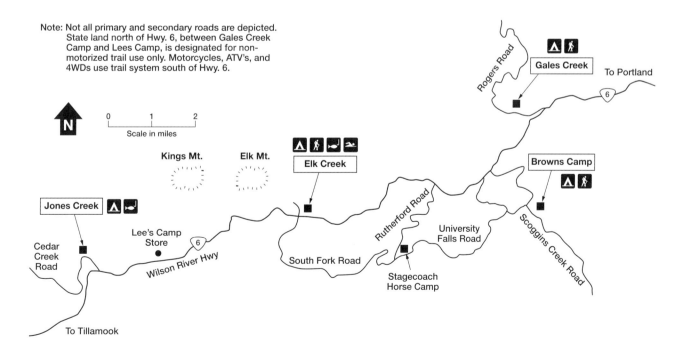

Highway (S.R. 6) off Elk Creek Road. *Activities:* These shaded sites lie where Elk Creek flows into the Wilson River and offer access to swimming, fishing, and trailhead access to three trails.

3. **Gales Creek** (32 campsites): Located 41 miles west of Portland. To reach this creekside campground take the Wilson River Highway to Gales Creek via posted signs. *Activities:* The Gales Creek Trail takes off from the campground entrance and begins the 25-mile section of developed hiking trails through the Forest.

4. **Jones Creek** (35 campsites): Go one-half mile west of Lees Camp Store off S.R. 6, about 54 miles west of Portland. Turn north and cross the bridge over the Wilson River. The shaded campground lies just north of the highway. *Activities:* Campers will find good fishing access and swimming.

For more information contact:

Tillamook State Forest
Northwest Oregon Area
801 Gales Creek Road
Forest Grove, OR 97116-1199
(503) 357-8005

U.S. Army Corps of Engineers Campgrounds —

Oregon features numerous large, multiple-purpose projects built by the U.S. Army Corps of Engineers for hydroelectric power production, flood control, navigation, and recreation. Most of these projects offer a full range of recreation facilities operated by the Corps and other federal, state, or local agencies. Campgrounds, picnic areas, boat ramps, hiking trails, and marinas are a few of the facilities provided.

A unique feature of the Oregon projects is one of the Corps' main activities, fishery management on the Columbia and Snake rivers. Many Corps projects include fish ladders to enable salmon and other fish to complete their migration upstream. Visitors can learn more about this program, and often see salmon during their migration, in special fish viewing rooms at project visitor centers. Tours of some of the nation's largest hydroelectric plants and fish hatcheries are also popular.

The following information can help you take advantage of camping opportunities at a Corps recreation area.

For more information contact:

Public Affairs Office
U.S. Army Engineer District, Portland
P.O. Box 2946
Portland, OR 97208-2946
(503) 326-6021

Area (see map at right)	Campsites w/electricity	Campsites w/o electricity	Showers	Dump Station	Marina	Visitor Center
1. Applegate Lake		•		•		
2. Blue River Lake		•				
3. Bonneville Lock, Dam & Lock		•		•	•	•
4. Cottage Grove Lake		•	•	•		
5. Cougar Lake		•				
6. Dalles Lock & Dam/Lake Celilo	•	•	•	•	•	•
7. Detroit Lake	•	•	•	•		•
8. Dorena Lake		•	•	•		
9. Fall Creek Lake		•				
10. Fern Ridge Lake		•	•		•	
11. Foster Lake		•	•	•		
12. Green Peter Lake		•				
13. Hills Creek Lake		•				
14. John Day Lock & Dam/Lake Umatilla	•	•	•	•	•	
15. Lookout Point Lake		•				
16. Lost Creek Lake	•	•	•	•	•	•
17. McNary Lock & Dam/Lake Wallula	•	•	•	•	•	•

All facilities listed above have restrooms, drinking water, boat ramps, and picnic/day-use areas. This list only includes Corps projects with camping facilities.

U.S. Fish and Wildlife Service ————

One of the great experiences of camping is seeing wildlife in its natural habitat. Outdoor enthusiasts will find the wildlife of Oregon just as diverse as its terrain and limate. Whether you are a photographer, birdwatcher, angler, or nature-lover, you will find wonderful wildlife viewing opportunities throughout the state.

The Pacific Region of the U.S. Fish and Wildlife Service (USFWS) includes six states including Oregon. The region encompasses 92 national wildlife refuges and 19 national fish hatcheries. About 41%, or 224 species, of U.S. endangered fish, wildlife, and plant species are found in this region. Oregon contains approximately 18 USFWS managed facilities. Most of these facilities offer recreation and education opportunities. For example, wildlife obser-

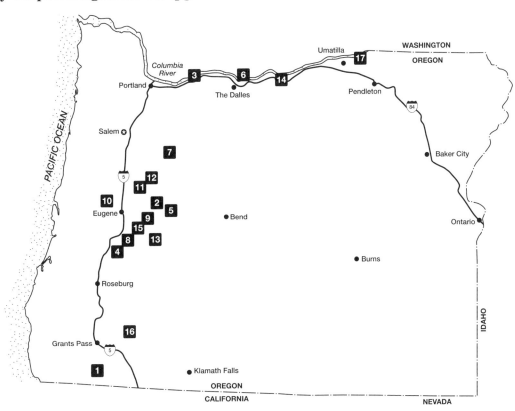

vation, study and photography; fishing; interpretive exhibits; pheasant, migratory, and waterfowl hunting; resident and big game hunting; fish hatchery tours; hiking; and camping.

Although there is only one refuge in Oregon that allows camping, most refuges have camping facilities nearby. Hart Mountain National Antelope Refuge in south-central Oregon, 68 miles northeast of Lakeview, offers primitive camping facilities. Pronghorn antelope, California bighorn sheep, mule deer, and sage grouse are among the more common species of wildlife seen here. The 241,104 acres of refuge is located between elevations of 4,500 and 8,065 feet. Besides observing wildlife, activities include big game hunting and limited stream fishing.

Available for purchase is the Oregon Wildlife Viewing Guide. This unique 80-page, full-color publication lists 123 individual viewing sites with 13 section maps, specific directions to each site, and information about tourist facilities at or near each location. For more information on refuges and wildlife management areas contact:

U.S. Fish and Wildlife Service
911 NE 11th Avenue
Portland, OR 97232-4181
(503) 231-6828

Important Contacts

American Youth Hostels	(503) 683-3685
Bed and Breakfast Directories	(503) 476-2932
Fishing/Hunting Licenses	(503) 229-5403
Mt. Hood Recreation Association	(503) 622-3162
Oregon Bicycle Program	(503) 378-3432
Oregon Charterboat Association	(503) 563-3973
Oregon Guides and Packers	(503) 683-9552
Oregon Highway Division	(503) 378-6546
Oregon Paragliding Association	(503) 389-5411
Oregon Tourism	1-800-547-7842
	(503) 373-7307 (FAX)
Oregon Trail Coordinating Council	(503) 228-7245
Road Condition Report	(503) 889-3999
Rockhounding/Fossil Information	(503) 255-5135
Ski Industry Association	(503) 622-4822
State Parks Campsite	
(Information)	(503) 378-6305
(Reservations)	(503) 731-3411
Snow Report:	
Mt. Bachelor	(503) 382-2442
Mt. Hood	(503) 227-7669
Weather Service	(503) 236-7575

Federal Recreation Passport Program

Some federal parks, refuges, and facilities can be entered and used free of charge. Other areas and facilities require payment of entrance fees, user fees, special recreation permit fees, or some combination. A brochure published by the U.S. Department of the Interior entitled *Federal Recreation Passport Program* explains the entrance pass programs. Briefly stated, the passports most beneficial to park visitors are described below.

Passports are obtainable at all National Park System areas where entrance fees are charged, all National Forest Service supervisors' offices, and most Forest Service ranger station offices.

Note: The Golden Eagle, Golden Age, Golden Access, annual Parks Pass, Duck Stamp, single-visit entrance fees, recreation use fees, or special recreation permit fees do not cover charges by private concessionaires or other contractors operating within federal recreation areas.

Golden Eagle Passport

The Golden Eagle Passport is an annual entrance pass to federally operated parks, such as national parks, monuments, historic sites, recreation areas, and national wildlife refuges. It admits the permit holder and accompanying persons in a private, noncommercial vehicle. For those not traveling by private car, it admits the permit holder and family group. The pass costs $25, and is good for one calendar year from the date of purchase. The passport permits unlimited entries to all federal entrance fee areas.

Golden Age Passport

The Golden Age Passport is a lifetime entrance pass for citizens or permanent residents of the United States who are 62 years or older. There is a one-time fee of $10 for the passport. It admits the permit holder and any accompanying passengers in a single, private, noncommercial vehicle. Where entry is not by private car, the passport admits the permit holder, spouse, and children. It provides a 50% discount on federal use fees charged for facilities and services except those provided by private concessionaires. It must be obtained in person, with proof of age.

Golden Access Passport

The Golden Access Passport is a free lifetime entrance pass for citizens or permanent residents of the U.S. who have been medically determined to be blind or permanently disabled and, as a result, are eligible to receive benefits under federal law. It offers the same benefits as the Golden Age Passport, and must be obtained in person with proof of eligibility.

Park Pass

The Park Pass is an annual entrance permit to a specific park, monument, historic site, or recreation area in the National Park System that charges entrance fees. The pass admits the permit holder and any accompanying passengers in a single, private, noncommercial vehicle. Where entry is not by private vehicle, the pass admits the holder, spouse, children, and parents. The Park Pass does not cover use fees, such as fees for camping or parking. It is valid for entrance fees only. It is good for one calendar year and permits unlimited entries only to the park unit where it is purchased.

Federal Duck Stamp

Officially known as the Migratory Bird Hunting and Conservation Stamp and still required of waterfowl hunters, the federal Duck Stamp now also serves as an annual entrance fee permit to national wildlife refuges that charge entrance fees. The Duck Stamp is valid for entrance fees only and does not cover use fees. There is an annual cost for the stamp, which is good from July 1 through June 30 of the following year. The stamp permits unlimited entries to all national wildlife refuges that charge entrance fees and can be purchased at most post offices. The Federal Duck Stamp can be purchased at most post offices and many national wildlife refuges. Some sporting goods stores may carry them as a service to their customers. They may also be purchased through the mail from the U.S. Postal Service, Philatelic Sales Division, Washington, D.C. 20265-9997 for the price of the stamp plus $.50 postage and handling.

Trails lead to a world of lush forests, enchanting waterfalls, and inspiring mountains.

Backcountry Ethics

Spectacular backcountry areas throughout the United States await park campers. Rules for backcountry camping are common sense rules and important to control actions that may damage natural resources or take away from the enjoyment of an outdoor experience. In recent years, the term "going light" has taken on new meaning. To a backpacker, "going light" is the skill of paring down the load and leaving at home every ounce that can be spared. Today, "going light" also means sparing the land and traveling and camping by the rules of "low impact." The U.S. Forest Service suggests the following low impact rules. Although these suggestions were written for the hiker and backpacker, they are quite appropriate for anyone camping, whether traveling by foot, boat, bicycle, or horse.

General Information

▲ Keep noise to a minimum (exceptions may exist for areas inhabited by bears).
▲ Respect other campers' space and privacy.
▲ Do not short-cut trails or cut across switchbacks. Trails are designed and maintained to prevent erosion.
▲ Trampling meadows can obscure trails and damage vegetation.
▲ Do not pick flowers, dig up plants, or cut branches from live trees. Leave them for others to enjoy.
▲ Remember, it is unlawful to take, damage, or deface any park objects: rocks, plants, and artifacts.
▲ It is unlawful and dangerous to feed animals, large or small.

Planning a Trip

▲ Keep camping groups small.
▲ Take a gas stove to help conserve firewood.
▲ Bring sacks to carry out trash.
▲ Take a light shovel or trowel to help with personal sanitation.
▲ Carry a light basin or collapsible bucket for washing.
▲ Before traveling, study maps of the area, get permits if necessary and learn the terrain.
▲ Check on weather conditions and water availability.

Setting Up Camp

▲ Pick a campsite that does not require clearing away vegetation or leveling a tent site.
▲ Use an existing campsite, if available.

▲ Camp 300 feet from streams or springs. Law prohibits camping within ¼ mile of an only available water source.
▲ Do not cut trees, limbs, or brush to make camp improvements. Carry tent poles.

Breaking Camp

▲ Before leaving camp, naturalize the area. Replace rocks and scatter needles, leaves, and twigs around the campsite.
▲ Scout the area to be sure nothing is left behind. Everything packed into camp should be packed out. Try to make it appear as if no one has been there.

Campfires

▲ Even when campfires are permitted, use gas stoves when possible to conserve dwindling supplies of firewood.
▲ If a campfire is needed and allowed, use an existing campfire site. Keep it small.
▲ If new fire site is needed, select a safe spot away from rock ledges that would be blackened by smoke; away from meadows where it would destroy grass and leave a scar; away from dense brush, trees and duff, where it would be a fire hazard.
▲ Clear a circle of all burnable materials. Dig a shallow pit for the fire. Keep the sod intact.
▲ Use only fallen timber for firewood. Even standing dead trees are part of the beauty of wilderness, and are important to wildlife.
▲ Put fires out before leaving. Let the fire burn down to ashes, mix the ashes with dirt and water. Feel it with your hand. If it is cold out, cover the ashes in the pit with dirt, replace the sod, and naturalize the disturbed area.

Pack It In—Pack It Out

▲ Bring trash bags to carry out all trash that cannot be completely burned.
▲ Aluminum foil and aluminum-lined packages will not burn completely in a fire. Compact it and pack it out in trash bags.
▲ Cigarette butts, pull-tabs, and gum wrappers are litter too. They can spoil a campsite and trail.
▲ Do not bury trash! Animals dig it up.
▲ Try to pack out trash left by others. A good example may catch on!

Keep The Water Supply Clean

▲ Wash yourself, dishes, and clothes away from any source of water.

▲ Pour wash water on the ground away from streams and springs.

▲ Food scraps, toothpaste, even biodegradable soap will pollute streams and springs. Remember, it is your drinking water too!

▲ When deemed necessary, boil water or treat water before drinking it.

Disposing of Human Waste

▲ When nature calls, select a suitable spot at least 100 feet from open water, campsites, and trails. Dig a hole 4 to 6 inches deep. Try to keep the sod intact.

▲ After use, fill in the hole, completely burying waste. Then tramp in the sod.

Emergency Items

▲ According to conditions, carry rain gear, extra warm clothing such as a windbreaker, wool jacket, hat, and gloves. Sunscreen lotion is important to use in both warm and cold conditions.

▲ Keep extra high-energy foods like hard candies, chocolate, dried fruits, or liquids accessible. Do not overload yourself, but be prepared.

▲ Travel with a first-aid kit, map, compass, and whistle. Know how to use them.

▲ Always leave a trip plan with a family member or a friend. File a trip plan with park rangers.

▲ Mishaps are rare, but they do happen. Should one occur, remain calm. In case of an accident, someone should stay with the injured person. Notify appropriate officials.

Camping/Backpacking Supplies Checklist

Camping Equipment Checklist

The following checklists are designed to guide you in planning your next camping trip. Your needs will vary according to the type, length, and destination of your trip, as well as personal preferences, number of persons included, season of the year, and budget limitations.

Obviously, all items on the checklists aren't needed on any one trip. Since using checklists helps you think more methodically in planning, these extensive lists should serve merely as a reminder of items you may need.

When using these checklists to plan a trip, the item may be checked (√) if it needs to be taken. Upon returning, if the item was considered unnecessary, a slash could be used: ⅄. If a needed item was forgotten, a zero could be used (0); if the item has been depleted and needs to be replenished, an encircling of the check could be used; Ⓥ. This is of particular importance if you camp regularly and keep a camping box packed with staples that can be ready to go on a moment's notice.

Cooking equipment needs are quite dependent on the menu—whether you plan to cook and eat three balanced meals a day or whether you plan to eat non-cooked meals or snacks the entire trip. Many campers find it helpful to jot down the proposed menu for each meal on a 4″ × 6″ index card to help determine the grocery list as well as the equipment needed to prepare the meal. By planning this way, you'll avoid taking equipment you'll never use and you won't forget important items.

Typical Menu with Grocery and Equipment Needs

MEAL: Saturday breakfast	Number of Persons: 5	
MENU	GROCERY LIST	EQUIPMENT
orange juice	Tang	camp stove
bacon	10 slices bacon	gasoline, funnel
eggs	8 eggs	folding oven
(scrambled)	1 can biscuits	frying pan
biscuits	peach jelly	baking pan
	honey	pitcher
	margarine	mixing bowl
	salt	cooking fork, spoon
	pepper	

Shelter/Sleeping:

____ Air mattresses

____ Air mattress pump

____ Cots, folding

____ Cot pads

____ Ground cloth

____ Hammock

____ Mosquito netting

____ Sleeping bag or bed roll

____ Tarps (plastic & canvas)

____ Tent

____ Tent stakes, poles, guy ropes

____ Tent repair kit

____ Whisk broom

A catch for the campfire!

Extra Comfort:

_____ Camp stool
_____ Catalytic heater
_____ Folding chairs
_____ Folding table
_____ Fuel for lantern & heater
_____ Funnel
_____ Lantern
_____ Mantels for lantern
_____ Toilet, portable
_____ Toilet chemicals
_____ Toilet bags
_____ Wash basin

Clothing/Personal Gear:

_____ Bathing suit
_____ Boots, hiking & rain
_____ Cap/hat
_____ Facial tissues
_____ Flashlight (small), batteries
_____ Jacket/windbreaker
_____ Jeans/trousers
_____ Pajamas
_____ Pocket knife
_____ Poncho
_____ Prescription drugs
_____ Rain suit
_____ Sheath knife
_____ Shirts
_____ Shoes
_____ Shorts
_____ Socks
_____ Sweat shirt/sweater

_____ Thongs (for showering)
_____ Toilet articles (comb, soap, shaving equipment, tooth brush, toothpaste, mirror, etc.)
_____ Toilet paper
_____ Towels
_____ Underwear
_____ Washcloth

Safety/Health:

_____ First-aid kit
_____ First-aid manual
_____ Fire extinguisher
_____ Insect bite remedy
_____ Insect repellant
_____ Insect spray/bomb
_____ Poison ivy lotion
_____ Safety pins
_____ Sewing repair kit
_____ Scissors
_____ Snake bite kit
_____ Sunburn lotion
_____ Suntan cream
_____ Water purifier

Optional:

_____ Binoculars
_____ Camera, film, tripod, light meter
_____ Canteen
_____ Compass
_____ Fishing tackle
_____ Frisbee, horseshoes, washers, etc.

_____ Games for car travel & rainy day
_____ Hobby equipment
_____ Identification books: birds, flowers, rocks, stars, trees, etc.
_____ Knapsack/day pack for hikes
_____ Magnifying glass
_____ Map of area
_____ Notebook & pencil
_____ Sunglasses

Miscellaneous:

_____ Bucket/pail
_____ Candles
_____ Clothesline
_____ Clothespins
_____ Electrical extension cord
_____ Flashlight (large), batteries
_____ Hammer
_____ Hand axe/hatchet
_____ Nails
_____ Newspapers
_____ Pliers
_____ Rope
_____ Saw, bow or folding
_____ Sharpening stone/file
_____ Shovel
_____ Tape, masking or plastic
_____ Twine/cord
_____ Wire
_____ Work gloves

Good planning makes for relaxing enjoyment!

Cooking Equipment Checklist

Food Preparation/ Serving/Storing:

_____ Aluminum foil
_____ Bags (large & small, plastic & paper)
_____ Bottle/juice can opener
_____ Bowls, nested with lids for mixing, serving & storing
_____ Can opener
_____ Colander
_____ Fork, long-handled
_____ Ice chest
_____ Ice pick
_____ Knife, large
_____ Knife, paring
_____ Ladle for soups & stews
_____ Measuring cup
_____ Measuring spoon
_____ Pancake turner
_____ Potato & carrot peeler
_____ Recipes
_____ Rotary beater
_____ Spatula
_____ Spoon, large
_____ Tongs
_____ Towels, paper

_____ Water jug
_____ Wax paper/plastic wrap

Cooking:

_____ Baking pans
_____ Charcoal
_____ Charcoal grill (hibachi or small collapsible type)
_____ Charcoal lighter
_____ Coffee pot
_____ Cook kit, nested/pots & pans with lids
_____ Fuel for stove (gasoline/kerosene/liquid propane)
_____ Griddle
_____ Hot pads/asbestos gloves
_____ Matches
Ovens for baking:
_____ Cast iron dutch oven
_____ Folding oven for fuel stoves
_____ Reflector oven
_____ Tote oven
_____ Skewers
_____ Skillet with cover
_____ Stove, portable

_____ Toaster (folding camp type)
_____ Wire grill for open fire

Eating:

_____ Bowls for cereal, salad, soup
_____ Cups, paper
_____ Forks
_____ Glasses, plastic
_____ Knives
_____ Napkins, paper
_____ Pitcher, plastic
_____ Plates (plastic, aluminum, paper)
_____ Spoons
_____ Table cloth, plastic

Clean-Up:

_____ Detergent (Bio-degradable soap)
_____ Dish pan
_____ Dish rag
_____ Dish towels
_____ Scouring pad
_____ Scouring powder
_____ Sponge

Hiking/Backpacking Checklist

This list is not meant to be all inclusive or necessary for each trip. It is a guide in choosing the proper gear. Although this list was prepared for the hiker/backpacker, it is quite appropriate for anyone using the backcountry, whether they are traveling by foot, canoe, bicycle, or horse. Parentheses indicate those optional items that you may not want to carry depending upon the length of the trip, weather conditions, personal preferences, or necessity.

Backpacking doesn't get any better than this. Oregon has hundreds of miles to trek for any level of hiking skill.

Ten Essentials for Any Trip:

___ Map
___ Compass
___ First-aid kit
___ Pocket knife
___ Signaling device
___ Extra clothing
___ Extra food
___ Small flashlight/extra bulb & batteries
___ Fire starter/candle/waterproof matches
___ Sunglasses

Day Trip (add to the above):

___ Comfortable boots or walking shoes
___ Rain parka or 60/40 parka

___ Day Pack
___ Water bottle/canteen
___ Cup
___ Water purification tablets
___ Insect repellant
___ Sun lotion
___ Chapstick
___ Food
___ Brimmed hat
___ (Guide book)
___ Toilet paper & trowel
___ (Camera & film)
___ (Binoculars)
___ (Book)
___ Wallet & I.D.
___ Car key & coins for phone
___ Moleskin for blisters
___ Whistle

Overnight or Longer Trips (add the following):

___ Backpack
___ Sleeping bag
___ Foam pad
___ (Tent)
___ (Bivouac cover)
___ (Ground cloth/poncho)
___ Stove
___ Extra fuel
___ Cooking pot(s)
___ Pot scrubber
___ Spoon (knife & fork)
___ (Extra cup/bowl)
___ Extra socks
___ Extra shirt(s)
___ Extra pants/shorts
___ Extra underwear
___ Wool shirt/sweater
___ (Camp shoes)
___ Bandana

___ (Gloves)
___ (Extra water container)
___ Nylon cord
___ Extra matches
___ Soap
___ Toothbrush/powder/floss
___ Mirror
___ Medicines
___ (Snake bite kit)
___ (Notebook & pencil)
___ Licenses & permits
___ (Playing cards)
___ (Zip-lock bags)
___ (Rip stop repair tape)
___ Repair kit—wire, rivets, pins, buttons, thread, needle, boot strings

Map Symbols

 AIRPORT

 BACKCOUNTRY CAMPSITE

 BOAT LAUNCH

 CAMPGROUND

 FISHING

 FOOD

 FUEL

 GROUP CAMPING

 GENERAL STORE

 HANDICAP ACCESS

 HIKING TRAIL

 HORSEBACK TRAIL

 INFORMATION

 INTERPRETIVE TRAIL

 LODGING

 MARINA

 PARKING

 PICNIC

 RANGER STATION

 RESTROOMS

 SWIMMING

 TRAILER SANITATION STATION

F.R.= Forest Road Service
C.R.= County Road
S.R.= State Route or Highway
I= Interstate Route or Highway

*Recreation sites scattered throughout the region. See BLM map on page 34 for site locations.

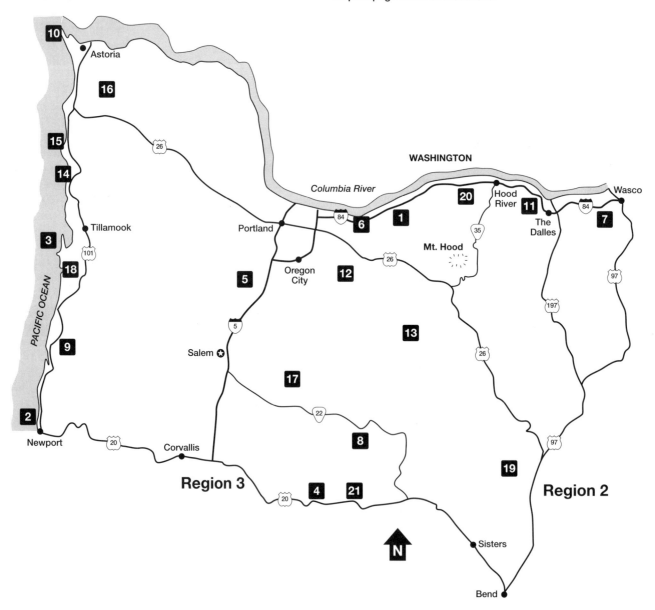

Ainsworth State Park

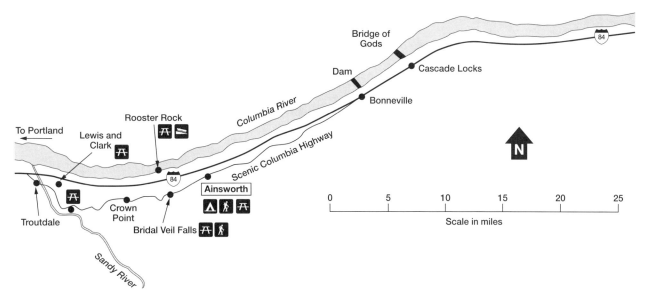

For Information

Ainsworth State Park
c/o Columbia River Gorge District Office
P.O. Box 100
Corbett, OR 97019
(503) 695-2261
FAX—695-2226

Location

Ainsworth State Park is located near Multnomah Falls at the foot of St. Peter's Dome in the spectacular Columbia River Gorge National Scenic Area. Just 37 miles east of Portland, take Exit 35 off I-84 to reach the park. Providing great access to other points of interest in the area, the park covers 156 acres in a fir and hemlock forest. Elevation is 100 feet. *Note:* See Columbia River Gorge National Scenic Area Map (page 37) for location of park.

Facilities and Activities

The campground is open mid-April through late October and operates on a first-come, first-served basis.

45 RV campsites w/full hookups (60' maximum length)	flush toilets
pull-through sites	tables
showers	fire pits
drinking water	trailer dump station
	9 picnic sites
	hiking/sightseeing

Ainsworth is a perfect base camp to see the spectacular features of the Columbia River Gorge National Scenic Area such as Multnomah Falls, North America's second highest.

Beverly Beach State Park

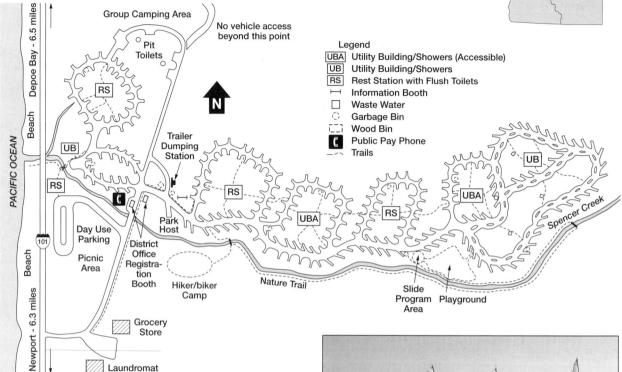

Legend

UBA	Utility Building/Showers (Accessible)
UB	Utility Building/Showers
RS	Rest Station with Flush Toilets
⊢	Information Booth
□	Waste Water
○	Garbage Bin
⌐	Wood Bin
ℂ	Public Pay Phone
---	Trails

For Information

Beverly Beach State Park
198 NE 123rd Street
Newport, OR 97365
(503) 265-4560
FAX—265-8917

Adventures are endless.

Location

Located on the east side of U.S. 101, 7 miles north of Newport, Beverly Beach State Park features a campground and picnic facility convenient to several miles of sandy ocean beaches and a variety of coastal recreation attractions. The park has dense shore pine and covers 130 acres. Among many nearby attractions, the Oregon Coast Aquarium features North America's largest walk-through Seabird Aviary. The tufted puffin and roughly 100 other seabirds native to the Oregon coast can be seen here.

Facilities and Activities

The campground is open year-round. Reservations are accepted from Memorial Day weekend through Labor Day.

53 RV campsites w/full hookups (65′ maximum length)
75 RV campsites w/ electric & water only
151 tent campsites/5 group tent areas
hiker/biker camp area
    pull-through sites
    showers
    drinking water
    flush toilets
    tables
playground/swimming
beachcombing/fishing
hiking/trails
slide program
grocery store/laundromat near park entrance
accessible campsites/restrooms/showers for
    people with disabilities

Bureau of Land Management Recreation Sites

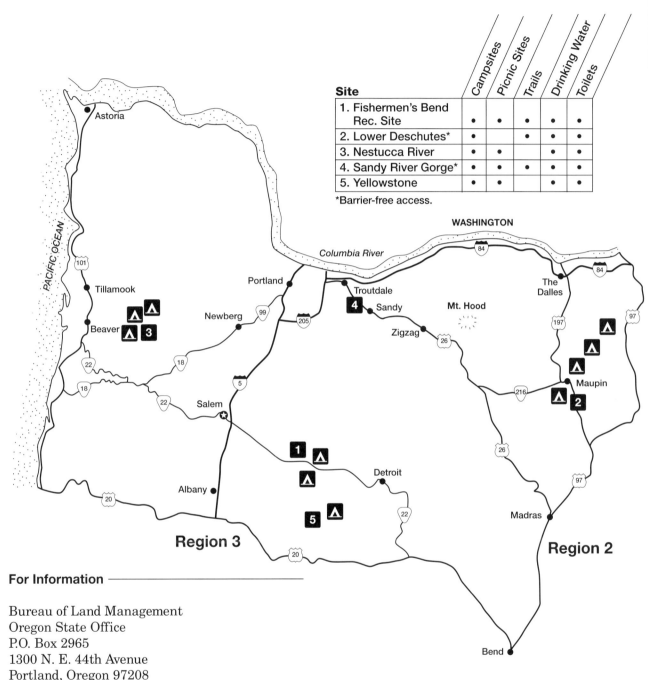

Site	Campsites	Picnic Sites	Trails	Drinking Water	Toilets
1. Fishermen's Bend Rec. Site	•	•	•	•	•
2. Lower Deschutes*	•		•	•	•
3. Nestucca River	•	•		•	•
4. Sandy River Gorge*	•	•	•	•	•
5. Yellowstone	•	•		•	•

*Barrier-free access.

For Information

Bureau of Land Management
Oregon State Office
P.O. Box 2965
1300 N. E. 44th Avenue
Portland, Oregon 97208
(503) 280-7001

Site Descriptions/Activities

1. **Fishermen's Bend Recreation Site:** Nestled along a forested curve of the North Santiam River, this site is highly developed. *Activities:* Interpretive trails for hiking, boating/rafting, and fishing.

2. **Lower Deschutes Wild and Scenic River:** The river presents a wide variety of activities for adventurous visitors. At Shears Falls, traditional Native Americans lean from tall platforms over the river to dipnet steelhead and salmon. The Scenic Byway runs on an old railroad grade for 36 miles of the river. Numerous

drive-in campsites await visitors to this beautiful river setting. A State Waterways Boater Pass is required for boating on the river. *Activities:* Boating, rafting, fishing, hunting, wildlife viewing, historic sightseeing, ORV playing, hiking, and swimming.

3. **Nestucca River:** The upper Nestucca River is an Oregon Scenic Waterway segment paralleled by the Nestucca River Back Country Byway. Visitors can drive or ride through the lush forests of Oregon's Coast Range. Four BLM sites are available along the river. *Activities:* Fishing, hunting, observing wildlife, and exploring a historic site.

4. **Sandy River Gorge:** The Sandy Wild and Scenic River winds its way through this spectacular 800-foot-deep, heavily forested gorge. Low-elevation old-growth forests, riparian woodlands and fern- and moss-laden cliffs dominate the landscape. Facilities are available at Multnomah County's Oxbow Park, a highly developed recreation area along the Sandy River. *Activities:* Boating/rafting, fishing, wildlife viewing, geological sightseeing, hiking, and swimming.

5. **Yellowstone:** Oregon's oldest trees enshroud the steep slopes surrounding Crabtree Lake. Quartzville Wild and Scenic River flows gently into a placid arm of the 10-mile-long Green Peter Reservoir. *Activities:* Boating/rafting, fishing, hunting, viewing wildlife, botanical sightseeing, hiking, mineral collecting, and swimming.

Cape Lookout State Park

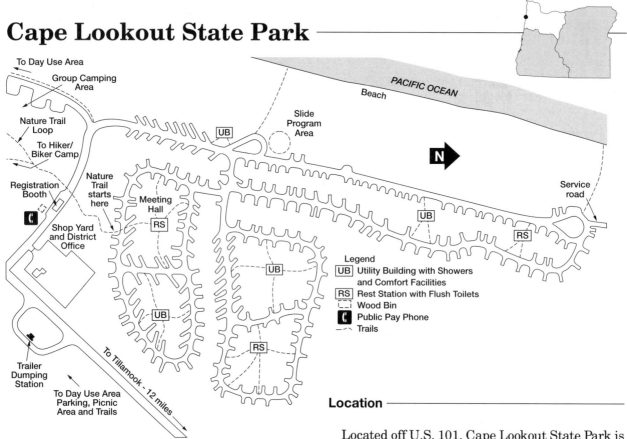

For Information

Cape Lookout State Park
13000 Whiskey Creek Road W.
Tillamook, OR 97141
(503) 842-3182
FAX—842-3647

Location

Located off U.S. 101, Cape Lookout State Park is just 12 miles SW of Tillamook (known for its cheese factory and salmon/steelhead fishing). The park covers 2,014 acres where coastal rain forest, rugged cliffs, sandy beaches, and pristine Netart's estuary form the backdrop for a variety of recreational pursuits. Cape Lookout is one of several interesting attractions along the Three Capes Scenic Drive. Cape Meares, Three Arches National Wildlife Refuge, and Netart's Bay are nearby attractions.

Cape Lookout State Park *(continued)*

Facilities and Activities

Open year-round, reservations are accepted from Memorial Day weekend through Labor Day.

54 RV campsites w/full hookups (62′ maximum
   length)
   showers
   drinking water
   flush toilets
   tables
   wood stoves
   trailer dump station
1 RV campsite w/electric & water only
195 tent campsites/4 group tent areas
hiker/biker camp area
121 picnic sites/beachside day-use
swimming/beachcombing
hiking/5.5 miles of trails
sightseeing/geology
slide program/nature study
accessible campsites/restrooms/showers for
   people with disabilities

*Fly a kite, build a sand castle, or hunt for agates—
broad, sandy beaches invite fun for all.* ▶

Cascadia State Park

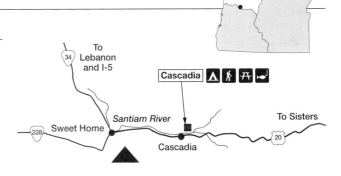

For Information

Cascadia State Park
c/o Armitage State Park
P.O. Box 7515
Eugene, OR 97401
(503) 686-7592
FAX—686-7925

Location

Just 14 miles east of Sweet Home on U.S. 20, Cascadia State Park is located on the banks of the South Santiam River in the western foothills of the Cascade Mountains. Heavily timbered with fir, the park covers 258 acres at an elevation of 860 feet. Cascadia provides wonderful access to river swimming and fishing, and a scenic waterfall.

Facilities and Activities

The campground is open mid-April through late October. It operates on a first-come, first-served basis except for group camping. To make reservations for group picnic and camp facilities, call the park.

26 unimproved tent campsites w/limited nearby
   facilities
1 group tent area
   drinking water
   flush toilets
   tables
134 picnic sites
3 group picnic sites
play area/swimming/fishing
hiking/2 miles of trails
accessible restrooms for people with disabilities

Champoeg State Park

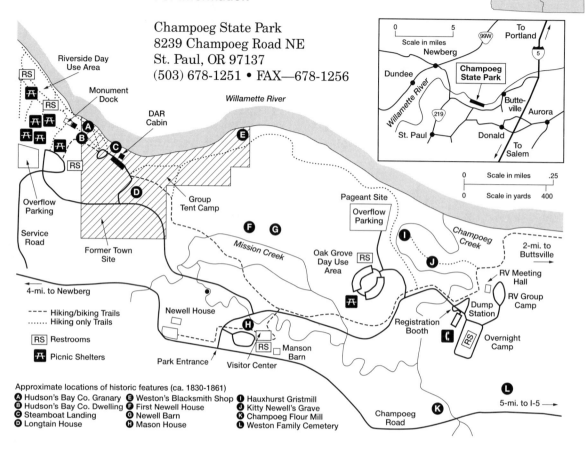

For Information

Champoeg State Park
8239 Champoeg Road NE
St. Paul, OR 97137
(503) 678-1251 • FAX—678-1256

Approximate locations of historic features (ca. 1830-1861)
- **A** Hudson's Bay Co. Granary
- **B** Hudson's Bay Co. Dwelling
- **C** Steamboat Landing
- **D** Longtain House
- **E** Weston's Blacksmith Shop
- **F** First Newell House
- **G** Newell Barn
- **H** Mason House
- **I** Hauxhurst Gristmill
- **J** Kitty Newell's Grave
- **K** Champoeg Flour Mill
- **L** Weston Family Cemetery

Location

Champoeg State Park is located off U.S. 99W, 7 miles east of Newberg; Exit 278 off I-5. The park is located on the Willamette Valley site where the provisional government for the region's first American commonwealth was founded in 1843. The visitor center museum traces the past history of a Kalapooya Indian community, a pioneer townsite, and a steamboat port located on the Willamette River. There is an annual Champoeg Historical Pageant held in July at the 2,700-seat amphitheater. The visitor center also offers an interpretive store and group meeting room. Other points of interest include a log cabin museum, a townsite archaeological dig, and a historic barn restoration. The park provides an extensive biking/hiking trail system along the river. Private boat docks are located 5 miles from the park.

Facilities and Activities

The campground is open year-round and operates on a first-come, first-served basis. Reservations are available for the group picnic area, the RV group camp area, and the meeting hall.

48 RV campsites w/electric & water only (32' maximum length)
RV group camp
30 overflow spaces
6 primitive tent campsites
utility shelters w/electric & water
  showers
  drinking water
  flush toilets
  wood stoves
  tables
  trailer dump station
group meeting hall
510 picnic sites
13 group picnic sites
courtesy dock/boating/fishing/waterskiing
hiking/trails/bicycling
museum/history/visitor center
accessible campsites/restrooms/showers for people with disabilities

Columbia River Gorge National Scenic Area

For Information

Columbia River Gorge National Scenic Area
Suite 200
902 Wasco Avenue
Hood River, Oregon 97031
(503) 386-2333
(503) 695-2220 (Wind & Weather)

Location

The first of its kind, Columbia River Gorge National Scenic Area was so designated in 1986 to preserve an 80-mile portion of the spectacular gorge of the Columbia River between Oregon and Washington. Just a 20-minute drive east of Portland, the Scenic Area encompasses 253,500 acres between Troutdale and the Deschutes River in Oregon, and Washougal and Wishram in Washington. Five bridges connect Washington's scenic and historic Lewis and Clark Highway 14 with the more heavily used I-84 in Oregon. Back-road excursions on both sides of the river are exceptional. Two sections of the Columbia River Scenic Highway offer dramatic panoramic views from the Oregon side.

Points of Interest

▲ The gorge is a historical transportation corridor dating from the Lewis and Clark Expedition and Oregon Trail to the present Columbia River Highway.
▲ It is the only sea level route through the rugged Cascade Mountains.
▲ The area is renowned for outstanding scenery and spectacular waterfalls including the famous Multnomah and Latourell Falls.
▲ The region abounds with American Indian cultural sites.
▲ Exceptional recreation opportunities include hiking, camping, birding, and excellent fishing; the gorge is world-renowned for windsurfing.
▲ Adjacent areas include Columbia Wilderness and the White Salmon and Klickitat Wild and Scenic Rivers.

Facilities and Activities

338 RV and tent campsites
1 group shelter
3 group campsites
picnicking
hiking
boating, boat ramps
rafting (on adjoining rivers)
sailing, windsurfing
swimming
fishing
biking
horseback riding
berry picking
auto touring
visitor centers, exhibits, and museums
ranger stations

Columbia River Gorge National Scenic Area (*continued*)

WASHINGTON

OREGON

Campgrounds	Total Sites	RVs	Tents	Fees	Drinking Water	Toilets Flush	Sanitary Dump
Ainsworth State Park* (OPR)	45	•	•	•	•	F	•
Beacon Rock (WPR)	35	•	•	•	•	F	•
Cascade Locks Marine Park (city)	35	•	•	•	•	F	
Eagle Creek (NFS)	20	•	•	•	•	F	
Horsethief Lake (WPR)	14	•	•	•	•	F	
Memaloose State Park* (OPR)	110	•	•	•	•	F	
Oxbow Park (county)	45	•	•	•	•	F	
Viento State Park* (OPR)	63	•	•	•	•	F	
Wyeth (NFS)	14	•	•	•	•	F	
Group Campgrounds Eagle Creek Overlook**	1	•	•	•	•	F	
Wyeth (OPR)	3	•	•	•	•	F	
Horsecamp† Herman Creek	7	•	•	•	•	F	

*Showers, water, sewer, electricity available.
**One shelter available.
Campground operated by: OPR = Oregon Parks and Recreation; NFS = National Forest Service; WPR = Washington Parks and Recreation.
†Loading dock and corral, no hook-ups, trailers up to 24′ only.

General Information

▲ Fees are charged for camping in designated parks.
▲ Visitor centers, displays, exhibits and scenic overlooks are located at several points of interest.

▲ Noteworthy places on the map, but not inclusive of all sites are:

In Oregon:
Ⓐ Ranger station (maps, information, publications)
Ⓑ Portland Women's Forum State Park (major viewpoint)
Ⓒ Crown Point (exceptional 30-mile vista, visitor center)
Ⓓ Latourell Falls (spectacular waterfall, hiking trail)
Ⓔ Multnomah Falls (620′ waterfall, displays, hiking trails)
Ⓕ Cascade Locks (marine park and historical museum)
Ⓖ The Dalles (staging area for Oregon trail, museum, and windsurfing mecca)
Ⓗ Deschutes River State Recreation Area

In Washington:
Ⓘ Beacon Rock State Park (historical landmark, viewpoint)
Ⓙ Bonneville Lock and Dam (visitor center, displays)
Ⓚ Bridge of the Gods (Pacific Crest Trail crossing, historical)
Ⓛ Wishram (railroad town, Celilo Falls Monument, Viewpoint overlooking the flooded site of an historic Native American fishing ground)

▲ Campgrounds are typically opened from April through October. They operate on a first-come, first-served basis. Fees are charged per night and vary according to facilities provided. Method of registration will vary depending on the operating agency.

Columbia River Gorge National Scenic Area *(continued)*

▲ RV and trailer lengths are limited at some campgrounds: Eagle Creek-30'; Herman Creek-24'; Wyeth-32'.

▲ Group campgrounds are available at Eagle Creek Overlook and Wyeth. Eagle Creek provides a 30' × 20' shelter with a fireplace, picnic tables and flush toilets. No electricity is available and the water system is closed during winter. Groups up to 150 people and 40 cars can be accommodated. Call the Columbia Gorge Ranger Station, 503-695-2276 for reservations. Wyeth campground has 3 group tent or trailer sites (up to 32') with no hook-ups. It is open from April to October with water and restrooms.

▲ Handicap accesses are typically available at restrooms, exhibits, and viewpoints.

▲ Windsurfing is excellent within the gorge. The Dalles, Hood River, and parks along the river are world-renowned for exceptional wind conditions. Parks and surrounding communities welcome boarders and provide excellent facilities and services for all skill levels.

Deschutes River State Recreation Area

Hold on!

For Information

Deschutes River State Recreation Area
89600 Biggs-Rufus Highway
Wasco, OR 97065
(503) 739-2322
FAX—739-2221

Location

Deschutes River State Recreation Area is located off I-5, 17 miles east of The Dalles. This attractive river recreation complex is on the banks of the Deschutes River near its confluence with the mighty Columbia River. High basalt cliffs tower above this 80-acre park that is filled with planted shade and poplar trees in the developed sections. At an elevation of 200 feet, the park offers riverside hiking and biking trails that lead from the primitive-site campground. There is a boat ramp located at Heritage Landing day-use park across the river from the park. It has an Oregon Trail interpretive shelter near the point where the river was forded by pioneer wagon trains.

Facilities and Activities

The campground is open mid-April through late October and operates on a first-come, first-served basis.

33 primitive tent campsites (25' maximum RV
  length)
  drinking water
  flush toilets
  stoves
  tables
25 picnic sites
fishing/boating
hiking/biking/trails

Detroit State Park

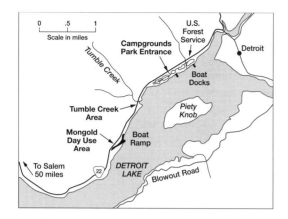

For Information

Detroit State Park
c/o Silver Falls State park
20024 Silver Falls Hwy.
Sublimity, OR 97385
(503) 873-8681
FAX—873-8925

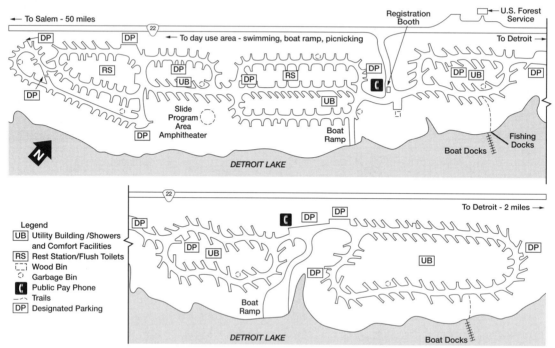

Location

Covering 104 acres, Detroit Lake State Park is located on S.R. 22, 50 miles east of Salem and 2 miles west of the the community of Detroit. The park is on the shore of the scenic reservoir in North Santiam river canyon, which is located on the western slope of the Cascade mountains. Here campers get an excellent view of nearby Mt. Jefferson. The park, elevation 1,580 feet, is forested with second-growth Douglas fir. Nearby attractions include a fishing resort and private boat rentals.

Facilities and Activities

The campground is open mid-April through late October. Reservations are accepted Memorial Day weekend through Labor Day.

107 RV campsites w/full hookups (35–40′ maximum length)
70 RV campsites w/ electric & water only
134 tent campsites
   showers
   drinking water
   flush toilets
   wood stoves & electric stoves
   tables
   trailer dump station
72 picnic sites (1 mile west of campground)
boat ramp/moorage dock/fishing dock
swim area/waterskiing
sightseeing/slide program
accessible campsites/restrooms/fishing dock for
   people with disabilities

Devil's Lake State Park

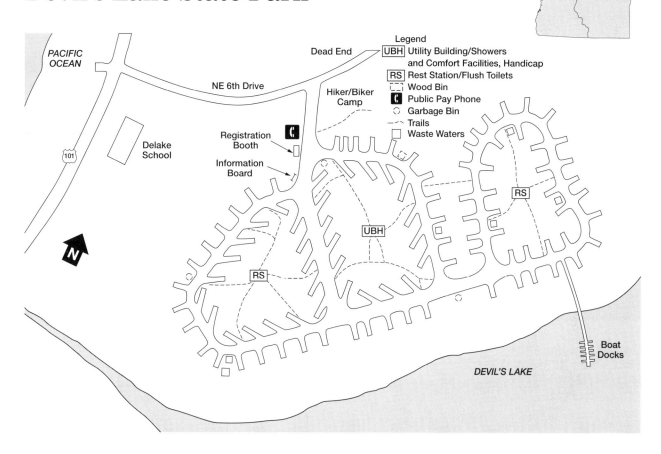

For Information

Devil's Lake State Park
c/o Beverly Beach State Park
198 NE 123rd Street
Newport, OR 97365
(503) 265-4560
FAX—265-8917

Location

Devil's Lake State Park, east of U.S. 101 in Lincoln City, is located on a quiet freshwater lake separated from the roaring ocean surf by the 100-foot-long "D" River, known as the "shortest river in the world." The park, 109 acres in size, is on the southwest shore of the lake and one-quarter of a mile from ocean beach. The picnic area is located just off East Devil's Lake Road (2.75 miles south of the campground) and features restrooms, picnic tables, and a boat ramp. "D" River State Wayside, within walking distance of the campground along Highway 101, provides access to the beach, restroom, and a tourist information center. Nearby activities are numerous along the "20 Miracle Miles" of U.S. 101, from

Neskowin to Depoe Bay. Recreational opportunities include horseback riding, boating, beachcombing, swimming, waterskiing, and golf. Freshwater and ocean fishing are excellent in the vicinity of Devil's Lake.

Facilities and Activities

The campground is open year-round. Reservations are accepted from Memorial Day weekend through Labor Day.

32 RV campsites w/full hookups (35′ maximum
    length)
100 tent campsites
    showers
    drinking water
    flush toilets
    tables
19 picnic sites
boat ramp (east side of lake)
boat dock/boating/fishing
waterskiing/swimming/beachcombing
accessible campsites/restrooms/showers/fishing
    dock for people with disabilities

Fort Stevens State Park

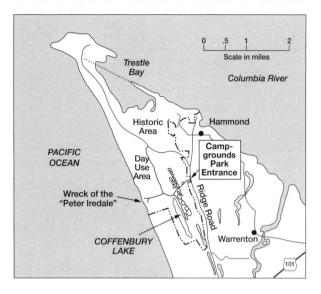

For Information

Fort Stevens State Park
Hammond, OR 97121
(503) 861-3170
FAX—861-1672

Location

Fort Stevens State Park is 10 miles west of Astoria off U.S. 101. It fronts the Pacific Ocean and mouth of the Columbia River. This 3,670-acre historical park is the site of an ex-military fort built during the Civil War to guard the mouth of the Columbia River. Visitors can explore the abandoned gun batteries and a military museum. The nearby commander's station provides a scenic view of the Columbia and South Jetty. The South Jetty, built in the late 1800's, is a good spot to see birds, whales, and big ships crossing the river bar. Fish such as sea perch, ling cod, and salmon can be caught from the jetty. The park provides access to miles of ocean beach with sand dunes. The remains of a wrecked British sailing ship (1906) is a major beach attraction just one mile west of the campground. Guided tours of the underground Battery Mishler and the back of a restored 1954 "deuce-and-a-half" army truck are also available in the summer.

Facilities and Activities

The campground, largest in the Oregon State Parks System, is open year-round. Reservations are accepted from Memorial Day weekend through Labor Day.

213 RV campsites w/full hookups (50′ maximum
    length)
130 RV campsites w/electric & water only
261 tent campsites
8 tent group areas
hiker/biker camp
    pull-through sites (36)
    showers
    drinking water
    flush toilets
    wood stoves
    tables
    trailer dump station
225 picnic sites
2 group picnic areas (by reservation)
play area/swim area/beachcombing
boat ramp/boating/fishing
windsurfing/swimming
hiking/9 miles of trails
bicycling/8.5 miles of trails
sightseeing/birdwatching/wildlife viewing
museum/slide program/tours/history
gift shop
accessible restrooms for people with disabilities

Oregon's coastal and inland waters teem with anglers' dreams.

Memaloose State Park

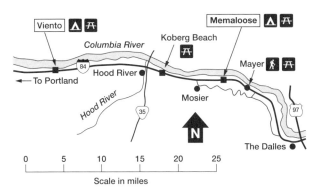

For Information

Memaloose State Park
c/o Columbia River Gorge District Office
P.O. Box 100
Corbett, OR 97019
(503) 695-2261
FAX—695-2226

Location

Memaloose State Park is 11 miles west of The Dalles on I-84. This 337-acre park is located on the steep, rocky riverbank in Columbia River Gorge National Scenic Area (high point at 532 feet above river). Surrounded by scattered ponderosa pine, Douglas fir, and oak, the park is directly accessible only to westbound traffic; eastbound traffic must exit 3 miles east of the park and return on the freeway to the park entrance. The campground overlooks the gorgeous Columbia River and an island that was once used as an ancient Indian burial ground. There is a swimming area and boat launch located at Mayer day-use park, 10 miles east of the campground. *Note:* See Columbia River Gorge National Scenic Area Map on page 38 for location of park.

Facilities and Activities

The campground is open mid-April through late October and operates on a first-come, first-served basis.

43 RV campsites w/full hookups (60′ maximum
   length)
   showers
   drinking water
   flush toilets
   tables
   trailer dump station
67 tent campsites
sightseeing/history

The Columbia River Gorge is renowned for its breathtaking scenery and windsurfing.

Milo McIver State Park

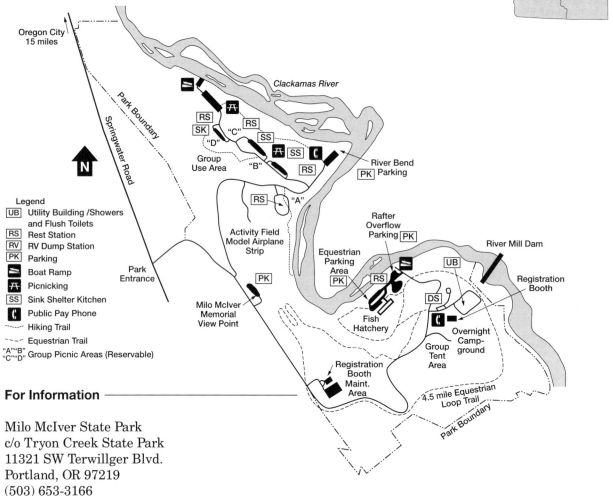

Legend
- **UB** Utility Building /Showers and Flush Toilets
- **RS** Rest Station
- **RV** RV Dump Station
- **PK** Parking
- **⬗** Boat Ramp
- **⛱** Picnicking
- **SS** Sink Shelter Kitchen
- **☎** Public Pay Phone
- **····** Hiking Trail
- **‑‑‑‑** Equestrian Trail
- "A""B" "C""D" Group Picnic Areas (Reservable)

For Information

Milo McIver State Park
c/o Tryon Creek State Park
11321 SW Terwilliger Blvd.
Portland, OR 97219
(503) 653-3166
FAX—653-3225

Location

Milo McIver State Park is located five miles northwest of Estacada off Springwater Road (S.R. 211). The scenic park provides a variety of recreational opportunities for visitors. Only 20 miles from Portland, it is a popular spot for picnickers from the metropolitan area, as well as a convenient camping place. The park comprises 937 acres of lawns and wooded areas on a series of natural terraces above the Clackamas River. A memorial viewpoint near the entrance provides a panoramic view of three prominent mountain peaks: Mt. St. Helens, Mt. Adams, and Mt. Hood. The Clackamas River offers great variety for rafting and fishing. The Oregon State Department of Fish and Wildlife fish hatchery is located in the south park day-use area. The fish hatchery annually raises and releases over one million Chinook salmon. A store and restaurant are located one mile from the campground.

Facilities and Activities

The campground is open mid-April through late October on a first-come, first-served basis.

42 RV campsites w/electric & water only (60′ maximum length)
3 group tent area
  showers
  drinking water
  flush toilets
  wood stoves
  tables
  trailer dump station
364 picnic sites
5 group picnic sites (by reservation)
boat ramp/boating/fishing
hiking/trails
horseback riding/4.5 miles of trails
scenery and wildlife viewing
accessible campsites/restrooms/boat ramp for
  people with disabilities

Mt. Hood National Forest

See charts on pages 47-52 for descriptions of numbered campgrounds

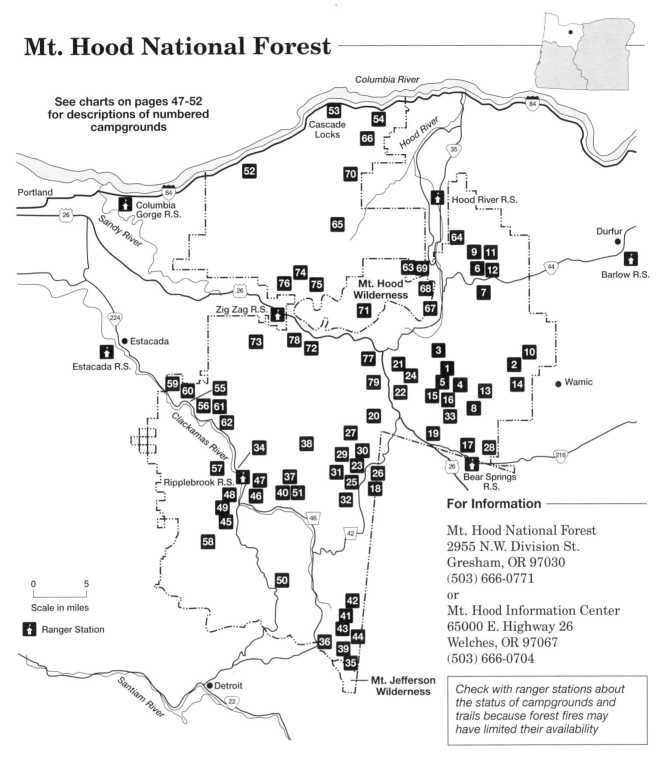

For Information

Mt. Hood National Forest
2955 N.W. Division St.
Gresham, OR 97030
(503) 666-0771
or
Mt. Hood Information Center
65000 E. Highway 26
Welches, OR 97067
(503) 666-0704

Check with ranger stations about the status of campgrounds and trails because forest fires may have limited their availability

Location

Located in northwest corner of Oregon, Mt. Hood National Forest straddles the Cascade Mountains from the spectacular Columbia River Gorge to the secluded beauty of Mt. Jefferson Wilderness Area just north of Detroit. Dominated by Oregon's tallest mountain and dormant volcano, Mt. Hood, the Forest is easily accessed for year-round recreation from I-84, U.S. 26, and S.R. 224, 22, and 216.

Points of Interest

▲ Outstanding fishing, breathtaking scenery, limitless recreation opportunities, and a wide diversity of plant and animal life can all be found in the Mt. Hood National Forest. Just one hour from Portland, Mt. Hood stands 11,235 feet high like the centerpiece of the forest. There visitors can find a multitude of alpine adventures to enjoy—winter and summer skiing (five ski areas);

Mt. Hood National Forest (continued)

spectacular sightseeing tours; hiking; climbing; biking; fishing; and historical sites including the Oregon Trail.

▲ Throughout the forest there are striking scenes of colorful wildflowers, inspiring wildlife, and spectacular waterfalls. Five wilderness areas feature fantastic opportunities for camping and hiking in solitude and beauty.

▲ Special places of interest include: the Columbia River Gorge National Scenic Area (described separately in **Region 1**); Multnomah Falls, the second highest in the country, dropping 620 feet; waterfalls at Wahkeena, Oneonta, Horsetail and Eagle Creek; lakes such as Wahtum, Lost, Trillium, Clear, Little Crater, and Timothy; the historic Timberline Lodge on Mt. Hood; Clackamas River Drive; Olallie Lake Scenic Area; the Cloud Cap area on the north side of Mt. Hood; and Bagby Hot Springs.

Wilderness Areas

Badger Creek Wilderness, 24,000 acres in size, is about 45 miles southwest of The Dalles and 67 miles east of Portland. Glacial features such as steep-walled, wide, U-shaped valleys contribute to the extensive geological and ecological diversity of this area. Lookout Mountain is the highest point in the wilderness. Forty-five miles of trails include the Badger Creek National Recreation Trail. The crest of Lookout Mountain provides commanding views of the Cascade Range and the eastern high desert country. Within the last few hundred years, the native tribes of the Wasco, Tenino, and Molalla have used the area for root digging, berry picking, and hunting. Three major access points are: F.R. 44 and 4410 via S.R. 35; F.R. 27 and 2710 via U.S. 97; and F.R. 48 and 4811. For more information contact: Barlow Ranger District—(503) 467-2291.

Bull of the Woods Wilderness, 34,900 acres in size, is located 68 miles southeast of Portland and 65 miles east of Salem. The Willamette National Forest administers 8,500 acres of the wilderness. The steep, mountainous slopes that make up the wilderness are deeply cut by a number of streams. Dense stands of giant trees cover most of the slopes. More than a dozen lakes are located in the wilderness, but are isolated from one another by steep, high ridges. For more information contact: Estacada Ranger District—(503) 630-6861.

Columbia Wilderness, 39,000 acres in size, is located about 30 miles east of Portland, and 8

miles west of Hood River. It offers a wide variety of scenic and natural features. On the north side, rugged and steep mountainsides exhibit spectacular basalt cliffs, rocky slopes, and rock outcroppings. Visitors can wander past talus slopes, waterfalls, lakes, and mountain peaks. All three main creeks of the wilderness, Tanner Creek, Eagle Creek, and Herman Creek, flow north to join the Columbia River. There are approximately 96 miles of trails within the wilderness that offer hiking, beautiful scenery, and good backcountry camping. One of the best known and most heavily-used trails is the Pacific Crest National Scenic Trail, which crosses Benson Plateau in the western portion of the wilderness. Another heavily-used trail is the Eagle Creek Trail which provides access to many popular scenic attractions and camping spots like Punch Bowl Falls, Tunnel Falls, and Wahtum Lake. Two primary access points for entry into the Wilderness are I-84 in the Columbia Gorge on the north, and Wahtum Lake on the southeast side. For more information contact: Hood River Ranger District—(503) 352-6002.

Mt. Hood Wilderness consists of 47,100 acres located about 23 miles east of Sandy and 45 miles east of Portland. The elevation ranges from 2,000 feet at the lowest point to 11,235 feet at the summit of Mt. Hood. Permanent glaciers cloak the top of Mt. Hood, and glacial-fed streams, high lakes, and alpine meadows acclaimed for their late summer tapestry of bright wildflowers, surround the mountain peak. This heavily used wilderness contains 112 miles of trails including the Pacific Crest National Scenic Trail, which traverses the wilderness. Elk Meadows, Ramona Falls, Elk Cove, Paradise Park, and the Timberline Trail offer special attractions and have the greatest recreation use. Various high lakes dotting the foothills of Mt. Hood also attract many visitors. Two primary access points include F.R. 18 and 50 via U.S. 26, and F.R. 3555 and 3512 via S.R. 35. For more information contact: Zigzag Ranger District—(503) 666-0704; or Hood River Ranger District—(503) 352-6002.

Mt. Jefferson Wilderness is located on the Mt. Hood, Willamette, and Deschutes national forests. It contains the second highest peak in Oregon, Mt. Jefferson (10,497 feet). Although nearly 3,000 feet smaller, Three-Fingered Jack (7,841 feet) is also a spectacular site for hikers and horseback riders in the area. Both mountains are extinct volcanoes. The wilderness area contains 111,177 acres that are 62% timber. Within the boundaries there are 150 lakes with about 60 of these lakes providing habitat for eastern brook and/or rainbow trout. There are nearly 194 miles of trails. Key access points are located on all sides of the wilderness, some beginning in the Deschutes National Forest, others in the Willamette National Forest, and one in the Mt. Hood National Forest. Approximately 36 miles of the Pacific Crest National Scenic Trail run through the Mt. Jefferson Wilderness (accessed from U.S. 20 in the south and from Breitenbush Lake in the north). The hiking season usually extends from July 1 to October 1; trails can be blocked with snow banks throughout June and early July. Animals in the wilderness include deer, elk, black bear, and coyotes. For more information contact: Clackamas Ranger District—(503) 630-4256.

Salmon-Huckleberry consists of 44,560 acres and lies about 15 miles southeast of Sandy, and 55 miles southeast of Portland. Most of this area is covered with trees. Volcanic plugs, pinnacles, cliffs, and steep and sharply cut slopes add to the ruggedness of this area. Its main attraction is the nationally designated Wild and Scenic Salmon River and the associated Salmon River National Recreation Trail. The trail follows the river and offers a variety of scenic attractions such as waterfalls within the Salmon River Gorge. The western part of the Wilderness contains such trails as Eagle Creek Trail, Wildcat Mountain Trail, and Huckleberry Mountain Trail. U.S. 26 and Salmon River Road, S.R. 224 and Abbot Road, and F.R. 2613 provide the main access points to the Wilderness. For more information contact: Zigzag Ranger District—(503) 666-0704.

Barlow Ranger District

For Information

Barlow Ranger district
P.O. Box 67
Dufur, OR 97021
(503) 467-2291

Campground Locations/Activities

1. **Badger Lake:** Access via F.R. 4860. *Activities:* Hiking and fishing.

2. **Bonney Crossing:** 10 mi. W of Wamic via C.R. 226 and F.R. 48, 4890, and 4891. Also accessible 35 mi. E of Government Camp via U.S. Hwy. 26 and F.R. 35, 48, 4890, and 4891. *Activities:* Hiking and horseback riding (horse facilities/trails/wilderness).

3. **Bonney Meadows:** 26 mi. W of Wamic via C.R. 226 and F.R. 48, 4890, and 4891. *Activities:* Hiking (trails) and scenery.

4. **Boulder Lake** (Hike-in primitive road): Access F.R. 4880 and Trailhead #463. *Activities:* Hiking and scenery.

5. **Camp Windy:** West end of Badger Creek Wilderness. Access via F.R. 3550 and primitive road. *Activities:* Hiking and scenery.

6. **Eight Mile Crossing:** 17 mi. SW of Dufur via C.R. 1 and F.R. 44. *Activities:* Hiking and fishing.

7. **Fifteen Mile:** North border of Badger Creek Wilderness. Access via F.R. 2730 then a primitive road. *Activities:* Hiking and scenery.

Campground (see map on page 45)	Elevation (Feet)	Tent Sites	Tent/Trailer Sites	Trailer Length (Feet)	Fees	Drinking Water
1. Badger Lake	4,500	15				
2. Bonney Crossing	2,200		8	16	•	
3. Bonney Meadows	4,800		5	22		
4. Boulder Lake	4,560	4 (W)				
5. Camp Windy	4,800	2				
6. Eight Mile Crossing	4,200		24	30		
7. Fifteen Mile	4,600		3	16		
8. Forest Creek	3,000		8	22		
9. Knebal Springs Horse Camp	4,000		4	22		
10. Little Badger	2,200		15	16		
11. Lower Crossing	3,800		3	16		
12. Pebble Ford	4,000		4	16		
13. Post Camp	4,000		4	16		
14. Rock Creek*	2,200		33	26	•	•

(W) Walk-in campsites only.
*Barrier-free recreational opportunities.

8. **Forest Creek:** 20 mi. SW of Wamic via C.R. 226 and F.R. 48, 4885, and 3530. *Activities:* Hiking.

9. **Knebal Springs Horse Camp:** 21 mi. W of Dufur via C.R. 1 and F.R. 44, 4430, and 1720. *Activities:* Hiking and horseback riding (horse facilities/trails/spring water).

Barlow Ranger District *(continued)*

10. **Little Badger:** Entry into the southeast corner of Badger Creek Wilderness via F.R. 2710. *Activities:* Hiking and scenery.
11. **Lower Crossing:** Access via F.R. 4440 and primitive road. *Activities:* Hiking.
12. **Pebble Ford:** 18 mi. SW of Dufur via C.R. 1, on F.R. 44. *Activities:* Hiking.
13. **Post Camp:** Access via F.R. 4860 and Post Camp Road. *Activities:* Hiking.
14. **Rock Creek Reservoir:** 7.5 mi. W of Wamic via C.R. 226 and F.R. 48. *Activities:* Fishing (barrier-free), boating (no motors), swimming.

Bear Springs Ranger District

For Information

Bear Springs Ranger District
Route 1, Box 222
Maupin, OR 97037
(503) 328-6211
TDD 328-6292

Campground Locations/Activities

15. **Barlow Creek:** 29 mi. SE of Government Camp via U.S. 26 and F.R. 42 and 141. *Activities:* Fishing.
16. **Barlow Crossing:** 12 mi. SE of Government camp via U.S. 26 and F.R. 43. *Activities:* Fishing.
17. **Bear Springs:** 25 mi. W of Maupin via S.R. 216. *Activities:* Picnicking (shelters for reservation).
18. **Clackamas Lake:** 23 mi. SE of Government Camp via U.S. 26 and F.R. 42 and 4270. *Activities:* Fishing (artesian spring and natural fault caused this lake), Historic Guard Station, and horseback riding (horse facilities).
19. **Clear Creek Crossing:** 30 mi. W of Maupin via S.R. 216 and F.R. 2130. *Activities:* Fishing.
20. **Clear Lake:** 11 mi. SE of Government Camp via U.S. 26. *Activities:* Boating (no speed limit on lake), waterskiing, swimming, and fishing. (Depth of lake decreases during irrigation season and in summer time).
21. **Devil's Half Acre:** Located on Barlow Road. Access via F.R. 3530. *Activities:* Hiking.
22. **Frog Lake:** 8.5 mi. SE of Government Camp via U.S. 26. *Activities:* Boating, fishing, and swimming.
23. **Gone Creek:** 26.5 mi. S of Government Camp via U.S. 26 and F.R. 42 and 57. *Activities:* Boating, swimming, and fishing.
24. **Grindstone:** Located on Barlow. Access via F.R. 3530. *Activities:* Hiking.
25. **Hoodview:** 27 mi. S of Government Camp via U.S. 26 and F.R. 42 and 57. *Activities:* Boating, swimming, and fishing on Timothy Lake.

Campground (see map on page 45)	Elevation (Feet)	Tent Sites	Tent/Trailer Sites	Trailer Pad Length	Fees	Drinking Water
15. Barlow Creek	3,100	5				
16. Barlow Crossing	3,100	5				
17. Bear Springs*†	3,200		21	32	•	•
18. Clackamas Lake*	3,400		46	32	•	•
19. Clear Creek Crossing	3,000	5				
20. Clear Lake*	3,600		28	32	•	•
21. Devil's Half Acre	3,600	5				
22. Frog Lake*	3,800		33	22	•	•
23. Gone Creek*	3,200		50	32	•	•
24. Grindstone	3,400	3				
25. Hoodview*	3,200		43	32	•	•
26. Joe Graham Horse Camp	3,300		14	28	•	•
27. Little Crater Lake*	3,200		16	22	•	•
28. McCubbins Gulch	3,000	5				
29. Meditation Point	3,200	4 (W/B)				
30. Oak Fork†	3,200		47	32	•	•
31. Pine Point*†	3,200		25	32	•	•
32. Summit Lake	4,000	6				
33. White River Station	3,000	5				

(W/B) Walk-in, boat-in campsites only.
*Barrier-free recreational opportunities.
†Concessionaire operated.

26. **Joe Graham Horse Camp:** 23 mi. SE of Government Camp via U.S. 26 and F.R. 42. *Activities:* Horseback riding (horse facilities).
27. **Little Crater Lake:** 24 mi. SE of Government Camp via U.S. 26 and F.R. 42, 4280, and 58. *Activities:* Natural artesian spring and natural fault line create this wonder.

28. **McCubbins Gulch:** 25 mi. NW of Maupin via S.R. 216 and F.R. 2110. *Activities:* Picnicking and hiking.
29. **Meditation Point** (Hike-in, boat-in only): Located on north side of Timothy Lake, about 28 mi. S of Government Camp via U.S. 26 and F.R. 42 and 57. *Activities:* Hiking, fishing, boating, and swimming.
30. **Oak Fork:** 26.5 mi. S of Government Camp via U.S. 26 and F.R. 42 and 57. *Activities:* Boating and fishing on Timothy Lake.
31. **Pine Point:** 27 mi. S of Government Camp via U.S. 26 and F.R. 42 and 57. *Activities:* Hiking, boating, and fishing.
32. **Summit Lake:** 29 mi. SE of Government Camp via U.S. 26 and F.R. 42 and 141. *Activities:* Boating.
33. **White River Station:** Located on Barlow Road. 14 mi. SE of Government Camp via U.S. 26, S.R. 35, and F.R. 48 and 3530. *Activities:* Fishing.

Clackamas Ranger District

For Information

Clackamas Ranger District
Ripplebrook Ranger Station
Estacada, OR 97023
(503) 630-4256
TDD 834-2275 (also for local calls)

Campground Locations/Activities

34. **Alder Flat:** Access via S.R. 224 about 25 mi. SE of Estacada. *Activities:* Hike through old-growth forest to get to campground.
35. **Breitenbush Lake:** Located in Olallie Scenic Area. 64 mi. SE of Estacada via S.R. 224 and F.R. 46, 4690, and 4220. *Activities:* Boating, fishing, and hiking.
36. **Camp Ten:** 63.1 mi. SE of Estacada via S.R. 224 and F.R. 46, 4690, and 4220. *Activities:* Boating, fishing, and hiking.
37. **Hideaway Lake:** 43 mi. SE of Estacada via S.R. 224 and F.R. 57, 58, and 5830. *Activities:* Boating, swimming, fishing, and hiking.
38. **Highrock Springs:** 46 mi. SE of Estacada via S.R. 224 and F.R. 57 and 58. *Activities:* Huckleberry picking in the fall.
39. **Horseshoe Lake:** Located in Olallie Scenic Area. 62 mi. SE of Estacada via S.R. 224 and F.R. 46, 4690, and 4220. *Activities:* Hiking and fishing.
40. **Lake Harriet:** 34.5 mi. SE of Estacada via S.R. 224, F.R. 57, and W on F.R. 4630. *Activities:* Boating (no motors), swimming, and fishing.
41. **Lower Lake:** Located in Olallie Scenic Area. 61.5 mi. SE of Estacada via S.R. 224 and F.R. 46, 4690, and 4220. *Activities:* Hiking.

Campground (see map on page 45)	Elevation (Feet)	Tent Sites	Tent/Trailer Sites	Trailer Pad Length	Fees	Drinking Water
34. Alder Flat*	3,200	6 (W)				
35. Breitenbush Lake	5,500	20				
36. Camp Ten	4,900		7	16		
37. Hideaway Lake	4,500		9	16		
38. Highrock Springs	4,400	7				
39. Horseshoe Lake	5,200	4				
40. Lake Harriet*	2,500		13	30	•	•
41. Lower Lake	4,600		9	16		
42. Olallie Meadows	4,500		5	16		
43. Paul Dennis	5,000		15	16	•	•
44. Peninsula*	4,900		35	24	•	•
45. Raab*	1,500		27	22		
46. Rainbow*†	1,400		17	16	•	•
47. Ripplebrook*†	1,500		13	16	•	•
48. Riverford*	1,500	10				
49. Riverside*†	1,400		16	22	•	•
50. Round Lake	3,750	6				
51. Shellrock Creek	2,300		5	16		

(W) Walk-in campsites only.
*Barrier-free recreational opportunities.
†Concessionaire operated.

42. **Olallie Meadows:** Located in Olallie Scenic Area. 58.4 mi. SE of Estacada via S.R. 224 and F.R. 46, 4690, and 4220. *Activities:* Hiking.
43. **Paul Dennis:** 63.3 mi. SE of Estacada via S.R. 224 and F.R. 46, 4690, and 4220. *Activities:* boating, swimming, fishing, and hiking.
44. **Peninsula:** 63.6 mi. SE of Estacada via S.R. 224 and F.R. 46, 4690, and 4220. *Activities:* Boating, swimming, and fishing.

Clackamas Ranger District (continued)

45. **Raab:** 32 mi. SE of Estacada via S.R. 224 and F.R. 46 and 63. *Activities:* Fishing.
46. **Rainbow:** 27 mi. SE of Estacada via S.R. 224 and F.R. 46. *Activities:* Swimming, fishing, and hiking.
47. **Ripplebrook:** 26.5 mi. SE of Estacada via S.R. 224. *Activities:* Fishing.

48. **Riverford:** 31 mi. SE of Estacada via S.R. 224. *Activities:* Swimming, fishing, and hiking.
49. **Riverside:** 29.7 mi. SE of Estacada via S.R. 224. *Activities:* Fishing and hiking.
50. **Round Lake:** Access via F.R. 6370. *Activities:* Hiking and fishing.
51. **Shellrock Creek:** 35 mi. SE of Estacada via S.R. 224 and F.R. 57 and 58. *Activities:* Fishing.

Columbia Gorge Ranger District

For Information

Columbia Gorge Ranger District
31520 S.E. Woodard Road
Troutdale, OR 97060
(503) 695-2276

Campground Locations/Activities

52. **Eagle Creek:** West of Cascade Locks via I-84, exit 41, turn right. *Activities:* Swimming, fishing, hiking, and biking.
53. **Herman Creek Horse Camp:** 1.6 mi. E of Cascade Locks via I-84. *Activities:* Designed for equestrians, horse handling facilities.
54. **Wyeth:** 7 mi. E of Cascade Locks via I-84, exit 51. *Activities:* Swimming, fishing, and hiking.

Campgrounds (see map on page 45)	Elevation (Feet)	Tent/Trailer Sites	Trailer Pad Length	Fees	Drinking Water
52. Eagle Creek*	200	20	22	•	•
53. Herman Creek Horse Camp*	1,000	7	24	•	•
54. Wyeth*	400	17	32	•	•

*Barrier-free recreational opportunities.
Eagle Creek (reservations available) and Wyeth have group campsites.

Even in summer, there are winter sports to enjoy on Mt. Hood.

Estacada Ranger District

Campground (see map on page 45)	Elevation (Feet)	Tent/Trailer Sites	Trailer Pad Length	Fees	Drinking Water
55. Armstrong*†	900	12	16	•	•
56. Fish Creek*†	900	24	16	•	•
57. Indian Henry*†	1,100	86(R)	22	•	•
58. Kingfisher†	1,600	23	16	•	•
59. Lazy Bend†	800	21	16	•	•
60. Lockaby*†	900	30	16	•	•
61. Roaring River†	1,000	19	16	•	•
62. Sunstrip†	1,000	9	18	•	•

(R) Campsite reservations available through National Recreation Reservation System (1-800-280-CAMP).
*Barrier-free recreational opportunities.
†Concessionaire operated.

For Information

Estacada Ranger District
595 N.W. Industrial Way
Estacada, OR 97023
(503) 630-6861
TDD 630-6863

Campground Locations/Activities

55. **Armstrong:** Located on Clackamas River, 15.4 mi. SE of Estacada via S.R. 224. *Activities:* Fishing.

56. **Fish Creek:** Located on Clackamas River, 15.4 mi. SE of Estacada via S.R. 224. *Activities:* Fishing.

57. **Indian Henry:** 23.5 mi. SE of Estacada via S.R. 224. *Activities:* Hiking and fishing.

58. **Kingfisher:** 35 mi. SE of Estacada via S.R. 224 and F.R. 46, 63, and 70. *Activities:* Fishing, Hot Springs Fork of Collawash River.

59. **Lazy Bend:** 10.7 mi. SE of Estacada via S.R. 224. *Activities:* Fishing.

60. **Lockaby:** Located on Clackamas River, 15.3 mi. SE of Estacada via S.R. 224. *Activities:* Fishing.

61. **Roaring River:** Located at junction of Roaring and Clackamas Rivers, 18.2 mi. SE of Estacada via S.R. 224. *Activities:* Hiking and fishing.

62. **Sunstrip:** 19 mi. SE of Estacada via S.R. 224. *Activities:* Fishing.

Hood River Ranger District

For Information

Hood River Ranger District
6780 Highway 35 South
Mt. Hood-Parkdale, OR 97041
(503) 352-6002 (local)

Campground Locations/Activities

63. **Cloud Cap:** Located on Timberline Trail, 20 mi. S of Parkdale via S.R. 35 and F.R. 3512. *Activities:* Hiking and scenery.

64. **Gibson Prairie Horse Camp:** 15 mi. S of Hood River via S.R. 35 and F.R. 17. *Activities:* Horseback riding (horse facilities and trails).

65. **Lost Lake:** 28 mi. SW of Hood River via C.R. N22 and F.R. 13. *Activities:* Hiking, bicycling, boating, fishing, and swimming.

Campground (see map on page 45)	Elevation (Feet)	Tent Sites	Tent/Trailer Sites	Trailer Pad Length	Fees	Drinking Water
63. Cloud Cap	6,000	3				
64. Gibson Prairie Horse Camp			4	16		
65. Lost Lake*†	3,150		91(G)	24	•	•
66. Rainy Lake	4,100	4				
67. Robinhood*	3,600		24	18	•	•
68. Sherwood*	3,000		14	16	•	•
69. Tilly Jane	5,600	14(W)				
70. Wahtum Lake	4,000	5				

(G) Group sites available.
(W) Walk-in campsites.
*Barrier-free recreational opportunities.
†Concessionaire operated.

Hood River Ranger District *(continued)*

66. **Rainy Lake:** SW of Hood River via community of Dee and F.R. 2810 and 2820. *Activities:* Hiking and ⅛ mi. to lake for fishing.
67. **Robinhood:** 15 mi. SE of Parkdale via S.R. 35. *Activities:* Hiking and fishing.
68. **Sherwood:** 11 mi. SE of Parkdale via S.R. 35. *Activities:* Hiking and fishing.

69. **Tilly Jane:** 19.7 mi. SW of Parkdale via S.R. 35 and F.R. 3512. *Activities:* Hiking; historic area.
70. **Wahtum Lake:** 28 mi. SW of Hood River via community of Dee and F.R. 13 and 1310. *Activities:* Hiking, fishing, boating, and swimming.

Zigzag Ranger District

For Information

Zigzag Ranger District
70220 E. Hwy. 26
Zigzag, OR 97049
(503) 666-0704
(503) 622-3191

Campground Locations/Activities

71. **Alpine:** 5.4 mi. NE of Government Camp on S.R. 173. *Activities:* Hiking and scenery.
72. **Camp Creek:** 2.9 mi. SE of Rhododendron on U.S. 26. *Activities:* Hiking and fishing.
73. **Green Canyon:** 5.6 mi. S of Welches on F.R. 2618. *Activities:* Hiking (access into Salmon-Huckleberry Wilderness) and fishing.
74. **McNeil:** Across road from Riley Horse Camp near Sandy River; 5 mi. NE of Zigzag on F.R. 18. *Activities:* Bicycling, fishing, mushrooming, and exploring geologic features.
75. **Lost Creek:** 7 mi. NE of Zigzag via F.R. 18 and 1825. *Activities:* Hiking and fishing.
76. **Riley Horse Camp:** 6 mi. NE of Zigzag via F.R. 18, 1825, and 382. *Activities:* Fishing, hiking, and horseback riding (trails and horse facilities).
77. **Still Creek:** 1.7 mi. SE of Government Camp via U.S. 26. *Activities:* Hiking (Barlow trail) and fishing.
78. **Tollgate:** .5 mi. SE of Rhododendron on U.S. 26. *Activities:* Fishing and hiking (Barlow trail); historically restored CCC site.
79. **Trillium Lake:** 3.5 mi. SE of Government Camp via U.S. 26 and F.R. 2656. *Activities:* Boating, swimming, fishing, and bicycling.

Campground (see map on page 45)	Elevation (Feet)	Tent Sites	Tent/Trailer Sites	Trailer Pad Length	Fees	Drinking Water
71. Alpine†	5,600	16			•	•
72. Camp Creek*†	2,200		24(R)	22	•	•
73. Green Canyon*	1,600		15	22		
74. McNeil	2,000		34	22		
75. Lost Creek	2,000				•	•
75. Riley Horse Camp†	2,100		14(R)	16	•	•
76. Still Creek†	1,400	27(R)			•	•
77. Tollgate†	2,000		15(R)	16	•	•
78. Trillium Lake*†	3,600		39(R)	22	•	•

(R) Campsite reservations available through National Recreation Reservation System (1-800-280-CAMP).
 *Barrier-free recreational opportunities.
 †Concessionaire operated.

From any direction throughout the year, Mt. Hood graces the landscape with its majestic snow-capped peak.

Nehalem Bay State Park

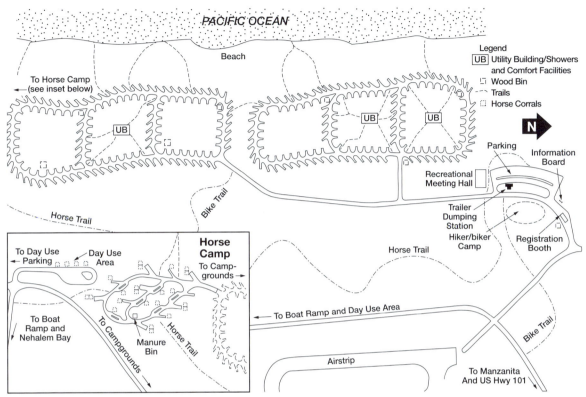

For Information

Nehalem Bay State [...]
c/o Cape Lookout S[...]
13000 Whiskey Cre[...]
Tillamook, OR 9714[...]
(503) 842-3182
FAX—842-3647

Location

Nehalem Bay State [...]
ning of a 4-mile sand [...]
Ocean from Nehalem [...]
101 at the Bayshore J[...]
halfway between Se[...]
beach extends the [...]
Nehalem Bay Spit and [...]
combers. Driftwood, a[...]
ing floats, and even [...] chunk of
beeswax from 16th Century Spanish merchant
ships can be found. Visitors can hike, bike, clam,
crab, and horseback ride in the park. A camp for
horseback riders and a recreational meeting hall
are available. Reservations for both are recom-

[...] ear-round, but are required during the
[...] (September-April). The Oregon Coast
[...] ery popular with hikers. Some of the
[...] stic views from the trail can be seen
[...] Falcon and Neah-Kah-Nie Mt., both of
[...] ocated in Oswald West State Park, just
[...] th of Nehalem Bay on Highway 101.
[...] ay State Park is one of the few parks
[...] hat is accessible by air. The 2,400-foot
[...] irport is less than ¼ mile from the
[...] entrance.

Activities

[...] ound is open year-round on a first-
[...] rved basis. Reservations are avail-
[...] eting hall and horse camp corral.

291 RV campsites w/electric & water only (60′
  maximum length)
17 primitive horse campsites
6 primitive airport campsites
  showers
  tubs

[handwritten note:] Reservation Center $44.ºº 1-800 452-5687 Res. # 973786 B27 16th thru 18th www.PRD.State.OR.US

Nehalem Bay State Park (continued)

drinking water
flush toilets
wood stoves
tables
trailer dump station
37 picnic sites
meeting hall
beachcombing/swimming
boat ramp/boating/fishing
hiking/biking/2 miles of trails
horseback riding/7.5 miles of trails
accessible campsites/restrooms/boat ramp for
    people with disabilities

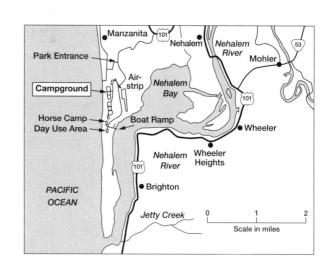

Oswald West State Park

For Information

Oswald West State Park
c/o Cape Lookout State Park
13000 Whiskey Creek Road West
Tillamook, OR 97141
(503) 842-3182
FAX—842-3647

Location

Oswald West State Park, located 10 miles south of Cannon Beach on U.S. 101, offers a unique camping experience within its 2,500 acres. The campground, accessible only by foot, is located ¼ mile by blacktop trail from the parking area (wheelbarrows are provided for equipment). Oswald actually lies

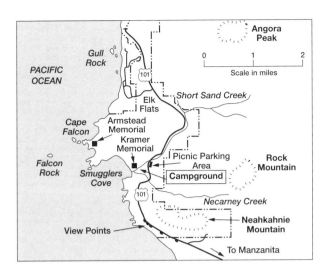

The Oregon Coast Trail offers superb sightseeing from the mouth of the Columbia River all the way to the California border.

on heavily forested slopes of the coastal mountain range and fronts more than 4 miles of ocean. Trails access cozy sandy beaches on a sheltered bay. A 13-mile segment of the Oregon Coast hiking trail leads through the park, to the summit of 1,700-foot Neah-Kah-Nie Mountain, and through primeval woods to the tip of Cape Falcon. Cape Falcon, a well-known navigational landmark, is the home of a dense old-growth sitka spruce forest with trees that measure more than 12 feet in diameter and 200 feet tall. Neah-Kah-Nie Mountain is rich in folklore. The name means "place of fire" or "home of fire." Local native Americans regularly burned the mountain to provide better grazing habitat for herds of deer and elk, their primary source of food. During the spring and fall migratory season, California grey whales can be viewed from the many highway turn-outs on Neah-Kah-Nie.

Facilities and Activities

The park's campsites are open mid-April through late October on a first-come, first-served basis.

36 primitive walk-in tent campsites
   drinking water
   flush toilets
   stoves
   tables
68 picnic sites
beachcombing/clamming/fishing
swimming/surfing/kayaking
photography/birdwatching/whale watching
sightseeing/wildlife viewing/geology
hiking/Oregon Coast Trail
One-quarter-mile blacktop trail leads to
   campsites from parking areas

"Digging for treasure" along the coast takes on a different meaning for many beachcombers.

Oswald West State Park 55

Saddle Mountain State Park

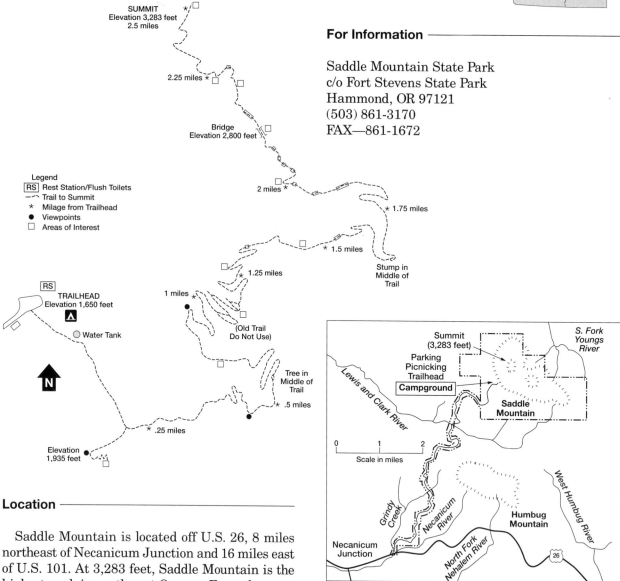

SUMMIT
Elevation 3,283 feet
2.5 miles

2.25 miles

Bridge
Elevation 2,800 feet

2 miles

1.75 miles

1.5 miles

Stump in
Middle of
Trail

1.25 miles

1 miles

(Old Trail
Do Not Use)

Legend
RS Rest Station/Flush Toilets
- - Trail to Summit
* Milage from Trailhead
● Viewpoints
□ Areas of Interest

RS
TRAILHEAD
Elevation 1,650 feet

Water Tank

N

Tree in
Middle of
Trail

.5 miles

.25 miles

Elevation
1,935 feet

**Summit
(3,283 feet)**

Parking
Picnicking
Trailhead
Campground

Saddle
Mountain

S. Fork
Youngs
River

Lewis and Clark River

Grindy Creek

Necanicum River

North Fork Nehalem River

Humbug
Mountain

West Humbug River

Necanicum
Junction

26

0   1   2
Scale in miles

For Information

Saddle Mountain State Park
c/o Fort Stevens State Park
Hammond, OR 97121
(503) 861-3170
FAX—861-1672

Location

Saddle Mountain is located off U.S. 26, 8 miles northeast of Necanicum Junction and 16 miles east of U.S. 101. At 3,283 feet, Saddle Mountain is the highest peak in northwest Oregon. From the summit, visitors have a panoramic view of Nehalem Bay and the Pacific Ocean to the west, the Columbia River to the north, and many of the snow-capped peaks in the Cascade Range to the east. Although the park encompasses 2,921 acres, the primitive-site campground is small. A 3-mile trail leads from the campground to the summit of Saddle Mountain. Wildlife seeking refuge in the park include deer, elk, coyotes, and squirrels. The forested area provides nesting for many species of birds including great-horned owls, nuthatches, and rufous humming-birds. The mountain top protects many rare plant species: Saddle Mountain bittercress and saxifrage, alpine lily, pink fawn-lily, hairy-stemmed sidalcea, sedge, and trillium.

Facilities and Activities

The campground is open mid-April through late October on a first-come, first-served basis.

10 primitive tent campsites
    drinking water
    flush toilets
    wood stoves
    tables
31 picnic sites
hiking/3-mile trail to summit
sightseeing/wildlife viewing
nature study/geology

Silver Falls State Park

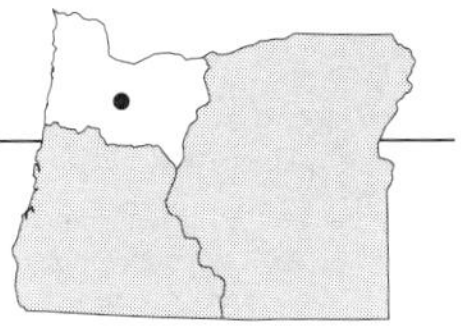

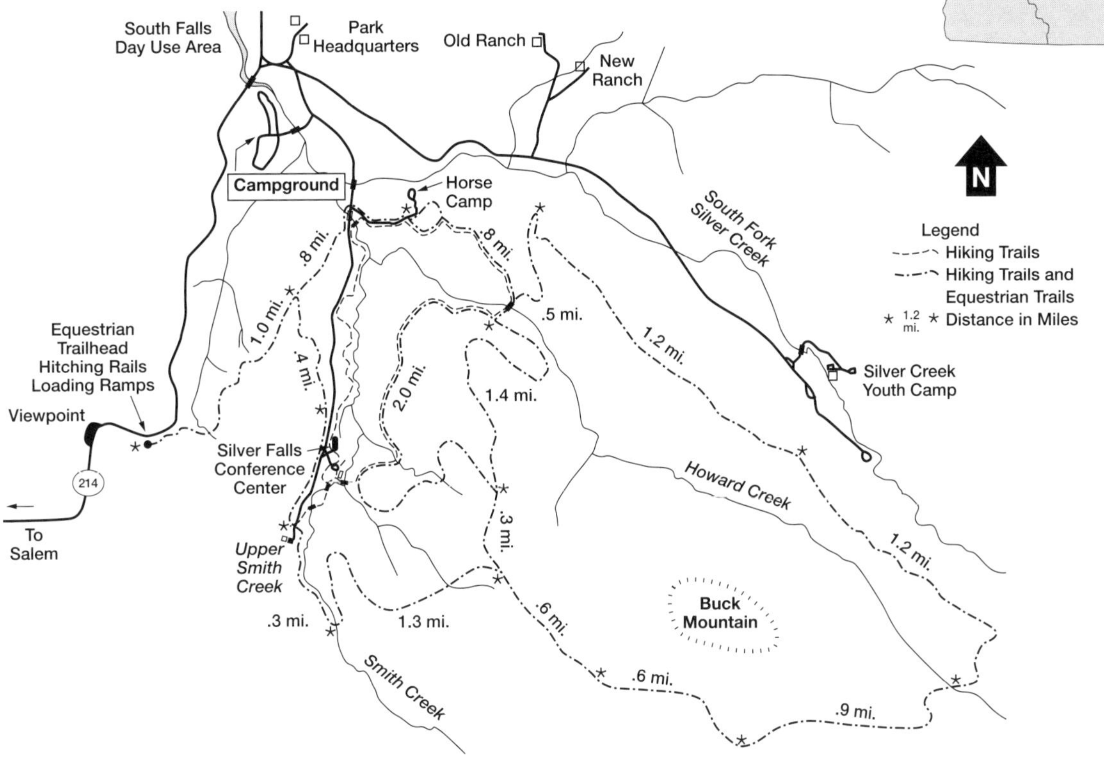

For Information

Silver Falls State Park
20024 Silver Falls Highway
Sublimity, OR 97385
(503) 873-8681
FAX—873-8925

Location

Silver Falls State Park, largest park in the state park system, is located on S.R. 214, 26 miles east of Salem. The park's 8,706 acres encompass two deep, densely forested canyons in the foothills of the Cascade Mountains. There is a 7-mile hiking trail that winds through canyons to ten waterfalls, five over 100 feet high (highest is 177-foot South Falls). Silver Falls State Park also features a 4-mile paved bicycle trail and a 14-mile equestrian trail. There is a horse camp and a variety of overnight group facilities. The Day Lodge, located above South Falls, and South Falls viewpoint are listed on the National Register of Historic Places. The lodge helps visitors appreciate the park's history, wildlife, plantlife, and geography. A swimming area was created in Silver Creek near the picnic area. A sandy beach on the east bank of the creek provides ample room for visitors to enjoy a cool refreshing dip or relax in the sun. There is a playground with rustic log structures and nearby restrooms.

Facilities and Activities

The campground is open mid-April through late October on a first-come, first-served basis. The conference center is open year-round. Other group lodging facilities are available March through November, weather permitting. Reservations are available for all group activities.

53 RV campsites w/electric & water only (for all sizes of RVs)
51 tent campsites
3 group tent areas
group trailer camp
rustic group lodges
horse camp
conference center w/food service/overnight lodging
day-use lodge
meeting hall
   showers
   tubs
   drinking water

Silver Falls State Park (*continued*)

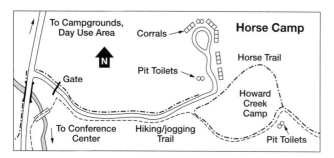

flush toilets
tables
trailer dump station
209 picnic sites
2 group picnic sites
swim area/sightseeing/nature study
fishing/nature study/geology
hiking/7 miles of trails
bicycling/4 miles of trails
horseback riding/14 miles of trails/corrals
small food concession

Siuslaw National Forest (North Half)

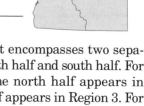

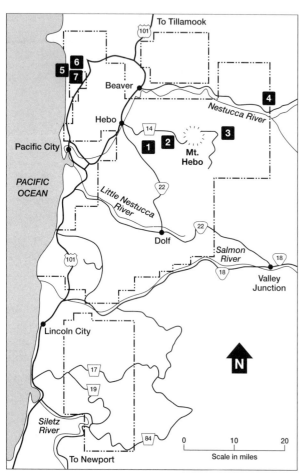

Location

Siuslaw National Forest encompasses two separate land portions, the north half and south half. For purposes of this guide, the north half appears in Region 1 and the south half appears in Region 3. For detailed information on the Siuslaw National Forest, the south half, and campgrounds in Alsea, Mapleton, and Waldport Ranger Districts, see page 187 of this *Camper's Guide*.

The 630,395-acre Siuslaw National Forest is located in the Coast Mountain Range of Oregon and extends from Tillamook to Coos Bay. U.S. 101 provides access to a dense Douglas-fir forest that is complemented by lush, green vegetation and miles of sand dunes. The Pacific Ocean creates a moderate climate over the Forest and constantly changes its mood. Expect summer fog. Temperatures remain mild year-round.

Points of Interest

Visitors find a variety of things to do including camping, beachcombing, whale watching, fishing, crabbing, hiking, boating, and sand dune touring. The forest offers diversity in hiking opportunities ranging from walks on the beach to lengthy hikes on wilderness trails. All offices provide information on regulations and activities such as plant gathering, off-road-vehicle use, fire precautions, hunting, and fishing.

See Region 3 "Points of Interest" in the south half of Siuslaw National Forest for details on Oregon Dunes National Recreation Area and Cape Perpetua Scenic Area.

Wilderness Areas

Cummins Creek Wilderness covers approximately 9,173 acres and offers camping, fishing,

For Information

Siuslaw National Forest
4077 S.W. Research Way
P.O. Box 1148
Corvallis, OR 97339-1148
(503) 750-7000

and hiking. Accessible from U.S. 101, the wilderness is 11 miles south of Waldport. The wilderness preserves the last remaining virgin stands of Sitka spruce, western hemlock, and Douglas fir in Oregon's coast lands. The Cummins Ridge Trail, 6.2 miles, leads east along Cummins Ridge through dense Sitka spruce and Douglas fir stands. For more information contact: Waldport Ranger District—(503) 563-3211.

Drift Creek Wilderness, about 5,800 acres in size, contains one of the largest stands of old-growth forest in the Coast Range Mountains. Hiking trails provide access to the unique terrain of this wilderness. Horses and pack animals are not allowed within the wilderness due to sensitive soils. For more information contact: Waldport Ranger District—(503) 563-3211.

Rock Creek Wilderness encompasses approximately 7,400 acres of steep and brushy terrain. Hiking trails provide access through the wilderness. For more information contact: Waldport Ranger District—(503) 563-3211.

Hebo Ranger District

For Information

Hebo Ranger District
P.O. Box 324
Hebo, OR 97122
(503) 392-3161

Campground Locations/Activities

1. **Castle Rock:** 5 mi. SE of Hebo via S.R. 22. *Activities:* Fishing.
2. **Hebo Lake:** 5 mi. E of Hebo via S.R. 22, then F.R. 14. *Activities:* Picnic shelter, small lake, and fishing.
3. **Mt. Hebo:** 10 mi. E of Hebo via S.R. 22, then F.R. 14. *Activities:* About 2 mi. E of Mt. Hebo viewpoint. Hiking. Trailhead for portion of Pioneer-Indian Trail.
4. **Rocky Bend:** 13 mi. SE of Beaver via C.R. 858, then F.R. 85. *Activities:* On Nestucca River, fishing.
5. **Sandbeach:** Access is 6 mi. N of Pacific City via C.R. 871 and 872. *Activities:* ORV play area, sand dunes, beachcombing, area entry reservation required on summer holiday weekends; dump station available.
6. **Sandbeach East:** 10 mi. N of Pacific City. *Activities:* Fee per vehicle. Area entry reservations required on summer holiday weekends; ORV, play area.
7. **Sandbeach West:** 10 mi. N of Pacific City. *Activities:* Fee per vehicle. Area entry reservations required on summer holiday weekends; ORV, play area.

Campground	Elevation (Feet)	Tent Sites	Tent/Trailer Sites	Fee	Water	Toilets F = Flush V = Vault
1. Castle Rock*	200	4			•	V
2. Hebo Lake	1,600	10		•	•	V
3. Mt. Hebo	3,000	4				V
4. Rocky Bend	600	9				V
5. Sandbeach**	50		101	•	•	F/V
6. Sandbeach East	50		100	•	•	F/V
7. Sandbeach West	50		75	•	•	F/V

*Walk-in camping from parking area.
**Picnic facilities available.
Sandbeach West and East are handicap accessible.

The Siuslaw National Forest is popular for its miles of sand dunes and beaches, a haven for ORV play.

The Cove Palisades State Park

Deschutes River Campground

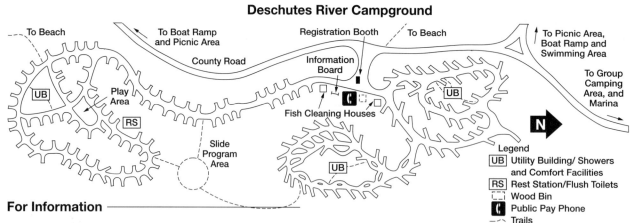

For Information

The Cove Palisades State Park
Route 1, Box 60 CP
Culver, OR 97734
(503) 546-3412
FAX—546-2220

Location

The Cove Palisades State Park is located in the famous Central Oregon recreation area of Lake Billy Chinook, formed in an impressive rim-rocked canyon by the Deschutes and Crooked rivers. The park can be accessed from U.S. 97, 15 miles southwest of Madras. Located at an elevation of 1,750 feet, the Cove Palisades' 4,119 acres include towering cliffs, gnarled junipers, and the waters of Lake Billy Chinook. There are two campgrounds in the park. The Crooked River Camp is located on the canyon rim of the Crooked River's east shore. The Deschutes River Camp is located just south of "The Island" that separates the two rivers. Besides the many water-sports to enjoy, the park features ancient Indian rock carvings, or petroglyphs, located at the base of the prominent rock formation known as "The Ship." Park services include a marina concession and general store. Houseboats can be rented nearby. Other attractions in the vicinity of the park are: Round Butte and Pelton Dams (contains the longest fish ladder in the world); the Warm Springs Indian Reservation; excellent trout fishing on the Lower Deschutes River; the scenic Metolius River Recreation Area and Suttle Lake west of Sisters; and a number of rockhounding areas throughout the region.

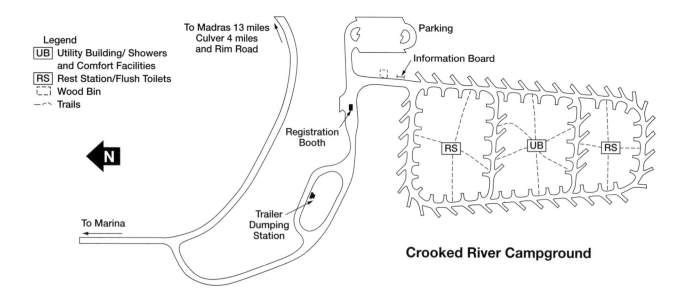

Crooked River Campground

Facilities and Activities

Campgrounds are open mid-April through late October. Reservations are accepted from Memorial Day weekend through Labor Day.

87 RV campsites w/full hookups (35′ maximum
   length)
   pull-through sites
   showers
   tubs
   drinking water
   flush toilets
   wood & electric stoves
   tables
   trailer dump station
94 tent campsites
91 tent campsites w/water nearby
3 group tent area
97 picnic sites
play area/swim area/waterskiing
boat ramp/boating/fishing
hiking/sightseeing
geology/rockhounding
accessible campsites/restrooms/showers/vault
   toilet at boat ramp for people with disabilities

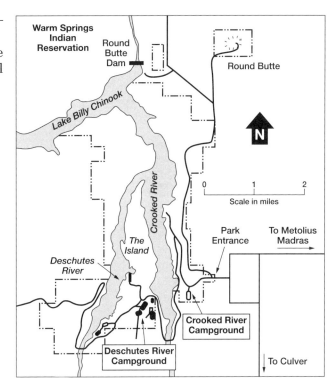

For biking, rockhounding, or just relaxing, campers won't be disappointed in their options for recreation anywhere in Oregon.

Viento State Park

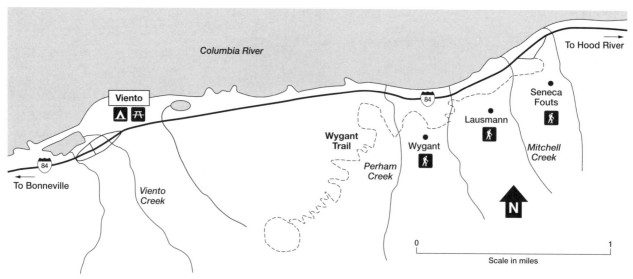

For Information

Viento State Park
c/o Columbia River Gorge District Office
P.O. Box 100
Corbett, OR 97019
(503) 695-2261
FAX—695-2226

Location

Viento State Park lies in a shaded area along Viento Creek in the spectacular Columbia River Gorge National Scenic Area. Located on I-84, 8 miles west of Hood River, the park has a short hiking trail to Viento Lake. The campground is located on the river side of the freeway. *Note:* See Columbia River Gorge National Scenic Area on page 38 for more information.

Facilities and Activities

The campground is open mid-April through late October on a first-come, first-served basis.

5 developed tent campsites
58 tent campsites w/water nearby
  showers
  drinking water
  flush toilets
  wood & electric stoves
  tables

19 picnic sites
hiking/ trails/sightseeing
accessible campsite/restrooms/showers for people
  with disabilities

A beautiful picnic spot is not hard to find along the Columbia River Gorge National Scenic Area.

Willamette National Forest

For Information

Willamette National Forest
211 East 7th Avenue
P.O. Box 10607
Eugene, OR 97440-2607
(503) 465-6521

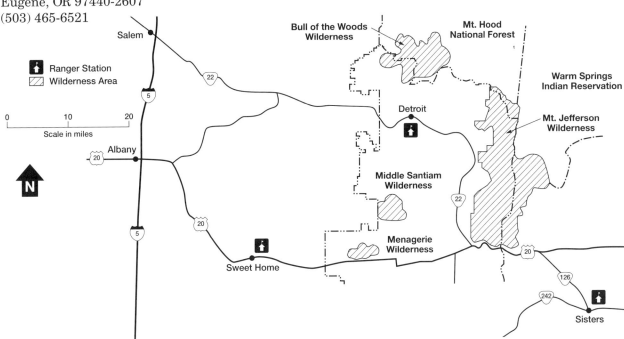

Location

For detailed information on campgrounds and maps in five ranger districts in the Willamette National Forest located south of U.S. 20, see page 212 of this *Camper's Guide*. Campgrounds in Detroit Ranger District only are described here since they are located north of U.S. 20, which is within Region 1.

East of Eugene, the Willamette National Forest stretches for 110 miles along the western slopes of the Cascades and extends from the Mt. Jefferson area east of Salem to the Calapooya Mountains northeast of Roseburg. The forest is 1,675,407 acres in size or about the size of the state of New Jersey. Access to the forest comes from four major highways, U.S. 20 and S.R. 22, 58, and 242. The nearest entry point to the Willamette National Forest is just 20 miles from the Eugene-Springfield area off S.R. 58.

Points of Interest

Recreation opportunities on the forest are numerous. There are over 80 campgrounds and picnic grounds containing some 1,200 units. Units are composed of a table, fireplace, and a tent site or trailer parking place (hookups are not available).

Nearly all campgrounds have water and either pit, vault, or flush toilets. Offered on a first-come, first-served basis, there are occupancy restrictions in most campgrounds ranging from 10–16 days. Some sites have a user's fee. Some sites and group areas are on the National Recreation Reservation System.

There are over 1,400 miles of trails in the forest for hikers. A number of these are low-elevation, easy-access trails for year-round hiking pleasure. Three very scenic, low-elevation trails have been designated National Recreation Trails. They are the McKenzie River Trail, Fall Creek Trail, and South Breitenbush Gorge Trail. The Fall Creek and McKenzie River Trails are within 50 miles of Eugene (bus service is available from Eugene to McKenzie Bridge). The South Breitenbush Gorge Trail is located 60 miles east of Salem.

For the fishing enthusiast, many kinds of trout are found in the forest's lakes and streams including brook, rainbow, brown, cutthroat, and bull trout. Kokanee salmon have been planted in some lakes.

Big game animals include Roosevelt elk, bear, and blacktailed and mule deer. The forest is open to hunting and fishing in regular season established by the Oregon Department of Fish and Wildlife and subject to its regulations.

Two developed ski areas, Hoodoo and Willamette Pass Ski Area, operate under special use permits from the Willamette National forest. Cross-country skiing is also popular, and many forest roads and trails lend themselves to this activity.

There are two snowmobile areas in the forest. One is located near Willamette Pass on Waldo Lake Road, and the other is located near Big Lake just off Santiam Pass on U.S. 20.

Rainfall on the Willamette National Forest varies from 40 to more than 150 inches a year, much of it in snow, which blankets the higher Cascades each year. The forest is blanketed with Douglas-fir, the most valuable timber species in the U.S. Producing about 8% of all timber cut on national forest lands, the Willamette National Forest is often the top timber producer among the 159 national forests in the U.S.

Brochures on hiking trails, snowmobile and cross-country ski trails, and maps of the forest and wilderness areas are available through the Forest headquarters or ranger district offices.

Wilderness Areas

The Willamette has eight Wilderness Areas totaling 380,805 acres. These areas, the majority of which encompass seven major mountain peaks in the Cascades, are popular with hikers, backpackers, and mountain climbers. See the Willamette National Forest in Region 3 for information on four of the eight Wilderness Areas located south of U.S. 20: Diamond Peak, Mt. Washington, Three Sisters, and Waldo Lake.

Some wildernesses have special area regulations. Check with the local ranger district office for further information and detailed maps. Following are descriptions of the four Wilderness Areas located within Region 1, north of U.S. 20.

Bull of the Woods Wilderness contains 34,885 acres with elevations that range from 2,500 to 5,700 feet. The major portion of the wilderness is located on the Mt. Hood National Forest (the Willamette section contains 7,463 acres). The country is characterized by very steep, mountainous terrain, dissected deeply by streams. Bull of the Woods Peak is the hub of a 68-mile trail system, complete with several loop opportunities. There are at least 12 lakes larger than one acre scattered throughout the wilderness, isolated from one another by high ridges. These lakes support fish populations. The lower slopes are typically steep, 30–60%, and covered with dense stands of timber. The upper slopes are very steep, 60–90%, and also mostly covered by dense timber. The area contains the major

headwaters of the Collawash, Breitenbush, and Little North Fork Santiam Rivers. Historically, prospecting has been an active use of the area. Some of the better huckleberry fields lie to the west of Beachie Saddle. The Bull of the Woods lookout still remains and commands a spectacular view of the surrounding areas. For information contact: Estacada Ranger District—(503) 630-6861 and Detroit Ranger District—(503) 854-3366.

Menagerie Wilderness, 5,033 acres in size, is characterized by steep, dissected slopes. Smaller areas of the wilderness have gentle, undulating, smooth slopes with a series of rock pinnacles that stand out above the surrounding landscape. Vegetation consists mainly of Douglas-fir, Western hemlock, Western red cedar, and associated species. This is a popular technical climbing area with mountaineers. Elevations range between 1,600 to 3,900 feet. There are two main trailheads that lead to Rooster Rock. For information contact: Sweet Home Ranger District—(503) 367-5168.

Middle Santiam Wilderness, 8,542 acres in size, has elevation ranges between 1,600 to 5,022 feet. A wide variety of topography occurs in this area ranging from steep slopes to high peaks and ridges. Vegetation varies from true fir associations at upper levels to Douglar-fir, Western hemlock associations at lower elevations. Upper slopes and ridge-tops in the middle portion have shallow, rocky soils derived from andesites and basalts. Dense stands of old-growth Douglas-fir are found at lower levels. Primary attractions are Donaca Lake and the Middle Santiam River, both with native fish populations. The wilderness is served by three trails. For more information contact: Sweet Home Ranger District—(503) 367-5168.

Mt. Jefferson Wilderness covers 111,177 acres with elevations ranges between 2,400 to 10,497 feet. Mt. Jefferson, 10,497 feet, is the predominant feature of this High Cascades area, along with Three Fingered Jack, 7,841 feet. Both of these areas are favorite climbing destinations for mountaineers. There are 190 miles of trails, including a 40-mile stretch of the Pacific Crest National Scenic Trail. Eighty-seven percent of the wilderness has vegetation cover with 62% of that being timber. There are over 150 lakes, approximately one-half of which are stocked with eastern brook trout and/or rainbow trout. Deer, elk, black bear, and coyotes are common. Other geographic features include steep talus slopes, rock outcrops, and alpine meadows. For information contact: Detroit Ranger District—(503) 854-3366 or Sisters Ranger District—(503) 549-2111.

Willamette National Forest *(continued)*

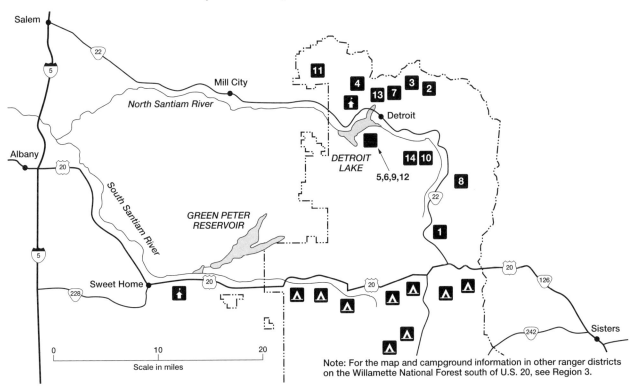

Note: For the map and campground information in other ranger districts on the Willamette National Forest south of U.S. 20, see Region 3.

Detroit Ranger District

For Information

Detroit Ranger Station
HC60 Box 320
Mill City, OR 97360
(503) 854-3366

1. **Big Meadows Horse Camp:** Off S.R. 22. Turn on F.R. 2267 for 1 mi., left on F.R. 2257 for .5 mi, 25 mi SE of Detroit. *Activities:* Hiking and fishing. Contact Detroit Ranger Station.

2. **Breitenbush:** Access via S.R. 22 off Breitenbush Road (F.R. 46), 10 mi. northeast of Detroit. *Activities:* Camping and fishing.

3. **Cleator Bend:** Access via S.R. 22 off Breitenbush Road (F.R. 46), 9 mi. northeast of Detroit. *Activities:* Camping and fishing.

4. **Elk Lake:** Access via S.R. 22 on Elkhorn-Elk Lake Road (F.R. 2209), 14 mi. north of Detroit. *Activities:* Camping, boating, swimming, fishing, and hiking.

5. **Hoover:** Access via S.R. 22. Located on south side of Detroit Reservoir, 5.5 mi. southeast of Detroit on Blowout Road (F.R. 10). *Activities:* Camping, hiking, boating, water skiing, fishing, and swimming. Adjacent group area.

Campground	Elevation (Feet)	Tent Sites	Tent/Trailer Sites	Fee	Water	Toilets F = Flush V = Vault
1. Big Meadows Horse Camp	3,600		9	•	•	V
2. Breitenbush	2,100		30	•	•	V
3. Cleator Bend	2,200		9	•	•	V
4. Elk Lake	3,700	12			•	V
5. Hoover*	1,600	2	35	•	•	F
6. Hoover Camp**	1,600	group of 50		•		V
7. Humbug	1,800		22	•	•	V
8. Marion Forks	2,500		15	•	•	V
9. Piety Island	1,600		11			V
10. Riverside	2,400		37	•	•	V
11. Shady Cove	1,500		11			V
12. Southshore†	1,600	8	24	•	•	V
13. Upper Arm	1,600	2	3			V
14. Whispering Falls	2,000		12	•	•	F

*Accessible to handicapped.
**Group areas/reservations required.
†Picnic sites available.

6. **Hoover Camp:** Access via S.R. 22. On Detroit Reservoir, 5.5 mi. southeast of Detroit on Blowout Road (F.R. 10). *Activities:* Fishing, boating, swimming, hiking, shelter with kitchen/dining area.
7. **Humbug:** Access via S.R. 22. Travel Breitenbush Road (F.R. 46), 5 mi. northeast of Detroit. *Activities:* Camping, fishing, and hiking.
8. **Marion Forks:** Access via S.R. 22, 16 mi. SE of Detroit. *Activities:* Picnicking, fishing, and hiking.
9. **Piety Lake:** Access via S.R. 22. Access by boat on Detroit Reservoir. *Activities:* Picnicking, boating, swimming, fishing, and waterskiing.
10. **Riverside:** Access via S.R. 22, 14 mi. SE of Detroit. *Activities:* Fishing.
11. **Shady Cove:** On Little North Santiam Road, 19 mi NE of Mehama. Access via S.R. 22. *Activities:* Picnicking and fishing.
12. **Southshore:** Access via S.R. 22. South side of Detroit Reservoir on Blowout Road (F.R.10), 8 mi. south of Detroit. *Activities:* Picnicking, boating, swimming, fishing, water skiing, and hiking.
13. **Upper Arm:** Access via S.R. 22. On Breitenbush Road (F.R. 46), on Detroit Reservoir, 1 mi. NE of Detroit. *Activities:* Picnicking, swimming, fishing, and boating.
14. **Whispering Falls:** Travel S.R. 22, 8 mi. southeast of Detroit. *Activities.* Camping and fishing.

Home to deer, elk, and bear, the Willamette National Forest is a recreation paradise year-round.

Region 2

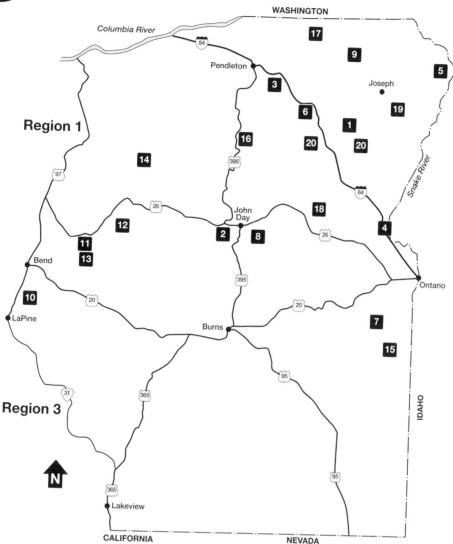

*—Bureau of Land Management Recreation
Sites, page 68
1—Catherine Creek State Park, page 70
2—Clyde Holliday State Park, page 71
3—Emigrant Springs State Park, page 72
4—Farewell Bend State Park, page 74
5—Hells Canyon National Recreation Area,
page 76
6—Hilgard Junction State Park, page 79
7—Lake Owyhee State Park, page 80
8—Malheur National Forest, page 82
9—Minam State Park, page 86
10—Newberry National Volcanic Monument,
page 87

11—Ochoco Lake State Park, page 89
12—Ochoco National Forest, page 90
   • Crooked River National Grassland,
   page 95
13—Prineville Reservoir State Park, page 98
14—Shelton State Wayside, page 100
15—Succor Creek State Park, page 101
16—Ukiah-Dale State Park, page 102
17—Umatilla National Forest, page 103
18—Unity Lake State Park, page 108
19—Wallowa Lake State Park, page 108
20—Wallowa-Whitman National Forest, page 110

*Recreation sites scattered throughout region. See BLM map
on page 68 for site locations.

Bureau of Land Management Recreation Sites

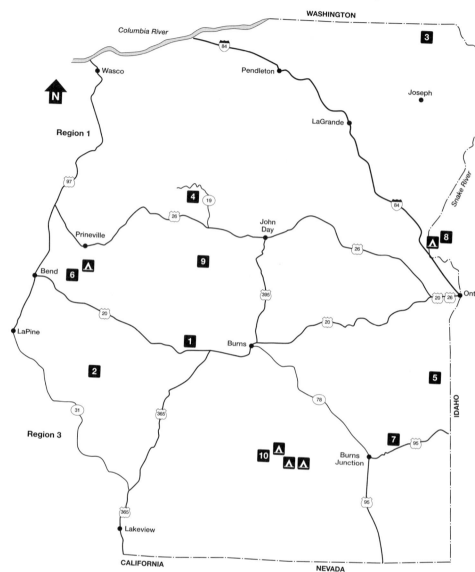

Site Descriptions/Activities

1. **Chickahominy Reservoir:** Located west of Burns along U.S. 20, this reservoir has an outstanding trout fishery. There are no designated campsites. Fishing season peaks in June and resumes in September as the hot summer weather ends. *Activities:* Fishing.

2. **Christmas Valley/Ft. Rock Basin:** Explore thousands of acres of sand dunes, a lost forest surrounded by desert, dramatic volcanic features, a two-mile crack in the ground, and wide open spaces as you travel the Christmas Valley Back Country Byway. *Activities:* Fishing, hunt-

Site	Campsites	Picnic Sites	Trails	Drinking Water	Toilets
1. Chickahominy Reservoir	•	•			
2. Christmas Valley/ Ft. Rock Basin	•	•			•
3. Grande Ronde	•				•
4. John Day River*	•				•
5. Leslie Gulch/ Succor Creek*	•	•		•	•
6. Lower Crooked	•			•	•
7. Owyhee	•	•	•	•	•
8. Spring Rec. Site*	•			•	•
9. South Fork John Day	•				
10. Steens Mountain*	•	•		•	•

*Barrier-free access.

ing, geological and botanical sightseeing; historic site investigating; and ORV playing.

3. **Grande Ronde National Wild and Scenic River:** For those who enjoy trees with their canyon geology, there is no better float than the one beginning at Minam on the Wallow River, drifting on to the Grande Ronde River, and finally, taking out at Hellers Bar on the Snake River. Elk, deer, bighorn sheep, and great trout, bass and steelhead fishing are all there for that trip of a lifetime. *Activities:* Boating/rafting, fishing, hunting, wildlife viewing, hiking, and swimming.

4. **John Day River:** This picturesque area includes both the North Fork and mainstem of the John Day River, which offer boaters several easy one-day float trips during late spring and early summer. The river basin is nationally known for its smallmouth bass fishing, though steelhead and trout fishing are also popular. There are three campgrounds. *Activities:* Boating/rafting, fishing, hunting, and swimming.

5. **Leslie Gulch/Succor Creek National Back Country Byway:** This byway takes you through some of the most rugged, spectacular landscapes in eastern Oregon. Amazing volcanic ash tuff formations, rare plants, watchable wildlife such as bighorn sheep, interesting history, and a multitude of recreational activities await the adventurer. Hiking adjacent to the byway is unparalleled. *Activities:* Boating/rafting, fishing, hunting, wildlife viewing, geological and botanical sightseeing, and hiking.

6. **Lower Crooked Wild and Scenic River:** Nationally known for its rainbow trout fly fishing, the Chimney Rock segment of this river has facilities for camping, swimming, hiking, and sightseeing. A paved portion of the 43-mile byway winds its way through a spectacular river canyon whose towering, reddish basalt canyon walls have given rise to the name "Palisades." *Activities:* Fishing, hunting, hiking, and swimming.

7. **Owyhee Wild and Scenic River:** Explore more than 120 miles of some of the most rugged, spectacular canyonlands you will ever see. Quiet pools interrupted by the sheer terror of the Widow Maker rapids will electrify thrill seekers. Farther on, boaters will see serene views of spires and cliffs towering a thousand feet overhead. Watch for golden eagles, bighorn sheep, and river otter. *Activities:* Boating/rafting, fishing, hunting, wildlife viewing, geological and

botanical sightseeing, historical sites, hiking, and swimming.

8. **Spring Recreation Site:** Brownlee Reservoir is known for its large channel catfish, abundant crappie, and good bass fishing. A recently renovated BLM fee recreation site on the shore of the reservoir offers a boat ramp, fish cleaning station, tent and trailer camping, and barrier-free access. *Activities:* Boating/rafting and fishing.

9. **South Fork John Day Wild and Scenic River:** The South Fork John Day River National Back Country Byway parallels the river through a scenic, narrow canyon. Wildlife such as mule deer, Rocky Mountain elk, bighorn sheep, and many species of birds can be seen along the river's tributaries. *Activities:* Primitive dispersed camping, fishing, hunting and hiking are popular activities in the canyon.

10. **Steens Mountain Recreation Lands:** This recreation area includes a 66-mile byway that provides spectacular views of deep glacial gorges and the opportunity to view pronghorn antelope, wild horses, bighorn sheep, raptors, and deer. There is excellent fishing in the Donner and Blitzen National Wild and Scenic River. Three free campgrounds and many picnic campsites are available. *Activities:* The Steens, along with nearby Pueblo and Trout Creek Mountains, offer high-altitude hiking, trophy big game hunting, redband trout fishing, sightseeing, wildlife viewing, and wildflower displays.

REGION 2

One of the best kept secrets for places to fish, hike, and camp in solitude—land administered by the Bureau of Land Management!

Catherine Creek State Park

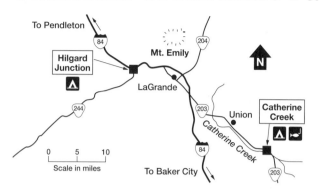

foothills of northeastern Oregon's Wallowa Mountains. The park stands at an elevation of 3,200 feet and encompasses 160 acres of trees that include ponderosa pine, cottonwood, and larch. This state park can be accessed from Oregon 203, just 8 miles southeast of Union.

For Information

Catherine Creek State Park
c/o Emigrant Springs State Park
P.O. Box 85
Meacham, OR 97859
(503) 983-2277
FAX—983-2279

Location

Catherine Creek State Park is located in a forested area along Catherine Creek in the western

Facilities and Activities

The campground is open from mid-April through late October and operates on a first-come, first-served basis. Group picnic reservations are available.

18 primitive tent campsites
   drinking water
   flush & pit toilets
   stoves
   tables
72 picnic sites
2 group picnic sites
hiking/trails
sightseeing/fishing

Oregon's inland waterways are a rich source for recreational opportunities.

Clyde Holliday State Park

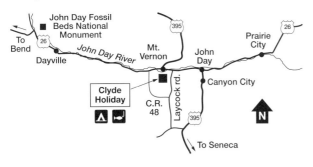

For Information

Clyde Holliday State Park
P.O. Box 9
Canyon City, OR 97820
(503) 575-2773
FAX—575-2016

Location

Clyde Holliday State Park is located on U.S. 26, 7 miles west of John Day. This lovely small park, with an elevation of 2,890 feet, covers 20 acres along the banks of the John Day River. The location of Clyde Holliday State Park makes it ideal for camping and taking day-trips to nearby points of interest. The park lies just 30 miles east of John Day Fossil Beds National Monument's Sheep Rock Unit and main visitor center (near the junction of U.S. 26 and S.R. 19). Other day-trips that will take you back in time and introduce you to the history of the West include: the quaint western town of Frenchglen and the Steens Mountains; Strawberry Mountain Wilderness Area; Magone lake; and Blue Mountain and Ritter Hot Springs.

Facilities and Activities

The campground is open from mid-April through late October on a first-come, first-served basis.

30 RV campsites w/electric & water only (35′ maximum length)
showers
   drinking water
   flush toilets
   stoves
   tables
   trailer dump station
23 picnic sites
swimming/fishing
history/geology

John Day Fossil Beds National Monument is just a short drive from Clyde Holliday State Park. Don't miss seeing the powerful geologic history of central Oregon exemplified at John Day and Newberry national volcanic monuments.

Emigrant Springs State Park

For Information

Emigrant Springs State Park
P.O. Box 85
Meacham, OR 97359
(503) 983-2277
FAX—983-2279

Location

Emigrant Springs State Park is located on I-84, 26 miles southeast of Pendleton near the camping site used by pioneer wagon trains when traveling

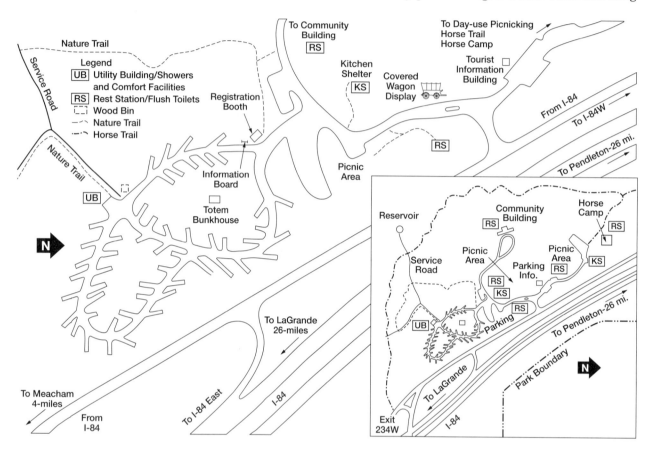

Pioneers traveled more than 2,200 miles from St. Louis to Astoria along the Old Oregon Trail. Here at Emigrant Springs, the first forested area reached along the journey, emigrants replenished their water barrels from a spring.

Emigrant Springs State Park *(continued)*

Today sojourners may camp in the Totem Bunkhouse year-round. Winter cross-country skiing is popular here.

the Old Oregon Trail over 150 years ago. Wagon trains camped here for several days and replenished their water barrels from a spring before completing their passage over the Blue Mountains. Today the park features campsites, a self-guided nature trail, a Totem Bunkhouse available year-round (used by cross-country skiers in winter), kitchen shelters, a community building with kitchen and dining facilities, a horse camp, and an Oregon Trail exhibit and covered wagon display. The Blue Mountains offer many recreational opportunities for hiking, fishing, and hunting.

Facilities and Activities

The campground is open mid-April through late October on a first-come, first-served basis. Reservations are available for the Totem Lodge and community building throughout the year.

18 RV campsites w/full hookups (60′ maximum length)
   showers
   tubs
   drinking water
   flush toilets
   wood & electric stoves
   tables
33 unimproved tent campsites
1 horse camp
1 overnight and day-use community building
1 Totem (bunkhouse) Lodge (2 four-person units)
138 picnic sites
1 group picnic site
play area/hiking/trails
sightseeing/history/Oregon Trail Exhibit

In 1843, almost a thousand people crossed the Blue Mountains in the first, large, emigrant wagon train.

Farewell Bend State Park

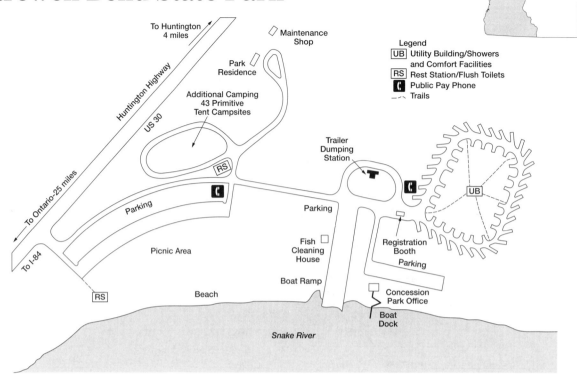

For Information

Farewell Bend State Park
Star Route
Huntington, OR 97907
(503) 869-2365
FAX—869-2457

Location

Located off I-84, just 25 miles northwest of Ontario, Farewell Bend State Park lies on the shore of Brownlee Reservoir formed by waters of the Snake River. Farewell Bend was named in the days of gold seekers, wagon trains, and pioneers. Early in the 1800s, explorers and trappers such as Wilson Price Hunt, Captain Bonneville, and John C. Fremont passed through the territory on what later became the Oregon Trail. In 1836, missionary Marcus Whitman assisted in guiding the first large wagon train through Farewell Bend. At this location, the Oregon Trail emigrants left the Snake River to head overland after following the river for nearly 330 miles; here they said "farewell" to the river. Remnants of the Oregon Trail can still be seen today traveling northward from Farewell Bend State Park toward the the old frontier town of Huntington on Highway 30. A small iron cross, visible from the highway, marks the location where Snake River

Shoshone Indians killed a number of unfortunate emigrants in October 1860. At the entrance to Farewell Bend State Park, the remains of an old pioneer wagon can be viewed. Today, the principal attractions in this desert-like region include fishing, hunting, boating, and relaxation.

Pioneers had to travel along the banks of the Snake River for nearly 330 miles before crossing its mighty waters here at Farewell Bend, now remembered with a state park.

Farewell Bend State Park *(continued)*

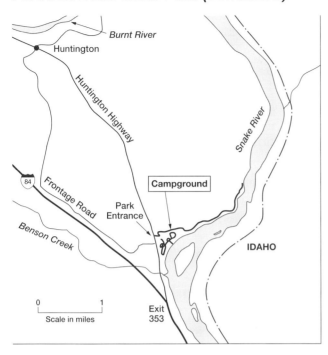

Facilities and Activities

The campground is open year-round on a first-come, first-served basis.

53 RV/tent campsites (24' maximum length)
43 unimproved tent campsites
2 group tent areas
   showers
   drinking water
   flush toilets
   wood & electric stoves
   tables
   trailer dump station
53 picnic sites
1 group picnic site
play area/swim area
boat ramp/boating/fishing/waterskiing
sightseeing/history/Oregon Trail Exhibit
accessible campsite/restrooms for people with disabilities

Today the Snake River is a principal attraction for boating, fishing, and camping.

Hells Canyon National Recreation Area

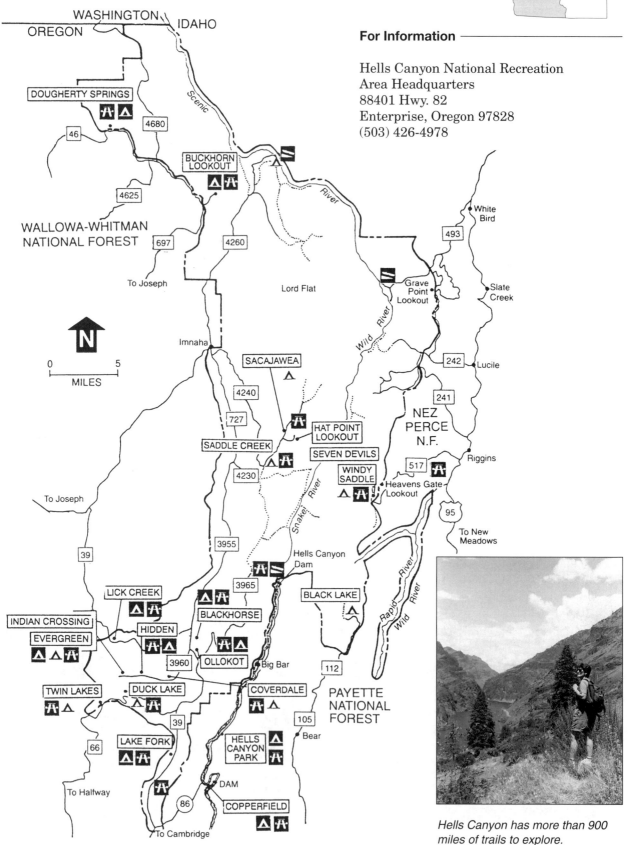

For Information

Hells Canyon National Recreation
Area Headquarters
88401 Hwy. 82
Enterprise, Oregon 97828
(503) 426-4978

WASHINGTON
IDAHO
OREGON

DOUGHERTY SPRINGS

4680

46

Scenic

BUCKHORN
LOOKOUT

4625

River

WALLOWA-WHITMAN
NATIONAL FOREST

697

4260

To Joseph

Lord Flat

White
Bird

493

Grave
Point
Lookout

Slate
Creek

Wild River

242

Lucile

N

0   5
MILES

Imnaha

SACAJAWEA

4240

727

241

NEZ
PERCE
N.F.

HAT POINT
LOOKOUT

SADDLE CREEK

4230

SEVEN DEVILS

WINDY
SADDLE

517

Riggins

Heavens Gate
Lookout

To Joseph

Snake River

95

To New
Meadows

39

3955

Hells Canyon
Dam

3965

LICK CREEK

BLACKHORSE

BLACK LAKE

Rapid River

Wild River

INDIAN CROSSING

HIDDEN

EVERGREEN

3960

OLLOKOT

Big Bar

112

TWIN LAKES

DUCK LAKE

39

COVERDALE

PAYETTE
NATIONAL
FOREST

105

Bear

66

LAKE FORK

HELLS
CANYON
PARK

86   DAM

To Halfway

COPPERFIELD

To Cambridge

*Hells Canyon has more than 900
miles of trails to explore.*

Campgrounds	Elevation (Feet)	Total Sites	RVs	Tents	Fee	Drinking Water	Toilets Flush/Vault	Sanitary Dump
Blackhorse	4,000	17	•	•	•	•	V	
Black Lake	7,200	4		•		□	V	
Buckhorn*	5,200	6		•		□	V	
Coverdale	4,300	10	•	•	•	•	V	
Dougherty Springs	5,100	10	•	•		□	V	
Duck Lake	5,200	2		•		□	V	
Evergreen**	4,500					□		
Hat Point*	6,982	2		•			V	
Hidden	4,400	13		•	•	•	V	
Indian Crossing*	3,200	14	•	•	•	•	V	
Lake Fork	3,200	10	•	•	•	•	V	
Lick Creek	5,400	12	•	•	•	•	V	
Ollokot	4,000	12	•	•	•	•	V	
Sacajawea	6,800	3		•		□	V	
Twin Lakes	6,500	6		•		□	V	
Seven Devils	7,200	9		•				
Saddle Creek	6,800	7		•				
Windy Saddle*	7,200	4		•				
Idaho Power Campgrounds†								
Copperfield Park		100	•	•	•	•	F	•
C. J. Strike		50		•		•	V	
Hells Canyon Park		60	•	•	•	•	F	•
McCormick		46	•	•	•	•	F	•
Woodhead		80	•	•	•	•	V	•

*Campground with horse ramp
**Group campground with no designated units
†Idaho Power campgrounds have electricity for RVs, showers, boat ramps and docks, and are open all year. See General Information for exceptions.
□ Pump, stream, or lake

Location

Hells Canyon National Recreation Area lies in the states of Oregon and Idaho, and within three national forests, Wallowa-Whitman, Payette and the Nez Perce. Administered by the Wallowa-Whitman National Forest in Oregon, the recreation area encompasses 652,488 acres that straddle the mighty Snake River. Sixty-seven miles of the river have been designated as "Wild and Scenic." This spectacular canyon can be reached by various routes from Idaho and Oregon. In Oregon, travel from Baker via State Route 86; from Joseph via State Route 350 and Forest Route 39; from Enterprise via County Roads 799 and 697 or several routes off State Route 3. From Idaho, access into Hells Canyon can be reached from U.S. 95. Three roads provide access to the Snake River. They are Forest Road 493 out of White Bird, Idaho and Forest Road 4260 from Imnaha, Oregon. Both of these roads are narrow, slick when wet, and not recommended for motorhomes or other large vehicles. The road to Hells Canyon Dam from either Cambridge, Idaho, or Halfway, Oregon, is paved, all-weather, and may be used by all types of vehicles.

Points of Interest

▲ Hells Canyon is the deepest gorge in North America, with elevations ranging from 9,393 feet atop the Seven Devils Mountains to 800 feet along the Snake River.

▲ Anglers, water-sport enthusiasts, backpackers, and hunters seldom go unrewarded in this recreation mecca.

▲ 420 miles of roads traverse the rugged and diverse terrain of the Canyon for excellent auto touring.

▲ Over 900 miles of trails provide access for hikers and horse riders.

▲ About 350 wildlife species (including elk, mountain goats, bighorn sheep and deer) spend all or part of the year in the recreation area.

▲ Steeped in rich cultural history, the area has many archeological sites, petroglyphs, and a 3.7-mile section of the Nee-Me-Poo Trail honoring the Nez Perce Indians' flight to freedom and the subsequent Nez Perce War.

Facilities and Activities

477 RV and tent campsites
group campsites
backcountry camping
20 picnic areas
hiking/backpacking
900+ miles of trails
fishing (bass, crappie, trout, steelhead, salmon)
boating/rafting ramps/docks
swimming
waterskiing
sailing/windsurfing
horseback riding
birdwatching
mountain and trail biking
interpretive signs
hunting (permits/restricted)
guide-services for fishing, rafting, horseback riding, and hunting

Hells Canyon National Recreation Area *(continued)*

General Information

▲ Roads accessing Hells Canyon may be rough and slippery. Some do not open until mid-summer because of snow. Check on current road conditions before entering the area.

▲ Fees are charged per night to camp at most campgrounds. See chart.

▲ Ranger stations are located in Baker, Oregon (503-523-6391); Enterprise, Oregon (503-426-4978); Clarkston, Washington (509-758-0616); and Riggins, Idaho (208-628-3916).

▲ All campgrounds operate on a first-come, first-served basis. Facilities and fees vary with sites. National forest campgrounds do not have electrical hook-ups or showers. Operating dates typically run from June to November. Idaho Power campgrounds operate year-round, charge a fee per night (except at C. J. Strike) and have electrical hook-ups and showers.

▲ RV hook-ups are available at Copperfield, Hells Canyon, McCormick, and Woodhead parks.

▲ Showers are available at Copperfield, McCormick, and Hells Canyon parks.

▲ Picnic areas are provided at North Pine Rest Stop, Rapid River Fish Hatchery, and 18 Idaho Power sites.

▲ Trail use is operated on a voluntary registration basis. Self-registration boxes are located at most major trailheads and at any office of the NRA.

▲ Party size for backcountry travel is limited to 8 people and 16 head of stock. Exceptions must be approved by the Forest Service.

▲ Rattlesnakes and poison ivy are common in the canyon. Visitors should take needed precautions. Snake-bite kits are recommended.

▲ Boat ramps are available at Dug Bar, Hells Canyon Creek Recreation Site, and Pittsburg Landing. Idaho Power campgrounds with boat ramps and docks include Hells Canyon, McCormick and Woodhead parks.

▲ Permits are required for all boating on the Wild and Scenic Snake River sections from Friday preceding Memorial Day weekend to September 15 annually. For information on reservations and permits call (208) 743-2297 (Lewiston, Idaho).

▲ Two fish hatcheries in the area, Rapid River and Oxbow, help replenish chinook salmon and steelhead populations. The public is welcome to tour the facilities and enjoy the picnic facilities.

▲ Fishing is strictly regulated by each state. Anglers on the Snake River need to have a license from one of the states and can fish the entire river from a boat. Anglers can only fish from the bank of the state where they have a license. Numerous outfitters provide transportation and guide services.

▲ For information on Idaho hunting and fishing licenses or regulations contact Idaho Department of Fish and Game at 1-800-635-7820. In Oregon contact the Department of Fish and Wildlife at (503) 229-5403.

▲ Outfitter guides provide many services including jet boat, float boat, auto tour, air tour, and pack trips into the recreation area. A list of outfitter names can be provided by writing the park headquarters.

▲ Daily updates on reservoir levels are offered year-round by calling Hells Canyon Recreation Report: in Idaho call 1-800-422-3143; from outside of Idaho call 1-800-521-9102.

▲ Travel and campground use is limited during inclement weather. Check for conditions before traveling.

The Snake River divides North America's deepest gorge and provides a multitude of recreational opportunities.

Hilgard Junction State Park

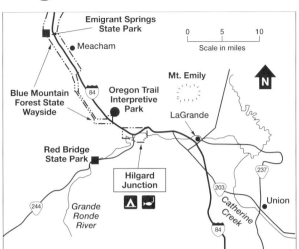

For Information

Hilgard Junction State Park
c/o Emigrant Springs State Park
P.O. Box 85
Meacham, OR 97859
(503) 983-2277
FAX—983-2279

The Oregon Trail Interpretive Park near Hilgard recounts days of the early wagon trains. Wagon ruts are still visible in many places along the Blue Mountain Crossing Interpretive Trail.

Location

Hilgard Junction State Park is located on the banks of the Grande Ronde River in the foothills of the Blue Mountains. This 233-acre park is easily accessed off I-84N, just 8 miles west of La Grande. Although the campsites are primitive, the park is a popular launching site for rafters. At an elevation of 2,900 feet, the cottonwood trees and ponderosa pine make it a scenic campground.

Facilities and Activities

The campground is open year-round on a first-come, first-served basis.

18 primitive RV/tent campsites (30′ maximum length)
   drinking water
   flush toilets
   stoves
   tables
   trailer dump station
30 picnic sites
rafting/fishing
Oregon Trail Exhibit nearby

Picnic or camp along the banks of the Grande Ronde River.

Lake Owyhee State Park

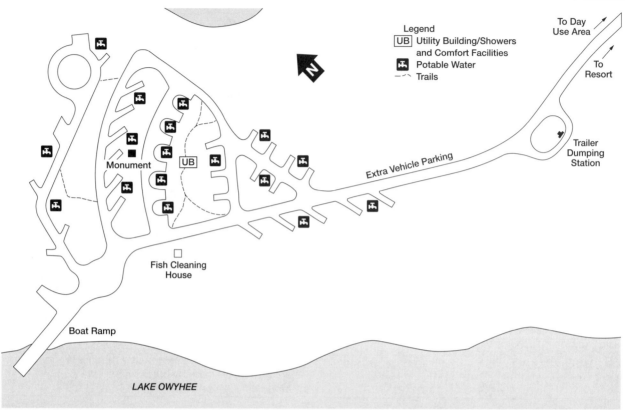

Legend
UB Utility Building/Showers and Comfort Facilities
Potable Water
Trails

To Day Use Area

To Resort

Trailer Dumping Station

Extra Vehicle Parking

Monument

UB

Fish Cleaning House

Boat Ramp

LAKE OWYHEE

For Information

Lake Owyhee State Park
c/o Farewell Bend State Park
Star Route
Huntington, OR 97907
(503) 869-2365
FAX—869-2457

Location

Lake Owyhee State Park, 730 acres in size at an elevation of 2,670 feet, is located off S.R. 201, 33 miles southwest of Nyssa and adjacent to Owyhee Reservoir. Scenic Lake Owyhee, formed by Owyhee Dam, is 53 miles long and lies beneath impressive rock formations in a colorful, steep-walled desert canyon. The lake offers excellent fishing for bass, crappie, catfish, and trout. In the summer, the area is popular for waterskiing, boating, and sightseeing. The trip up the lake from the park offers a unique opportunity to view the beauty and rugged terrain of the Owyhee mountains. Wildlife can be viewed in their natural habitat and include waterfowl, golden

For summer watersports, Lake Owyhee is a great destination in this sparsely populated area of the state.

Lake Owyhee State Park *(continued)*

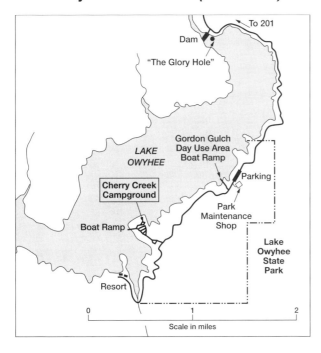

eagles, coyotes, pronghorn antelope, wild horses, and mule deer. On occasion, people also see California bighorn sheep, once nearly extinct in Oregon, and very rarely a mountain lion. In the fall, the surrounding mountains become a popular hunting ground for mule deer and chukars. Limited grocery items are available at a nearby resort, as well as a restaurant and lounge. Gasoline can also be purchased at the resort.

Facilities and Activities

The campground is open mid-April through late October on a first-come, first-served basis.

10 RV campsites w/electricity & water only (55′ maximum length)
30 tent campsites
   showers
   drinking water
   flush toilets
   wood and electric stoves
   tables
   trailer dump station
15 picnic sites
3 boat ramps
boating/fishing/waterskiing/swimming
sightseeing/birdwatching/wildlife viewing
rockhounding
marina w/boat moorage .5 mile from park
accessible restrooms/showers for people with disabilities

REGION 2

This semi-arid, high-desert country is home to wildlife such as the California bighorn sheep.

Malheur National Forest

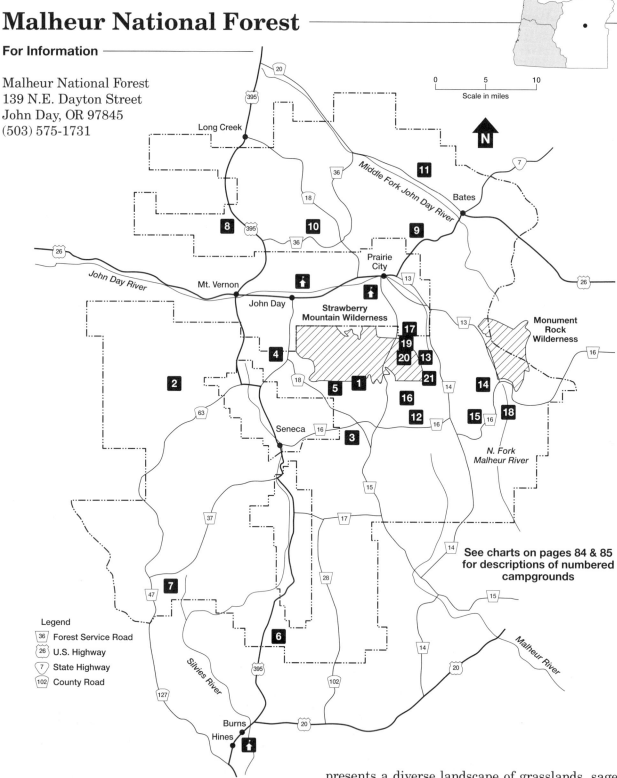

For Information

Malheur National Forest
139 N.E. Dayton Street
John Day, OR 97845
(503) 575-1731

Scale in miles
0   5   10

N

See charts on pages 84 & 85 for descriptions of numbered campgrounds

Legend
36 Forest Service Road
26 U.S. Highway
7 State Highway
102 County Road

Location

The 1,460,000-acre Malheur National Forest is located in the Blue Mountains of eastern Oregon. Forest headquarters in John Day can be reached by traveling U.S. 26, which traverses the forest from east to west, or U.S. 395 from the south. The forest presents a diverse landscape of grasslands, sage, juniper, and forests of pine, fir and other tree species, along with alpine lakes and meadows. Elevations vary from about 4,000 feet to the 9,038-foot summit of Strawberry Mountain. The Strawberry Mountain range extends east to west through the center of the forest. Year-round recreation opportunities abound.

Malheur National Forest (*continued*)

Points of Interest

▲ The Malheur is one of only two forests in the Northwest with a wild horse herd. The forest also supports the largest remaining wild runs of spring chinook and summer steelhead in northeast Oregon; it is one of three remaining wild runs in the Columbia River System. The forest also provides winter roost habitat for over 150 American bald eagles.

▲ Campers enjoy both developed campgrounds and traditional primitive campsites across the forest. Picnicking can be enjoyed among the beautiful wildflowers. There is outstanding scenery along 2,117 miles of forest roads. Hikers and horseback riders have more than 230 miles of trails to enjoy.

▲ Campgrounds are usually open on the forest between May 30 and October 15. Some of the campgrounds are accessible at other times of the year, but the water systems are likely to be shut off and no maintenance is provided. Campgrounds operate on a "pack-it-out" basis. Large garbage sacks are available free from Forest Service offices for packing garbage out.

▲ Winter weather begins in October, generally lasting through March. At higher elevations, snowpack varies from 4–8 feet deep. Snowmobiling, cross-country skiing, ice fishing, and sledding are all popular winter activities here.

▲ About April, fluctuating spring weather sets in. Although a late spring snowfall is not uncommon, roads and trails begin to open up by June. The fishing season is regulated by the state of Oregon; it usually begins in April, but stream fishing does not really become good until after the spring runoff, in May, June, and July.

Campgrounds in a national forest are well marked and provide great access to its many resources.

▲ By the end of June, summer temperatures have usually arrived, along with greater fire danger. Temperatures are often in the 90s at lower elevations, somewhat cooler in the mountains. Afternoon lightning storms are not uncommon.

▲ Fall brings huckleberries and hunters, and the campgrounds receive heavy use. Both mule deer and Rocky Mountain elk are hunted on the Forest along with a variety of other game. Hunting seasons and regulations are managed by the State of Oregon. Big game seasons are usually in October and November.

▲ The Strawberry Mountain Wilderness attracts backpackers and hikers who enjoy its alpine lakes and mountain scenery. More outstanding scenery and solitude are available in the Indian Rock-Vinegar Hill Scenic Area at the northeastern corner of the Forest and the Monument Rock Wilderness on the eastern boundary. Nipple Butte, Murderers Creek, and Dixie Mountain offer a true, wild experience and opportunity to view rich varieties of wildlife species even though they are not designated wilderness areas.

Wilderness Areas

Strawberry Mountain Wilderness consists of 68,303 acres and has an extensive trail system. There are seven mountain lakes. Strawberry Lake receives about 80% of the recorded use in the wilderness. Besides the Strawberry Lake trailhead, there are 14 other trailheads into the mountains. The skyline trail makes a complete east-west course across the range from Canyon Mountain to the John Day summit, above Prairie City. For information contact: Prairie City Ranger District—(503) 820-3311 or Bear Valley Ranger District—(503) 575-2110.

Monument Rock Wilderness encompasses 19,800 acres with 12 miles of trails. The wilderness is shared with Wallowa-Whitman National Forest and offers camping, fishing, and hiking. The Little Malheur River trail follows the river 8 miles through a forested canyon, from the southern end of the Forest up to Elk Flat. From Elk Flat a road leads to Table Rock Lookout and the wide, open top of Monument Rock Wilderness. A wander across the wildflower-strewn meadows at the top of the Monument Rock area offers views to the Steens in the south and Eagle Caps to the north. Ironsides and Castle Rock are prominent features nearby. For information contact: Prairie City Ranger District—(503) 820-3311.

Bear Valley Ranger District

For Information

Bear Valley Ranger District
528 E. Main
John Day, OR 97845
(503) 575-2110

Campground Locations/Activities

1. **Canyon Meadows:** 20 mi. SE of John Day on F.R. 1520. *Activities:* Hiking, hunting, fishing, non-motorized boating, picnicking, and access to Strawberry Mountain Wilderness.
2. **Oregon Mines:** 25 mi. SW of Mt. Vernon via U.S. 26 W, F.R. 21 and 2170. *Activities:* Stream fishing, picnicking, and hunting.
3. **Parish Cabin:** 11 mi. E of Seneca on F.R. 16. *Activities:* Group picnicking, stream fishing, and hunting.
4. **Starr:** 16 mi. S of John Day on U.S. Hwy. 395. *Activities:* Snow play area, picnicking, and hunting.

Campground (see map on page 82)	Elevation (feet)	Tent/Trailer Sites	Water**; S = Stream; PI = Piped; PU = Pump	Toilets V = Vault
1. Canyon Meadows*	5,100	18	PI	V
2. Oregon Mines*	4,300	4	S	V
3. Parish Cabin*	4,900	20	PI	V
4. Starr*	5,100	8	PI	V
5. Wickiup*	4,300	9	PI	V

*Picnic sites available.
**Only water from developed systems at recreation sites is maintained safe to drink. Stream and open water sources are easily contaminated and should not be drunk without proper treatment.

5. **Wickiup:** 18 mi. SE of John Day on F.R. 15. *Activities:* Stream fishing, hunting, group picnicking.

Burns Ranger District

For Information

Burns Ranger District
HC 74, Box 12870
Hines, OR 97738
(503) 573-7292

Exhibits of ancient fossils in nearby John Day Fossil Beds National Monument pique the imagination to wonder what this land looked like when dinosaurs roamed this very site.

Campground Locations/Activities

6. **Idlewild:** 17 mi. N of Burns on U.S. 395. *Activities:* Group picnicking and hunting. Excellent for bird watching during Spring.
7. **Yellowjacket:** 30 mi. NW of Burns on F.R. 3745. *Activities:* Boating, lake fishing, and hunting.

Campground (see map on page 82)	Elevation (feet)	Tent/Trailer Sites	Water**; S = Stream; PI = Piped; PU = Pump	Toilets V = Vault
6. Idlewild*	5,300	24	PI	V
7. Yellowjacket	4,800	20	PU	V

*Picnic sites available.
**Only water from developed systems at recreation sites is maintained safe to drink. Open water sources are easily contaminated and should not be drunk without proper treatment.

Long Creek Ranger District

For Information

Long Creek Ranger District
528 E. Main
John Day, OR 97845
(503) 575-2110

Campground Locations/Activities

8. **Beech Creek:** 17 mi. N of Mt. Vernon on U.S. 395. *Activities:* Hunting.
9. **Dixie:** On U.S. 26, 8 mi. NE of Prairie City. *Activities:* Group picnicking, berry picking, and hunting.
10. **Magone Lake:** 26 mi. N of John Day on F.R. 3620. *Activities:* Boat launch, swimming, hiking, fishing, and group picnicking.
11. **Middle Fork:** 9 mi. NW of Austin Jct. on C.R. 20. *Activities:* Primitive site—no water.

Campground (see map on page 82)	Elevation (feet)	Tent Sites	Tent/Trailer Sites	Water**; S = Stream; PI = Piped; PU = Pump	Toilets V = Vault
8. Beech Creek*	4,500	2	3	PI	V
9. Dixie*	5,000		11	PU	V
10. Magone Lake*	5,000	3	13	PI	V
11. Middle Fork	4,100	—Primitive—			V

*Picnic sites available.
**Only water from developed systems at recreation sites is maintained safe to drink. Open water sources are easily contaminated and should not be drunk without proper treatment. Magone Lake has one double trailer site and three barrier-free tent/trailer sites.

Prairie City Ranger District

For Information

Prairie City Ranger District
P.O. Box 156
Prairie City, OR 97869
(503) 820-3311

Campground Locations/Activities

12. **Big Creek:** 21 mi. E of Seneca on F.R. 815. *Activities:* Stream fishing and hunting.
13. **Crescent:** 17 mi. SE of Prairie City on F.R. 14. *Activities:* Stream fishing and hunting.
14. **Elk Creek:** 25 mi. SE of Prairie City on F.R. 16. *Activities:* Stream fishing and hunting.
15. **Little Crane:** 30 mi. SE of Prairie City on F.R. 16. *Activities:* Stream fishing and hunting.
16. **Murray:** 21 mi. E of Senea on F.R. 924. *Activities:* Stream fishing, hiking, and hunting.
17. **McNaughton Springs:** 8 mi. S of Prairie City on F.R. 6001. *Activities:* Stream fishing, hunting, and access to Strawberry Mountain Wilderness.
18. **N. Fork Malheur:** 29 mi. SE of Prairie City on F.R. 1675. *Activities:* Stream fishing and hunting.
19. **Slide Creek:** 9 mi. S of Prairie City on F.R. 6001. *Activities:* Stream fishing, hiking, horse corrals, hunting, and access to Strawberry Mountain Wilderness.
20. **Strawberry:** 11 mi. S of Prairie City on F.R. 6001. *Activities:* Stream fishing, hiking, horse corrals, hunting, and access to Strawberry Mountain Wilderness.
21. **Trout Farm:** 15 mi. SE of Prairie City on F.R. 14. *Activities:* Pond and stream fishing, group picnicking, and hunting.

Campground (see map on page 82)	Elevation (feet)	Tent Sites	Tent/Trailer Sites	Water**; S = Stream; PI = Piped; PU = Pump	Toilets V = Vault
12. Big Creek	5,100		14	PU	V
13. Crescent	5,200		4	S	V
14. Elk Creek	5,000		5	S	V
15. Little Crane	5,500		5	S	V
16. Murray	5,200		14	PU	V
17. McNaughton Springs	4,900		4	S	V
18. N. Fork Malheur	4,700		5	S	V
19. Slide Creek	4,800		1	S	V
20. Strawberry	5,700		11	PI	V
21. Trout Farm*	4,900	5	4	PI	V

*Picnic sites available.
**Only water from developed systems at recreation sites is maintained safe to drink. Open water sources such as streams are easily contaminated and should not be drunk without proper treatment.

Minam State Park

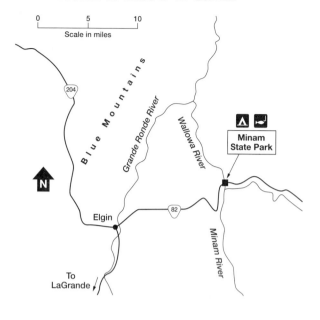

Scale in miles

204

Blue Mountains

Grande Ronde River

Wallowa River

Minam State Park

N

82

Elgin

Minam River

To LaGrande

Location

Located in a pine forest, Minam State Recreation Area can be accessed off S.R. 82, 15.5 miles northeast of Elgin. This 602-acre park fronts two miles of Wallowa River below the river's junction with Minam River. The area provides access for rafting and fishing.

Facilities and Activities

The campground is open mid-April through late October on a first-come, first-served basis.

12 primitive tent campsites
  pit toilets
  drinking water
  stoves
  tables
7 picnic sites
rafting/fishing

For Information

Minam State Recreation Area
c/o Wallowa Lake State Park
72214 Marine Lane
Joseph, OR 97846
(503) 432-8855
FAX—432-4141

Expect vistas, landmarks, and beauty that have awed travelers through northeastern Oregon since the first settlers journeyed here.

Newberry National Volcanic Monument

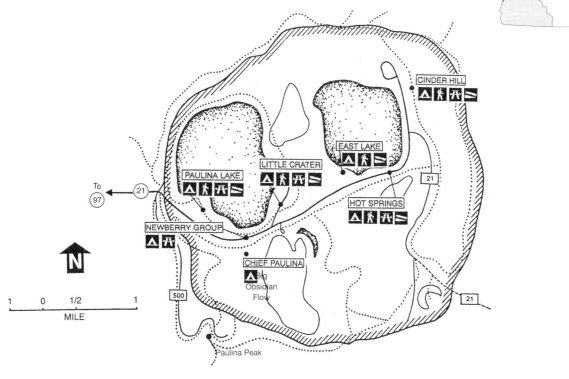

For Information

Newberry National Volcanic Monument
Deschutes National Forest
Fort Rock Ranger District
1230 N.E. 3rd, Suite A-262
Bend, Oregon 97701
(503) 383-4708

Campgrounds	Total Sites	RVs (no hook-ups)	Tents	Fee	Drinking Water	Toilets Flush/Vault	Sanitary Dump
Cinder Hill	110	•	•	•	•	F/V	•
East Lake	29	•	•	•	•	F/V	
Hot Springs**	42	•	•	•	•	F/V	
Little Crater	50	•	•	•	•	F/V	
Paulina	69	•	•	•	•	F/V	
Group Campground							
Newberry Group*	3	•	•	•	•	V	
Horse Camp							
Chief Paulina*			•	•	•		

*Reservations required by writing park headquarters or calling
(503) 388-5664

**Open only when use required

Three National Forest campgrounds are available in the vicinity. Prairie (16 units) and McKay (10 units) are on County Road 21 along Paulina Creek. Rosland (11 units) is off of County Road 43 west of La Pine.

Location

Nestled within the Deschutes National Forest, Newberry National Volcanic Monument is located in central Oregon off of Hwy. 97 between Bend and La Pine. It is the fourth national monument in the U.S. to be managed by the National Forest Service. The monument stretches across 28 miles and encompasses over 50,000 acres of an internationally significant volcanic region. Newberry Crater, the park's centerpiece, is 13 miles east of Hwy. 97 on County Road 21.

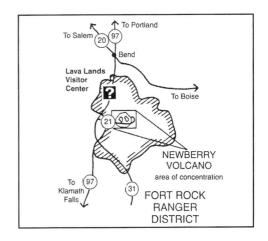

Map does not show actual Monument boundaries.

Newberry National Volcanic Monument *(continued)*

Points of Interest

▲ 95% of known volcanological features can be seen here.

▲ Newberry Crater is a caldera with two scenic lakes and volcanic flows of ash, pumice, and lava.

▲ Lava Butte depicts a classic volcanic cinder cone and rugged lava flow.

▲ Lava Cast Forest represents a frozen forest of tree molds in a lava flow.

▲ Lava River Cave is a 600-foot-long lava tube cave.

▲ The area provided major sources of obsidian for tool making and trade by early Native Americans.

Facilities and Activities

300 RV and tent campsites
3 group campsites
6 picnic areas
9 developed hiking trails
5 interpretive trails
boating/boat ramps
fishing
horseback riding trails and camping
bicycling (paved roads only)
snowmobiling/nordic skiing
2 visitor centers/exhibits/slide programs
amphitheater
interpretive/campfire programs
RV park with full hook-ups
showers and laundry
2 resorts with lodging
boat rentals and launching
restaurants, snacks
groceries, ice, public phones
camping and fishing supplies
winter services

General Information

▲ Fees are charged to camp in monument campgrounds. No park entrance fees are charged.

▲ Two visitor centers are operated seasonally. Lava Lands Visitor Center on Hwy. 97 (mid-March to late October) and Paulina Visitor Center in Newberry Crater (June to early September) provide exhibits, information, slide shows and programs for visitors. Maps and books are available for purchase. Contact Lava Lands at (503) 593-2421 for information.

▲ Naturalist activities are provided in the summer and include walks, flintknapping or arrowhead manufacture, and campfire programs.

▲ Campgrounds operate on a first-come, first-served basis. Sites provide an individual parking spur, table, and fireplace. All have drinking water, flush and/or vault toilets; most have boat launching facilities with loading docks.

▲ Group campsites offer drinking water and dumpsters for garbage. Newberry Group Campground offers group picnic areas, electrical outlets, tent areas, group fire pits, and paved parking pads. Reservations are required: (503) 388-5664.

▲ A horse camp offers units that accommodate 4, 8, or 12 horses. Reservations are required: (503) 388-5664.

▲ Day-use areas are located at Paulina Creek Falls, Big Obsidian Flow, Paulina Lake, Newberry Group Site, Paulina Peak, Little Crater, Hot Springs, and Cinder Hill.

▲ Handicap accesses are provided for some restrooms, visitor centers, and trails.

▲ Hiking trails vary in difficulty and length (⅞-mile at Big Obsidian Flow to 22 miles at Crater Rim). Horses are allowed on many trails.

▲ Fishing is excellent for stocked brown, rainbow, and brook trout. Kokanee have also been stocked in Paulina Lake. East Lake has been experimentally stocked with Atlantic Salmon. A state fishing license is required.

▲ Mountain bikes are permitted on roads open to vehicular traffic and on some trails.

▲ Public showers and laundry facilities are available for a fee at East Lake RV Park.

▲ Summer temperatures range from 60°–100°F in the day and 30°–50°F at night.

Walk through rugged lava flows and climb atop a classic volcanic cinder cone at La Butte.

Ochoco Lake State Park

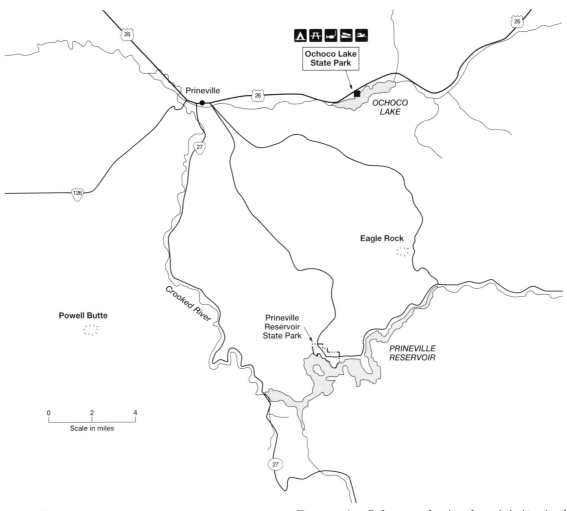

For Information

Ochoco Lake State Park
c/o Prineville Reservoir State Park
Prineville Lake Route
916777 Parkland Drive
Prineville, OR 97754
(503) 447-4363
FAX—447-1247

Location

Located on a juniper wooded lakeside promontory at an elevation of 3,140 feet, Ochoco Lake State Park offers boating, fishing, waterskiing, and swimming. Accessed from U.S. 26, 7 miles east of Prineville, this 10-acre park has primitive sites for camping. There are many outstanding recreation attractions in this part of Central Oregon that include the beautiful Ochoco National Forest and Prineville Reservoir. Other parks in the vicinity include Prineville Reservoir State Park, Painted Hills, Smith Rock, Cline Falls, and Ochoco and Ogden Waysides.

Facilities and Activities

The campground is open mid-April through late October on first-come, first-served basis.

22 primitive RV/tent campsites (35′ maximum
   length)
   drinking water
   flush toilets
   wood stoves
   tables
29 picnic sites
boat ramp/boating/fishing
waterskiing/swimming

Ochoco National Forest and Crooked River National Grassland

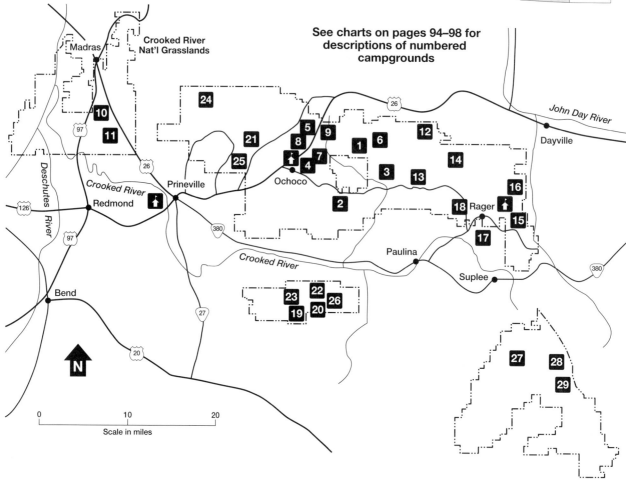

Crooked River Nat'l Grasslands

See charts on pages 94–98 for descriptions of numbered campgrounds

For Information

Ochoco National Forest and
Crooked River National Grassland
3000 E. Third Street
P.O. Box 490
Prineville, OR 97754
(503) 447-6247

Location

The Ochoco National Forest and Crooked River National Grassland occupy 959,290 acres around the geographic center of the state. Elevations range between 1,500 and 7,163 feet. Located at the western edge of the Blue Mountain Range, the forest is noted for its pine forests and the grassland is characterized by sagebrush/juniper areas often referred to as a "high desert." Both areas have picturesque rimrock vantage points, deep canyons, and other unique geologic landforms. The forest and grassland are accessible via S.R. 380 and U.S. 26 out of Prineville.

Points of Interest

▲ Camp and picnic sites have been developed throughout the forest and on the grassland. They are designed to blend with the environment and are located away from traffic and commercial developments. A parking space (most accommodate trailers averaging 22′ in length), table, fire pit, tent space and central water supply are typically provided at developed campgrounds. Most of the campgrounds have some type of vault toilet facility.

▲ The Ochoco encourages visitors to find their own special place for camping. Undeveloped campsites are available. Convenience facilities such as tables, fire pits, or drinking water are not pro-

Ochoco National Forest and
Crooked River National Grassland *(continued)*

vided at all these areas, so be prepared for "roughing it."

▲ Campgrounds are usually open from May 30 through Labor Day weekend. After Labor Day, many campgrounds remain open, but water systems are turned off and visitors are asked to pack their own trash out.

▲ Campsites are available on a first-come, first-served basis. The limit of stay varies from 1 to 14 days. Fees range from no fee to a per-day charge, and are paid at the campgrounds. For group camping and picnicking contact the district ranger stations for reservations.

▲ A well-developed forest and grassland road system provides access to much of the area. Small developed campgrounds, usually close to a small stream, are common. Many areas do not provide drinking water, so it is advisable to bring a supply with you. Delintment Lake, Antelope Reservoir, Walton Lake, and Haystack Reservoir offer fishing, camp facilities, and water recreation opportunities.

▲ Three wildernesses (Black Canyon, Mill Creek, and Bridge Creek) and three special management units (Silver Creek, Squaw Creek, and Lookout Mountain) provide many opportunities for backcountry camping, hiking, and horseback riding. Also, Deschutes Canyon and the National Grassland offer pristine canyon hiking and fishing opportunities.

▲ Two National Recreation Trails are also available for enjoyment: Round Mountain Trail (8.3 miles) and Twin Pillars Trail (9.0 miles). A trip into Black Canyon will take you to an area that is home for a herd of Rocky Mountain elk.

▲ Recreational attractions vary from hunting and fishing to rockhounding and cross-country skiing. The largest annual influx of visitors to the Ochoco occurs in late summer and fall when mule deer and elk attract large numbers of hunters. Other

"Ochoco" is derived from a Paiute word for willow. Like the Native Americans of 2,000 years ago, people still find the forest full of rich natural resources—especially for recreation.

Central Oregon, surrounded by natural beauty, is clearly the Northwest's year-round playground. Climbers come from around the world to scale the majestic spires of Smith Rock and its sheer walls above the Crooked River. It lies just north of Redmond.

wildlife includes antelope, a herd of wild horses, an occasional wildcat, and rarely a cougar. Golden and bald eagles are commonly sighted in the spring, though no bald eagle nesting sites are known in the forest. The Crooked River National Grassland supports a small herd of antelope, numerous mule deer, quail, and chukkars.

▲ Rockhounding is popular because of the unique geology of the area. In fact, the forest is in the center of one of the best known rockhound areas in the nation. Forest roads lead to several sites containing semi-precious quartz-family stones, such as thunder eggs, agates, jasper, limb casts, and petrified wood.

▲ Weather conditions in the summer are typically warm and sunny during the daytime, with cool nights. Frost can and does occur at higher elevations throughout the year. July and August are usually the warmest months.

Wilderness Areas

Black Canyon Wilderness is located approximately 57 miles east of Prineville and 35 miles west of John Day. Access is 11 miles out of Dayville on F.R. 74. Covering over 13,400 acres with elevations ranging between 2,850 and 6,483 feet, the wilderness is dominated by the steep canyons and sharp ridges formed by Black Canyon. Approximately 80% of the area exceeds a 30% slope gradient. Almost one-half of the area consists of openings that are usually located on ridge tops or south facing slopes. The timbered areas consist of mixed conifer and ponderosa pine old growth stands. Approximately 10 miles of streams drain the area and eventually enter the John Day River. Small native trout are found in the perennial streams and steelhead use them for spawning. The area serves as a year-long range for an abundance of wildlife including deer and elk. For more information contact: Paulina Ranger District— (503) 477-3713.

Bridge Creek Wilderness is located approximately 30 miles east-northeast of Prineville. This trailless wilderness covers 5,400 acres with elevation ranges between 4,360 and 6,607 feet. The wilderness' best access is 37 miles east of Prineville

Ochoco National Forest and
Crooked River National Grassland *(continued)*

Trout fishing is very popular in the Ochoco. Late spring and fall are the best times of the year to fill your creel.

on F.R. 22 via U.S. 26. Traveling F.R. 22 to F.R. 2200-150, then to 2630 will access the western corner of the wilderness. At this point the road becomes a limited maintenance road recommended for high-clearance vehicles only. More than half of the wilderness contains slopes of less than 30% gradient, although some extremely steep terrain is also present. The predominant timber type is mixed conifer with the remainder being lodgepole pine with small segments of ponderosa pine. Streams in the wilderness total 5.8 miles, and Bridge Creek is the domestic water source for the community of Mitchell. An abundance of wildlife occupies the area year-round. For more information contact: Big Summit Ranger District—(503) 447-9645.

Mill Creek Wilderness is located about 20 miles northeast of Prineville. The best access is from Wildcat Campground, 11 miles north of Ochoco Reservoir on F.R. 33. Covering 17,400 acres with elevation

ranges between 3,700 and 6,200 feet, the terrain varies from a steep, broken, lattice-type pattern of ridges and canyons southeast of Mill Creek to an almost flat plateau in the northwest corner. Two-thirds of the area has slopes exceeding 30% gradient. Fifteen percent of the area consists of openings, which are mostly barren ridge tops, but also includes some high-elevation meadows. A mix of conifer tree species dominates the forested area (84%). The northwest corner plateau area is mostly forested with lodgepole pine. Twenty-two miles of streams drain the area. Small rainbow trout are found in some of the perennial streams. Most of the area provides summer, spring, and fall range for an abundance of wildlife including deer and elk. Twin Pillars, a rather unique volcanic plug, is located in the northwest portion of the area. For more information contact: Prineville Ranger District—(503) 447-9641.

REGION 2

International climbers come to "America's Euro-Crag," Smith Rock, to enjoy the challenges of climbing within the 623-acre state park.

Big Summit Ranger District

Forest campsites provide lots of space for play and solace.

For Information

Big Summit Ranger District
348855 Ochoco Ranger Station
Prineville, OR 97754-9612
(503) 447-9645

Campground (see map on page 90)	Elevation (feet)	Campsites P = Primitive	Fees	Drinking Water	Vault Toilets
1. Allen Creek Horse Camp	4,200	5			•
2. Biggs Springs	4,800	3			•
3. Deep Creek	4,200	6			•
4. Ochoco Forest Camp*	4,000	6	•	•	•
5. Ochoco Divide	4,700	28	•	•	•
6. Scotts Camp	4,100	3		•	•
7. Walton Lake**	5,000	30	•	•	•
8. Whiterock	4,500	P			•
9. Wildwood	4,800	5			•

*Group picnic shelter reservation site/barrier-free.
**Group reservations/barrier-free.

Campground Locations/Activities

1. **Allen Creek Horse Camp:** 25 mi. E of Prineville to Ochoco Ranger Station, 19 mi. NE of Ranger Station on F.R. 22. *Activities:* Horseback riding; corrals, tables, and water for horses only.
2. **Biggs Springs:** E of Prineville 45 mi. via U.S. 26, SE of Ochoco Ranger Station 14 mi. on F.R. 42, S on F.R. 4215 for 5 mi. *Activities:* Camping (tables and fire rings).
3. **Deep Creek:** 49 mi. E of Prineville; along F.R. 42 , 4 mi. E of Big Summit Prairie. *Activities:* Camping (tables) and creek fishing.
4. **Ochoco Forest Camp:** E of Prineville 25 mi.; adjacent to Ochoco Ranger Station. Road access: F.R. 2610. *Activities:* Hiking, group picnicking, and fishing. Bike camp barrier-free facility.
5. **Ochoco Divide:** E of Prineville 30 mi. via U.S. 26; at summit of Ochoco Pass. *Activities:* Camping (tables and fire rings).
6. **Scotts Camp:** 25 mi. E of Prineville to Ochoco Ranger Station, then 22 mi. NE of Ranger Station on F.R. 22. *Activities:* Camping (tables).
7. **Walton Lake:** E of Prineville 31 mi.; NE of Ochoco Ranger Station, 7 mi. on F.R. 22. *Activities:* Boating (no motors), fishing, hiking, group camping.
8. **Whiterock:** 25 mi. from Prineville via U.S. 26, left on F.R. 3350, go 5 mi., then right on F.R. 300 to end. *Activities:* Very primitive camping (one table, fire rings and picnic area).
9. **Wildwood:** N of Prineville 27 mi. via U.S. 26, E on F.R. 2630 for 3 mi., N on F.R. 2210 for 3 mi. *Activities:* Camping (tables and fire rings).

Forest campgrounds are usually open from May 30 through Labor Day weekend. After Labor Day many campgrounds remain open, but water systems are turned off.

Crooked River National Grassland

Campground (see map on page 90)	Elevation (feet)	Campsites	Fees	Drinking Water	Flush Toilets
10. Haystack Reservoir	2,900	24	•	•	•
11. Cyrus Horse Camp	2,900	2			

For Information

Crooked River National Grassland
155 North Court, P.O. Box 687
Prineville, OR 97754-9117
(503) 447-9640

Managed by the Ochoco National Forest, the grassland includes much of the area homesteaded around the turn of the century; however, low rainfall and the depression of the 1930s caused many homesteaders to fail. The land became a part of the National Forest System in 1960 and today is the only grassland in Oregon and Washington administered by the Forest Service. The mission of the grassland is to demonstrate and promote sound grassland agriculture. Recreational opportunities within the grassland include camping, picnicking, hiking, horseback riding, boating, swimming, waterskiing, and fishing. For more information contact: Crooked River National Grassland, 155 North Court, P.O. Box 687, Prineville, OR 97754, (503) 447-9640.

Campground Location/Activities

10. **Haystack Reservoir:** 14 mi. S of Madras via U.S. 97; access via F.R. 1130, turn left on road 68, proceed .5 mi. to Haystack Reservoir. *Activities:* Swimming, fishing, waterskiing, (boat ramp), and picnicking (tables and fire rings).
11. **Cyrus Horse Camp:** 16 mi. N of Prineville via U.S. 26 to F.R. 7130. From 7130 turn left on F.R. 5750, proceed 1.3 mi. to camp. *Activities:* Horseback riding; 2 corrals that hold 4 horses each. Water for horses only. Tables and fire rings available.

Although the Crooked River National Grassland has been set aside to promote sound grassland agriculture, many recreational opportunities such as camping, hiking, boating, and horseback riding are available to visitors here and in the forest.

Paulina Ranger District

Many areas of the forest are suitable for cross-country skiing. The Bandit Springs area off Highway 26, and the Cram Creek area south of Round Mountain are ideal spots.

For Information

Paulina Ranger District
171500 Beaver Creek Road
Paulina, OR 97751-9706
(503) 477-3713

Campground Locations/Activities

12. **Barnhouse:** E of Mitchell 13 mi. on U.S. 26, then F.R. 12 for 5 mi. *Activities:* Camping.
13. **Big Springs:** 55 mi. E of Prineville, E of Ochoco Ranger Station 28 mi. on F.R. 42, then N on F.R. 4270 for 2 mi. *Activities:* Camping.
14. **Cottonwood:** E of Prineville 65 mi., E of Ochoco Ranger Station 35 mi. on F.R. 42, then N on F.R. 12 for 9 mi. *Activities:* Camping.
15. **Frazier:** SE of Prineville 87 mi. Take left fork 3 mi. E of Paulina to F.R. 58 to F.R. 511. *Activities:* Camping.
16. **Mud Springs:** SE of Prineville 90 mi., take left fork 3 mi. E of Paulina to F.R. 58. *Activities:* South Prong trailhead accessing Black Canyon Wilderness.

Campground (see map on page 90)	Elevation (feet)	Campsites	Fees	Drinking Water	Vault Toilets
12. Barnhouse	5,100	6			•
13. Big Springs	5,000	4			•
14. Cottonwood	5,700	6			•
15. Frazier	5,000	5			•
16. Mud Springs	5,820	4			•
17. Sugar Creek*	4,000	11	•	•	•
18. Wolf Creek	5,700	11		•	•

*Barrier-free facilities.

17. **Sugar Creek:** SE of Prineville 69 mi. Take left fork 3 mi. E of Paulina to F.R. 58. *Activities:* Fishing and swimming (barrier-free facilities).
18. **Wolf Creek:** SE of Prineville 68 mi., take left fork 3 mi. E of Paulina to F.R. 42. *Activities:* Fishing.

"No trace" camping ethic is easy to practice when you realize whose "homes" you are visiting.

Prineville Ranger District

For Information

Prineville Ranger District
155 North Court
P.O. Box 687
Prineville, OR 97754-9117
(503) 447-9641

Campground Locations/Activities

19. **Antelope Flat Reservoir:** 47 mi. SE of Prineville via S.R. 380 to F.R. 17 then F.R. 1700-600. *Activities:* Boating and fishing; black- top boat ramp, boat trailer parking lot; tables and fire rings.
20. **Double Cabin:** 48 mi. SE of Prineville via S.R. 380 to F.R. 17, then left on F.R. 16, then left on F.R. 1600-350. *Activities:* Primitive camping (tables); pond within .5 mi.
21. **Dry Creek Horse Camp:** 17 mi. NE of Prineville via U.S. 26 to Mill Creek Road, left on Mill Creek Road to F.R. 3370, then 2.5 mi. to F.R. 3370-200. *Activities:* Horseback riding (18 horse corrals, tables, fire rings, water for horses only).
22. **Elkhorn:** 37 mi. SE of Prineville via S.R. 380 to F.R. 16. *Activities:* Camping (tables and fire rings).
23. **Pine Creek:** 39 mi. SE of Prineville via S.R. 380 to F.R. 17, then left on F.R. 1750, then left on F.R. 1750-450. *Activities:* Camping (tables and fire rings).

Campground (see map on page 90)	Elevation (feet)	Campsites	Fees	Drinking Water	Vault Toilets
19. Antelope Flat Reservoir	4,600	24	•	•	•
20. Double Cabin	5,200	5			•
21. Dry Creek Horse Camp	3,900	5			•
22. Elkhorn	4,500	4		•	•
23. Pine Creek	5,750	2		•	•
24. Whistler	5,560	2			•
25. Wildcat	3,700	17	•	•	•
26. Wiley Flat	5,000	5		•	•

24. **Whistler:** 30 mi. NE of Prineville on McKay Road to F.R. 27, then F.R. 2700-500. *Activities:* Camping, hiking and horseback riding. Trailhead to Mill Creek Wilderness; one horse corral, fire ring, and table.
25. **Wildcat:** 20 mi. NE of Prineville via U.S. 26, on Mill Creek Road. *Activities:* Camping, hiking, fishing, and picnicking (tables and fire rings). Twin Pillars and Belknap trailheads access Mill Creek Wilderness.
26. **Wiley Flat:** 46 mi. SE of Prineville on S.R. 380 to F.R. 16, then F.R. 1600-400. *Activities:* Camping (tables and fire rings); lightly improved.

Snow Mountain Ranger District

For Information

Snow Mountain Ranger District
HC 74 Box 12870
Hines, OR 97738-9401
(503) 573-7292

Campground Locations/Activities

27. **Delintment Lake:** Post-Paulina Hwy. E of Prineville approximately 75 mi., then Suplee Road to F.R. 41. Well Signed. From Burns, N of Burns 48 mi. on F.R. 47. Left on F.R. 41 to lake. *Activities:* Camping, group picnicking, boating and fishing; boat ramp, accessible fishing dock; limited barrier-free access.

Campground (see map on page 90)	Elevation (feet)	Campsites	Fees	Drinking Water	Vault Toilets
27. Delintment Lake*	5,600	24	•	•	•
28. Emigrant	5,100	6		•	•
29. Falls	5,000	5		•	•

*Limited barrier-free access.

28. **Emigrant:** N of Burns 34 mi. on F.R. 47, then F.R. 43. *Activities:* Stream fishing.
29. **Falls:** N of Burns 30 mi. on F.R. 47, then F.R. 43. *Activities:* Stream fishing.

REGION 2

Prineville Reservoir State Park

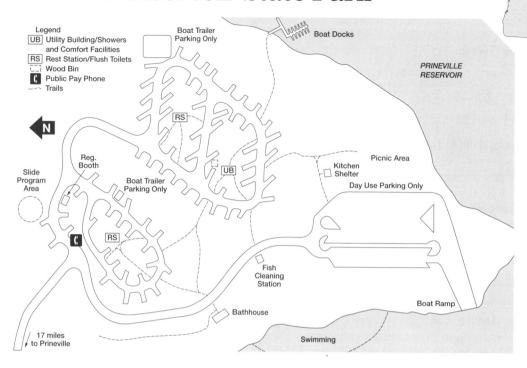

Legend
- **UB** Utility Building/Showers and Comfort Facilities
- **RS** Rest Station/Flush Toilets
- Wood Bin
- **C** Public Pay Phone
- Trails

N

Boat Trailer Parking Only
Boat Docks

PRINEVILLE RESERVOIR

RS

Reg. Booth

Slide Program Area

Boat Trailer Parking Only

UB

Kitchen Shelter

Picnic Area

Day Use Parking Only

RS

Fish Cleaning Station

Bathhouse

17 miles to Prineville

Swimming

Boat Ramp

For Information

Prineville Reservoir State Park
Prineville Lake Route
916777 Parkland Drive
Prineville, Oregon 97754
(503) 447-4363
FAX—447-1247

Location

Prineville Reservoir State Park covers 365 acres in a juniper-tree-covered area along the shore of Prineville Reservoir, which impounds the waters of the Crooked River. The park is near the geographical center of Oregon, which is known for its rockhounding opportunities. Many nearby areas

These red-tailed hawk chicks are a beautiful reminder of the delicate balance between wildlife and man that must be maintained to enjoy nature's gifts for generations to come.

Prineville Reservoir State Park *(continued)*

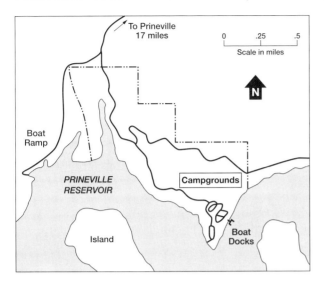

have been set aside for rock collectors where they can dig for their favorite rocks free of charge. Rockhounds from all over the country come to find agates with dendrites, white plume agates, various colored moss agates, green jasper, jasper interlaced with agate, Ochoco chalcendony, thunder eggs (the state rock), and petrified wood. There are many outstanding recreation attractions besides the excellent water activities to pursue on the reservoir. One of the best-known landmarks in this area is Stein's Pillar, located on Mill Creek Road, 15 miles northeast of Prineville. The beautiful Ochoco National Forest offers many sights and recreational opportunities, including good fishing and hunting. Petersen's Rock Garden and the Reindeer Farm near Redmond are two of the most popular tourist attractions in the area. There is a private marina that sells gas and groceries on the reservoir. A county park, primitive BLM camp, and private resort are located in the area.

Facilities and Activities

The campground is open mid-April through late October. Reservations are accepted from Memorial Day weekend through Labor Day.

22 RV campsites w/full hookups (40′ maximum
    length)
    showers
    drinking water
    flush toilets
    wood stoves
    tables
48 tent campsites
58 picnic sites
kitchen shelter/amphitheater
boat ramp/moorage docks (reservable)
boating/waterskiing/swim area
fishing/cleaning station
sightseeing/rockhounding
accessible campsite for people with disabilities

Rockhounds from all over the country may come to the area to find agates, jasper, thunder eggs and petrified wood; water-lovers come to play in the reservoir.

Shelton State Wayside

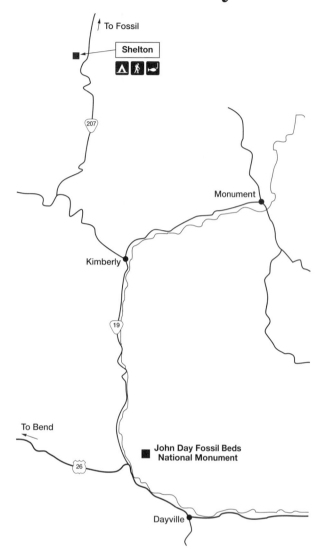

To Fossil

Shelton

207

Monument

Kimberly

19

To Bend

John Day Fossil Beds
National Monument

26

Dayville

For Information

Shelton State Wayside
c/o Clyde Holliday State Park
P.O. Box 9
Canyon City, OR 97820
(503) 575-2773
FAX—575-2016

Location

Shelton State Wayside is bordered by Service Creek in a gently sloping canyon on S.R. 19, 10 miles southeast of Fossil. This 180-acre park lies along S.R. 19, which leads through the heart of John Day Fossil Beds National Monument land. At an elevation of 3,500 feet, the park's landscape is dominated by old ponderosa pine trees and a scattering of juniper and Douglas fir.

Facilities and Activities

The campground is open from mid-April through late October, weather permitting. The park operates on a first-come, first-served basis.

36 primitive RV/tent campsites (50′ maximum
   length)
   pit toilets
   drinking water
   stoves
   tables
43 picnic sites
fishing/hiking/sightseeing

John Day Fossil Beds reveal an amazing span of time between the extinction of dinosaurs and the beginning of the Ice Age. Visitors will be intrigued by fossil exhibits of saber-toothed tigers, giant pigs, and three-toed horses.

37 MILLION YEARS AGO
UPPER CLARNO FORMATION

Succor Creek State Park

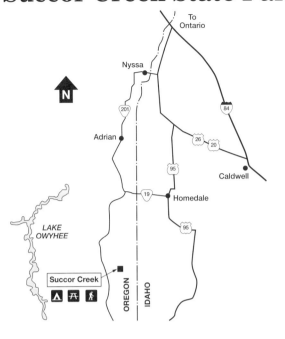

Location

Succor Creek State Park is located off Oregon 201, 30 miles south of Nyssa. Like many parks in the area, Succor Creek Recreation Area showcases significant geological events and oddities. There are massive formations and colorful pinnacles that rise from canyon walls in this area. Although the campsites are primitive, visitors have the opportunity to hike, picnic, and sightsee in the area.

Facilities and Activities

The campground is open on a first-come, first-served basis from mid-April through late October.

19 primitive RV/tent campsites
    flush toilets
    drinking water
    tables
picnic sites
hiking/trails
sightseeing/wildlife viewing

For Information

Succor Creek Recreation Area
c/o Farewell Bend State Park
Star Route
Huntington, OR 97907
(503) 869-2365
FAX—869-2457

Early risers have the best luck to observe wildlife.

REGION 2

Ukiah-Dale State Park

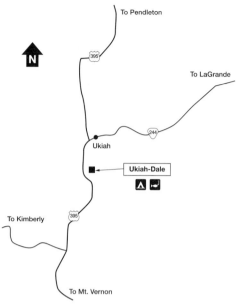

Location

Ukiah-Dale State Park is located on U.S. 395, 3 miles southwest of Ukiah. This 2,987-acre state park lies in a steep, forested canyon in the Blue Mountains along the banks of Camas Creek and the North Fork of John Day River. Originally established as a scenic roadside protection area, Ukiah-Dale State Park offers beautiful scenery and fishing for campers.

Facilities and Activities

The campground is open mid-April through late October on a first-come, first-served basis.

28 primitive tent campsites
   flush toilets
   drinking water
   stoves
   tables
hiking/fishing/sightseeing

For Information

Ukiah-Dale State Park
c/o Emigrant Springs State Park
P.O. Box 85
Meacham, OR 97859
(503) 983-2277
FAX—983-2279

Although hiker/biker camps are usually separated from the main campground, all park facilities such as restrooms and showers are available.

Umatilla National Forest

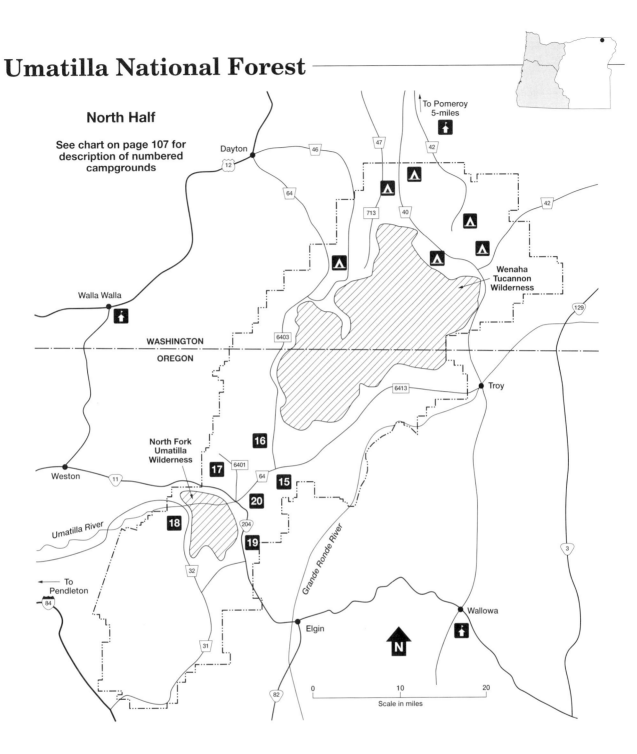

North Half

See chart on page 107 for description of numbered campgrounds

To Pomeroy 5-miles

Dayton

Walla Walla

WASHINGTON
OREGON

6403

Wenaha Tucannon Wilderness

Troy

6413

North Fork Umatilla Wilderness

Weston

16

17 6401

64 15

20

18 204

19

Umatilla River

32

To Pendleton

31

Grande Ronde River

Elgin

Wallowa

N

82

0   10   20
Scale in miles

For Information

Umatilla National Forest
2517 S.W. Hailey Avenue
Pendleton, OR 97801
(503) 278-3716

Location

The Umatilla National Forest, located in the Blue Mountains of southeast Washington and northeast Oregon, covers 1.4 million acres of diverse landscapes and plant communities. Parcelled in three sections, the forest is accessible from I-84, which runs through Pendleton and between the north section and the two south sections of the Umatilla. The Umatilla's north section extends into Washington and is partially bordered on the west by the Umatilla Indian Reservation and on the southeast by the Wallowa-Whitman National Forest. The south half is bordered by the Malheur National Forest. From Weston or Elgin, the forest is accessible via

Umatilla National Forest *(continued)*

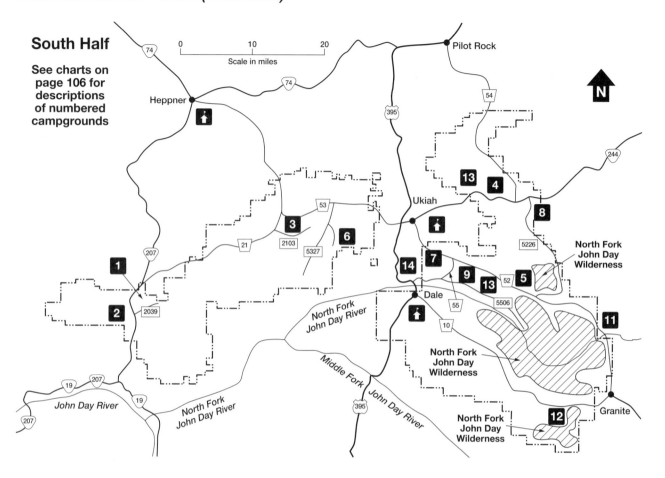

South Half

See charts on page 106 for descriptions of numbered campgrounds

Scale in miles
0   10   20

74   Pilot Rock

74

Heppner   54

395

13   4

Ukiah   8

244

53   North Fork John Day Wilderness

3   5226

21   2103   5327   6   7

207   1   14   9   13   52   5

5506   Dale   55   North Fork John Day Wilderness   11

2   2039   10

North Fork John Day River

19   207   North Fork John Day Wilderness   12   Granite

John Day River   19   North Fork John Day River   Middle Fork John Day River   395

207

S.R. 204. From Ukiah access is possible from U.S. 395 and S.R. 244. From Heppner, S.R. 207 crosses the forest. The far northern portions in Washington can be reached through Walla Walla, Dayton, Pomeroy, Asotin, and Clarkston.

Points of Interest

▲ Year-round recreation opportunities exist on the Umatilla including hiking, horseback riding, camping, skiing, and of course hunting and fishing. Approximately 35% of the forest's annual recreation use occurs during the big game hunting seasons, while camping is the second most popular activity. Sightseers may drive over 5,167 miles of forest roads, hike or ride over 715 miles of trails, float the Grande Ronde River, enjoy the most popular snowmobiling areas in Oregon, and select from over 20 campgrounds throughout the forest.

▲ Campgrounds provide some 316 campsites located away from traffic and commercial development where outdoor activities can be enjoyed. (See the

Camper's Guide to Washington for details and maps on the Pomeroy Ranger District, located in the state of Washington. There are six developed campsites, a portion of the Wenaha-Tucannon Wilderness, and many acres of scenic forest to explore in the Washington portion of the Umatilla). Camping is also allowed in most dispersed areas throughout the forest. Campgrounds are available on a first-come, first-served basis. They do not have electricity, showers, or sewage disposal. Holding tank waste disposal stations are located at Bull Prairie and Tollgate Guard Station. Where facilities and services are provided, a fee is charged for overnight use. Campers are welcome to stay at any campground for a maximum of 14 continuous days.

▲ Elevations in the forest range from 1,600 to 8,000 feet. Changes in weather are common, but summers are generally warm and dry with cool evenings. Cold and snowy winters and mild temperatures during spring and fall can be expected.

▲ During the winter months, skiing is a major sport on the Umatilla. Spout Springs Ski Area is

Umatilla National Forest *(continued)*

located near the Tollgate area in northeast Oregon, and Ski Bluewood is 20 miles south of Dayton, Washington. Cross-country skiing is also a popular sport with many marked ski trails in the forest.

▲ Over 250 miles of groomed snowmobile trails exist in the forest with abundant opportunities for all. Two snowmobile warming shelters are also available in the forest. One is located at Ruckle Junction and the other at Mt. Misery.

▲ Fishing opportunities abound throughout the forest with both lakes and streams available for variety. Many lakes and streams are stocked frequently with rainbow trout during the season. Steelhead and salmon are also present during their migration periods in many of the major rivers.

▲ Hunting is the most popular recreational activity in the forest, which supports one of the largest Rocky Mountain elk herds in the nation. There are also herds of mule and white-tailed deer. Rocky Mountain bighorn sheep can be found in the Wenaha-Tucannon Wilderness and a small population of California bighorn sheep can be found in the Cottonwood-Cummings Creek area. The forest supports 324 species of fish and wildlife.

▲ Other points of interest in the forest include Blue Mountain Scenic Byway, Vinegar Hill/Indian Rock Scenic Area, Ray Ridge Viewpoint, Stahl Canyon Overlook, Whitman Route Overlook, Table Rock Lookout, Potomus Point, and The Big Sink.

▲ The Umatilla, Indian word meaning "water rippling over sand," offers three wilderness areas for solitude and backcountry opportunities. Over 20% of the forest's 1.4 million acres is within designated wilderness.

Wilderness Areas

Wenaha-Tucannon Wilderness is located in the northern Blue Mountains and straddles the Oregon-Washington border. Encompassing 177,465 acres, most of the wilderness is characterized by rugged basaltic ridges and outcroppings separated by deep canyons with steep side slopes. The managed trail system within the wilderness totals over 200 miles. The normal hiking season is from June through November. Access to the wilderness can be gained in early spring along the Wenaha River near Troy, Oregon. Many higher elevation trailheads remain inaccessible through June. Most trails descend sharply into the rugged river canyons of the Wenaha and Tucannon rivers and their tributaries.

The Wenaha River, Crooked Creek, Rock Creek, and Butte Creek have cut deep canyons into the tablelands and left heavily timbered areas along the bottoms. The higher ridges are generally narrow with very steep side slopes. Elevations within the wilderness range from 2,000 feet on the Wenaha River to 6,401 feet at Oregon Butte. Wildlife includes Rocky Mountain elk and bighorn sheep, white-tail and mule deer, black bear, cougar, coyote, and pine martens. Both the Tucannon and Wenaha rivers provide good spawning habitat for Chinook salmon and steelhead. For more information contact: Pomeroy Ranger District in Washington—(509) 843-1891 or Walla Walla Ranger District in Washington—(509) 522-6290.

North Fork Umatilla Wilderness is located 30 miles east of Pendleton, the smallest wilderness in northeast Oregon. It encompasses only 10,144 acres, but provides opportunities for hiking, horseback riding, fishing, and hunting. The North Fork Umatilla River supports sizeable runs of anadromous fish, which makes this area a popular spot for anglers. There are also several streams within the wilderness that contain native trout, and a few streams support spawning steelhead. The terrain varies from gentle, sloping hills to extremely steep, timbered canyons. The elevation in the area ranges from 2,000 to 6,000 feet, assuring a good workout for hikers and equestrians using the 27-mile trail system. The wild, unpredictable weather of the Blue Mountains can also add to the challenge anytime of the year. For more information contact: Walla Walla Ranger District in Washington—(509) 522-6290.

North Fork John Day Wilderness, 121,800 acres, is located southeast of Ukiah and northwest of Baker, Oregon. It provides an abundance of natural diversity with its rolling benchlands to the granite outcrops of the Greenhorn Mountains. The wilderness is known primarily for its big game (Rocky Mountain elk and mule deer) and its anadromous fish habitat. There are over 130 miles of perennial streams, 40 miles of which provide spawning habitat for Chinook Salmon and steelhead. Over 100 miles of trails serve the area, which is popular for both hiking and horseback riding. The area is accessible from early spring to late fall from several trailheads located around the perimeter of the area. The highest peaks in the forest are located at the southern border of this wilderness. For more information contact: North Fork John Day Ranger District—(503) 427-3231.

REGION 2

Heppner Ranger District

For Information

Heppner Ranger District
P.O. Box 7
Heppner, OR 97836
(503) 676-9187

Campground (see map on page 104)	Elevation (feet)	Tent Sites	Tent/Trailer Sites	Fees	Drinking Water	Vault Toilets
1. Bull Prairie Lake*	4,000	2	26	•	•	•
2. Fairview*	4,300	1	4	•	•	
3. Penland Lake*	4,950	5	5			•

*Picnic sites available.

Campground Locations/Activities

1. **Bull Prairie Lake:** Access via S.R. 207. 36 mi. S of Heppner on F.R. 2039. *Activities:* Fishing, boating (non-motorized), and hunting.
2. **Fairview (RVs to 16'):** 34 mi. S of Heppner on S.R. 207. *Activities:* Hunting.
3. **Penland Lake:** Access via S.R. 207 and F.R. 5321. 26 mi. SE of Heppner off F.R. 21. *Activities:* Boating, swimming, fishing, and hunting.

North Fork John Day Ranger District

For Information

North Fork John Day Ranger District
P.O. Box 158
Ukiah, OR 97880
(503) 427-3231

Campground (see map on page 104)	Elevation (feet)	Tent Sites	Tent/Trailer Sites	Fees	Drinking Water	Vault Toilets
4. Bear Wallow Creek*	3,900	1	5			•
5. Big Creek	5,100	2				•
6. Divide Well	4,700	3				•
7. Drift Fence	4,250	3				•
8. Frazier*	4,300	5	27			•
9. Gold Dredge*	4,300	5	37			•
10. Lane Creek*	3,850		4			•
11. North Fork	5,200		5			•
12. Olive Lake*	6,000	3				•
13. Oriental Creek	3,500	5				•
14. Tollbridge	3,800		7	•	•	•

*Picnic sites available.

Campground Locations/Activities

4. **Bear Wallow Creek:** 10 mi. E of Ukiah on S.R. 244. *Activities:* Fishing, boating, and hunting. Interpretive trail.
5. **Big Creek:** Access via S.R. 244. 22 mi. SE of Ukiah on F.R. 52. *Activities:* Hiking, fishing, hunting, and access to wilderness.
6. **Divide Well:** Access via U.S. 395. 20 mi. W of Ukiah on F.R. 5327-290. *Activities:* Trail biking and hunting.
7. **Drift Fence:** Access via S.R. 244. 7 mi. SE of Ukiah on F.R. 52. *Activities:* Hunting.
8. **Frazier:** Access via S.R. 244. 16 mi. E of Ukiah on F.R. 5226. *Activities:* Trail biking, fishing, and hunting. Hot springs.
9. **Gold Dredge:** Access via S.R. 244. 7 mi. E of Dale on F.R. 5506. *Activities:* Trail biking, fishing, and hunting.
10. **Lane Creek:** Access via S.R. 244. 9 mi. E of Dale on S.R. 244. *Activities:* Fishing and hunting. Hot springs.
11. **North Fork:** Access via S.R. 244. 36 mi. SE of Ukiah on F.R. 52. *Activities:* Fishing, hunting, and wilderness access. Trailhead facility.
12. **Olive Lake:** Access via U.S. 395. 24 mi. SE of Dale on F.R. 10. *Activities:* Hiking, fishing, boating, trail biking, and hunting.
13. **Oriental Creek:** Access via U.S. 395. 12 mi. E of Dale on F.R. 5506. *Activities:* Fishing, hunting, and wilderness access. Wild and Scenic River.
14. **Tollbridge:** Access via U.S. 395; .5 mi. E of U.S. 395 just N of Dale on F.R. 55. *Activities:* Fishing, floating (April–June), Wild and Scenic River, and hunting.

Walla Walla Ranger District

For Information

Walla Walla Ranger District
1415 West Rose Street
Walla Walla, WA 99362
(509) 522-6290

Campground Locations/Activities

The Walla Walla Ranger District is actually located in Washington; its campgrounds are located in the Oregon portion of the Umatilla National Forest.

15. **Jubilee Lake:** Access via S.R. 204 . 12 mi. NE of Tollgate on F.R. 64. *Activities:* Hiking, boating, swimming, fishing, and hunting.
16. **Mottet:** Access via S.R. 204. 14 mi. NE of Tollgate on F.R. 64 and 6403. *Activities:* Hiking and hunting.
17. **Target Meadows:** Access via S.R. 204. 2 mi. N of Tollgate on F.R. 6401. *Activities:* Hunting.
18. **Umatilla Forks:** Access via S.R. 11/I-84. 33 mi. E of Pendleton on F.R. 32. *Activities:* Hiking,

Campground (see map on page 103)	Elevation (feet)	Tent Sites	Tent/Trailer Sites	Fees	Drinking Water	Vault Toilets
15. Jubilee Lake*	4,800	4	47	•	•	•
16. Mottet*	5,200		7		•	•
17. Target Meadows*	4,800	4	16	•	•	•
18. Umatilla Forks*	2,400	7	8		•	•
19. Woodland*	5,200		7			•
20. Woodward*	4,950		18	•	•	•

*Picnic sites available.

horseback riding, trail biking, wilderness access, and hunting.
19. **Woodland:** 23 mi. E of Weston on S.R. 204. *Activities:* Hunting.
20. **Woodward:** 18 mi. E of Weston on S.R. 204. *Activities:* Mountain biking and hunting.

Hunting is the most popular recreational activity in the Umatilla. The forest supports mule and white-tailed deer, as well as one of the largest Rocky Mountain elk herds in the nation.

Unity Lake State Park

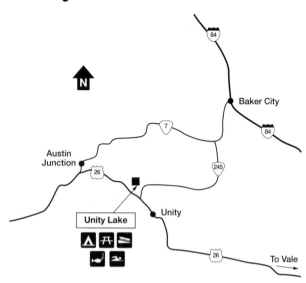

For Information

Unity Lake State Park
c/o Farewell Bend State Park
Star Route
Huntington, OR 97907
(503) 869-2365
FAX—869-2457

Location

Unity Lake State Park is located on S.R. 245, approximately 2 miles north of its junction with U.S. 26. It is 53 miles east of John Day, and 40 miles south of Baker City. This 39-acre park stands at an elevation of 3,866 feet on the shore of a reservoir formed by the damming of Burnt River. It occupies a generally flat, open terrain that provides a scenic view of the Blue Mountains to the north. This quaint park provides planted shade trees in a sagebrush environment.

Facilities and Activities

The campground is open mid-April through late October on a first-come, first-served basis.

RV campsites w/electric and water hookups (60′
   maximum length)
   pull-through sites
   showers
   drinking water
   flush toilets
   stoves
   tables
   trailer dump station
17 primitive tent campsites
hiker/biker camp
28 picnic sites
boat ramp/boating/fishing/swimming
sightseeing
accessible campsite/restrooms/showers for people
   with disabilities

Wallowa Lake State Park

For Information

Wallowa Lake State Park
72214 Marine Lane
Joseph, OR 97846
(503) 432-8855
FAX—432-4141

Location

Wallowa Lake State Park is located off S.R. 82, 6 miles south of Joseph on the shores of one of Oregon's most picturesque mountain lakes. Wallowa Lake is located in the heart of the Wallowa Mountains, often referred to as "The Switzerland of America." This heavily forested area provides wonderful outdoor recreation opportunities including horseback riding and hiking. Trails from the edge of the park lead into Eagle Caps Wilderness Area. Eagle Caps Wilderness consists of small, sparkling lakes nestled in beautiful alpine meadows at the base of rugged granite peaks reaching 9,000 to 10,000 feet in elevation. Just 12 miles south of Enterprise, headquarters for the Hells Canyon National Recreation Area, the park provides campers with access to many choices for recreating. Wallowa Lake is renowned

Wallowa Lake State Park *(continued)*

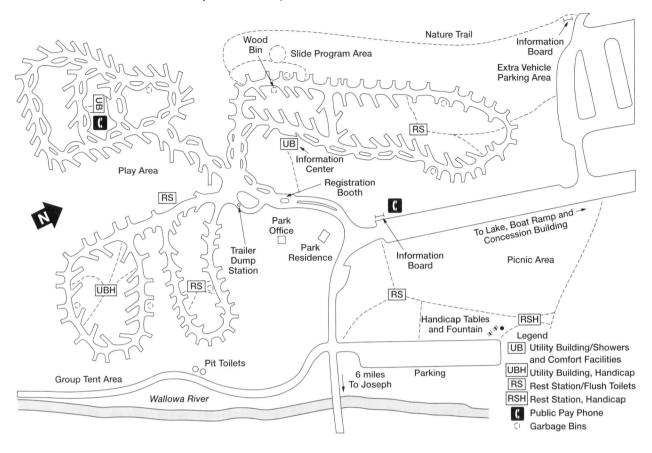

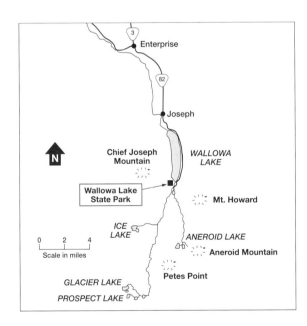

Legend

UB	Utility Building/Showers and Comfort Facilities
UBH	Utility Building, Handicap
RS	Rest Station/Flush Toilets
RSH	Rest Station, Handicap
C	Public Pay Phone
○	Garbage Bins

Facilities and Activities

The campground is open mid-April through late October. Reservations are accepted from Memorial Day weekend through Labor Day.

121 RV campsites w/full hookups (60′ maximum length)
   pull-through sites
   showers
   drinking water
   flush toilets
   wood stoves
   tables
   trailer dump station
89 tent campsites
3 group tent areas (club camping)
169 picnic sites
3 group picnic sites
swim area/fishing
boat ramp/boating/waterskiing
marina w/boat moorage (reservable)
hiking/horseback riding/trails
sightseeing/geology

for its rainbow and Dolly Varden trout, kokanee, and Mackinaw fishing. Fishing gear and water recreation equipment are available at the park's marina concession.

Wallowa-Whitman National Forest

Wallowa-Whitman National Forest
P.O. Box 907, 1550 Dewey Avenue
Baker City, Oregon 97814
(503) 523-6391

Location

Wallowa-Whitman National Forest covers 2,392,160 acres of country in northeastern Oregon. The forest encompasses the stately splendor of the Blue Mountains, the rugged grandeur of the Wallowa Mountains, and the spectacular canyon country of the Snake River. The forest, located in two separate sections, is accessible via I-84, which bisects the north and south halves.

Points of Interest

▲ "Wallowa" is a Nez Perce Indian word referring to the tripods placed in rivers to hold a pole lattice structure for catching fish. The Wallowa River Valley was the home of the elder Chief Joseph of the Nez Perce and his son of the same name, famous for his brilliant leadership in the Nez Perce war of 1877.

▲ Forest elevations range from 875 to 9,845 feet. Plant life varies from the desert-like country of Hells Canyon to the alpine vegetation of the Eagle Cap Wilderness and Seven Devils Mountains. A great variety of wildlife abounds in the forest, including more big-game species than any other forest in Oregon and Washington! Besides the elk, deer, mountain sheep, and mountain goats, the forest provides habitat for 88 species of mammals, 36 species of fish, and 236 species of birds. With all its recreational opportunities, the Wallowa-Whitman also encompasses North America's deepest gorge within Hells Canyon National Recreation Area. Some of the most dramatic scenery in the country is found along the Hells Canyon Scenic Byway on the Hells Canyon National Recreation Area. See Hells Canyon National Recreation Area under separate heading in Region 2 for more details.

▲ The forest provides wonderful settings for year-around recreation. In winter, cross-country skiing and snowmobiling are possible on numerous groomed and ungroomed trails. There is downhill skiing available at the Anthony Lakes Ski Area, 40 miles northwest of Baker City. Hells Canyon is beautiful in the springtime. There visitors can enjoy the 900 miles of hiking trails, white-water boating, mild temperatures, and colorful wildflowers. Swimming and fishing in the forest's many lakes, rivers, streams, and reservoirs can fill your summer. Backpacking is possible on a variety of hiking trails. With its four wilderness areas, there are over 1,660 miles of trails on the forest.

▲ Unique places to visit include Hat Point viewpoint (6,982 feet above the canyon), Pittsburgh Landing petroglyphs, Mason Dam viewpoint, numerous old gold mining towns, Mt. Howard tramway, Buck Point overlook (on primitive road), Buckhorn viewpoint, Hells Canyon dam, and many other scenic trails and sites.

▲ Weather patterns change from year to year, but generally winters are cold and snowy, spring and fall are mild, and summers are hot and dry.

Wilderness Areas

Eagle Cap Wilderness encompasses some 358,461 acres of land characterized by high alpine lakes and meadows, bare granite peaks and ridges, U-shaped glaciated valleys, thick timber in the lower valleys, and scattered alpine timber on the upper slopes. There are 509 miles of trails in the wilderness. Elevations range from 5,000 feet in the lower valleys to near 10,000 feet on the highest of the majestic peaks. Access is via several main routes; the most heavily used is S.R. 82 to Wallowa Lake, which is one mile from the wilderness boundary. Usually by July 4, most of the Eagle Cap Wilderness trails are snow free. For more information contact: Eagle Cap Ranger District—(503) 426-4978.

Hells Canyon Wilderness, located within Hells Canyon National Recreation Area, encompasses 215,233 acres of high mountain peaks, ominous canyon rim-rocks, breathtaking vistas, and quieting solitude. Elk, bear, bighorn sheep, mountain goats, and many other species of birds and animals are common here. Split by the Snake River into two distinct areas, the Hells Canyon Wilderness straddles the Idaho and Oregon state boundary. At lower elevations on the Idaho side, dry, barren, steep slopes break over into the Snake River Canyon. In the high country are the towering peaks, rock-faced slopes, and alpine lakes of the Seven Devils Mountain Range. Splendid mountain peaks rise to 9,845 feet. Lower elevations are at 875 feet. There are 141 miles of trails in Idaho with trailheads located

Wallowa-Whitman National Forest *(continued)*

at Black Lake, Windy Saddle, and Pittsburg Landing. There are 222 miles of trails in Oregon. The Oregon-side boasts expanses of grasslands at lower elevations to dense groupings of ponderosa pine and Douglas-fir trees at higher elevations. Popular Oregon-side viewpoints are McGraw, Hat Point, and Somers Point. Roads leading to wilderness trailheads and viewpoints for either area are mostly single lane, and suitable for low-speed use only. Access roads and trails begin to open in June, remaining open until September or October. For more information see Hells Canyon National Recreation Area, Region 2, of this guide or contact: Wallowa-Whitman National Forest Headquarters—(503) 523-6391 or Hells Canyon National Recreation Area—(503) 426-4978.

North Fork John Day Wilderness, shared with Umatilla National Forest, encompasses a total of 121,800 acres with 14,294 acres in the Wallowa-Whitman National Forest. Elevations range between 3,356 and 8,131 feet in the entire wilderness. Rolling benchlands, granitic outcrops of the Greenhorn Mountains, and the rugged gorge of the North Fork John Day River all provide an abundance of natural diversity in this wilderness. The area is known for its big game (Rocky Mountain elk and mule deer), and its anadromous fish habitat. There are over 130 miles of perennial streams, 40 miles of which provide spawning habitat for Chinook salmon and steelhead. There are three National Recreation Trails (Elkhorn, North Fork John Day, and Winom Creek) among the more than 130 miles of trails serving the area. There are 20 miles of trail on the

Wallowa-Whitman portion of the wilderness. The North Fork John Day drainage was a bustling gold and silver mining area in the middle to late 1800s. Old mining structures, building foundations, water-worn rock, ditches, and other traces of the thousands of people who removed an estimated $10 million in gold and silver are still visible. For more information contact: Baker Ranger District—(503) 523-6391.

Monument Rock Wilderness, shared with Malheur National Forest, consists of 19,600 total acres with 7,030 acres in the Wallowa-Whitman National Forest. The elevation ranges are between 5,120 on the Little Malheur River to 7,815 feet at Table Rock. The wilderness is located some 30 miles east of John Day, Oregon in the area that encompasses the headwaters of the Little Malheur River and the upper drainages of the South Fork of Burnt River. It has three prominent rock points. A fire lookout station, one of the entry points to the wilderness, is located on Table Rock just outside the wilderness boundary. Tree species include ponderosa pine, quaking aspen, Douglas-fir, white fir, and lodgepole pine. A trail system, 7 miles of trails on the Wallowa-Whitman, provides access to the area. The wilderness' diverse habitat is used by bear, deer, elk, grouse, hawks, badgers, and the rare wolverine. The "visiting season" runs between June and November. Hunting is the most popular activity, with hiking and backpacking increasing in popularity. For more information contact: Unity Ranger District—(503) 446-3351 or the Forest Headquarters—(503) 523-6391.

With its four wilderness areas, the forest has over 1,660 miles of trails for riding or hiking.

Baker Ranger District

For Information

Baker Ranger District
3165 10th Street
Baker City, OR 97814
(503) 523-4476

Campground Locations/Activities

1. **Anthony Lakes:** 30 mi. NW of Baker City via S.R. 30, C.R. 1146, F.R. 73. *Activities:* Hiking, climbing, fishing, boating, and swimming; group camping available.
2. **Deer Creek:** 28 mi. SW of Baker City via S.R. 7, C.R. 656, F.R. 6550 and 6530; last 4 mi. gravel. *Activities:* Hiking, fishing, and gold panning.
3. **Grande Ronde Lake:** 32 mi. NW of Baker via S.R. 30, C.R. 1146, F.R. 73; last 1 mi. gravel. *Activities:* Hiking, fishing, swimming, and winter sports.
4. **McCully Forks:** 33 mi. SW of Baker City via S.R. 7 and C.R. 410. *Activities:* Hiking, fishing, and gold panning.
5. **Millers Lane:** 27 mi. SW of Baker City via S.R. 7, C.R. 667, F.R. 2220; last 4 mi. gravel. *Activities:* Hiking, fishing, boating, and swimming.
6. **Mud Lake:** 31 mi. NW of Baker City via S.R. 30, C.R. 1146, and F.R. 73. *Activities:* Hiking, fishing, swimming, and winter sports.

Campground (see map on facing page)	Elevation (feet)	Tent Sites	Tent/Trailer Sites	Fees	Drinking Water	Service Level
1. Anthony Lakes*	7,100	21	16	•	•	(b)
2. Deer Creek	4,600	6				(a)
3. Grande Ronde Lake	6,800		8	•	•	(b)
4. McCully Forks	4,600	6				(a)
5. Millers Lane	4,120	3	4			(a)
6. Mud Lake	7,100	3	5	•	•	(b)
7. Southwest Shore	4,120		18			(a)
8. Union Creek*	4,120	12	58	•	•	(c)

*Picnic sites and group campsites available.
(a) Primitive, moderate use, no fee, no water, electricity, sewer or showers.
(b) Primitive, moderate use, fee, water, no electricity, sewer or showers.
(c) Modern, high use, fee, water, electricity, sewer, no showers.

7. **Southwest Shore:** 26 mi SW of Baker City via S.R. 7, C.R. 667, F.R. 2220; last 3 mi. gravel. *Activities:* Hiking, fishing, boating and swimming.
8. **Union Creek:** 20 mi. SW of Baker City via S.R. 7. *Activities:* Hiking, fishing, swimming, boating, waterskiing.

An estimated 10 million dollars in gold and silver were mined from the North Fork John Day drainage of the forest between the middle to late 1800s.

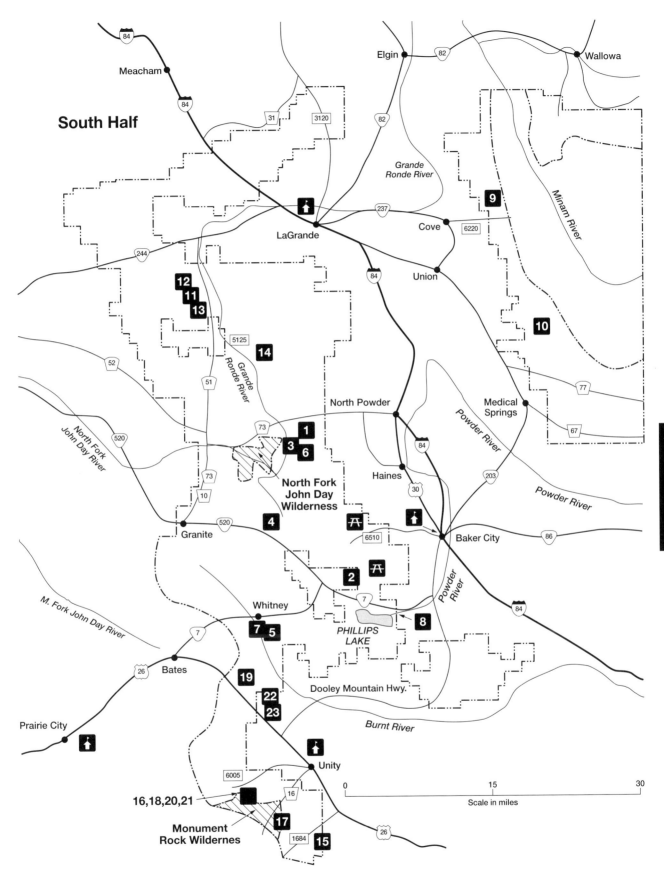

South Half

Meacham

Elgin

Wallowa

84

82

31

3120

82

Grande
Ronde River

Minam River

237

9

LaGrande

Cove

6220

244

12
11
13

5125

14

52

Union

84

10

51

Grande
Ronde River

77

North Powder

Medical
Springs

Powder River

67

North Fork
John Day River

520

73

1
3 6

North Fork
John Day
Wilderness

Haines

84

203

Powder River

73

10

Baker City

86

4

520

Granite

6510

2

M. Fork John Day River

Whitney

7 5

PHILLIPS
LAKE

7

8

Powder River

84

7

Bates

26

19

22
23

Dooley Mountain Hwy.

Burnt River

Prairie City

16,18,20,21

Monument
Rock Wildernes

6005

17

16

Unity

1684

15

26

0   15   30
Scale in miles

REGION 2

Wallowa-Whitman National Forest   113

La Grande Ranger District

For Information

La Grande Ranger District
Box 3502, Highway 30
La Grange, OR 97850
(503) 963-7186

Campground Locations/Activities

9. **Moss Springs:** 24 mi. E of La Grande via S.R. 82, Hwy. 237, F.R. 6220; last 10 mi. gravel and steep. *Activities:* Hiking (trailhead), and horseback riding (loading ramp and corrals).

10. **North Fork Cartherine Creek:** 29 mi. SE of La Grande via S.R. 203, F.R. 7785; last 6 mi. gravel. *Activities:* Hiking (trailhead), fishing, and horseback riding (loading ramp).

11. **River:** 32 mi. SW of La Grande via I-84, S.R. 244, and F.R. 51. *Activities:* Fishing and hiking.

12. **Spool Cart:** 27 mi. SW of La Grande via I-84, S.R. 244, and F.R. 51. *Activities:* Fishing and hiking.

13. **Time and A Half:** 30 mi. SW of La Grande via I-84, S.R. 244, and F.R. 51. *Activities:* Fishing and hiking.

14. **Woodley:** 40 mi. SW of La Grande via I-84, S.R. 244, and F.R. 5125; last 5 mi. gravel. *Activities:* Fishing and hiking.

Campground (see map on page 113)	Elevation (feet)	Tent Sites	Tent/Trailer Sites	Fees	Drinking Water	Service Level
9. Moss Springs*	5,400	11				(a)
10. North Fork Cartherine Creek	4,400		6			(a)
11. River*	3,800		6	•	•	(b)
12. Spool Cart	3,500		16			(a)
13. Time and A Half	3,700		5			(a)
14. Woodley*	4,500		7	•	•	(b)

*Picnic sites available.
(a) Primitive, moderate use, no fee, no water, electricity, sewer or showers.
(b) Primitive, moderate use, fee, water, no electricity, sewer or showers.
Note: Boulder Park and Two Color campgrounds, managed by La Grande Ranger District, are depicted in the North Half Map of the forest, page 116.

A great variety of wildlife abounds in the forest. Besides mountain goats, mountain sheep, elk, and deer, the forest provides habitat for 88 species of mammals, 36 species of fish, and 236 species of birds.

Unity Ranger District

For Information

Unity Ranger District
P.O. Box 38
Unity, OR 97844
(503) 446-3351

Campground Locations/Activities

15. **Eldorado:** 12 mi. S of Unity via U.S. 26 and F.R. 16. *Activities:* Fishing and hiking.
16. **Elk Creek:** 8 mi. W of Unity via S.R. 600 and F.R. 6005; last 4 mi. gravel. *Activities:* Fishing and hiking.
17. **Long Creek:** 10 mi. S of Unity via F.R. 1680. *Activities:* Fishing and hiking.
18. **Mammoth Springs:** 9 mi. W of Unity via S.R. 600 and F.R. 6005 and 2640; last 5 mi. gravel. *Activities:* Fishing and hiking.
19. **Oregon:** 12 mi. NW of Unity via U.S. 26. *Activities:* Hiking and ATV trails.
20. **South Fork:** 6 mi. W of Unity via S.R. 600 and F.R. 6005; last 2 mi. gravel. *Activities:* Fishing and hiking.
21. **Steven's Creek:** 7 mi. W of Unity via S.R. 600 and F.R. 6005; last 3 mi. gravel. *Activities:* Fishing and hiking.
22. **Wetmore:** 10 mi. NW of Unity via U.S. 26. *Activities:* Hiking (barrier-free trail to Yellow Pine).
23. **Yellow Pine:** 11 mi. NW of Unity via U.S. 26. *Activities:* Hiking (barrier-free trail to Wetmore).

Campground (see map on page 113)	Elevation (feet)	Tent Sites	Tent/Trailer Sites	Fees	Drinking Water	Service Level
15. Eldorado†	4,600	No sites designated				(a)
16. Elk Creek†	4,520	No sites designated				(a)
17. Long Creek†	4,430	No sites designated				(a)
18. Mammoth Springs†	4,550	No sites designated				(a)
19. Oregon*	4,880	3	8		•	(b)
20. South Fork*	4,400	2	12		•	(b)
21. Steven's Creek†	4,480	No sites designated				(b)
22. Wetmore*	4,320	4	12	•	•	(c)
23. Yellow Pine*	4,450		21	•	•	(c)

†Available for group picnicking and tent camping. Sites not designated.
*Picnic sites available.
(a) Very primitive, low use, no fee, no water, electricity, sewer or showers.
(b) Primitive, moderate use, no fee, no water, electricity, sewer or showers.
(c) Primitive, moderate use, fee, water, no electricity, sewer or showers.

A 67.5-mile stretch of the Snake River at the bottom of Hells Canyon is protected under the National Wild and Scenic Rivers System. This is a rafter's haven.

Eagle Cap Ranger District and Hells Canyon National Recreation Area

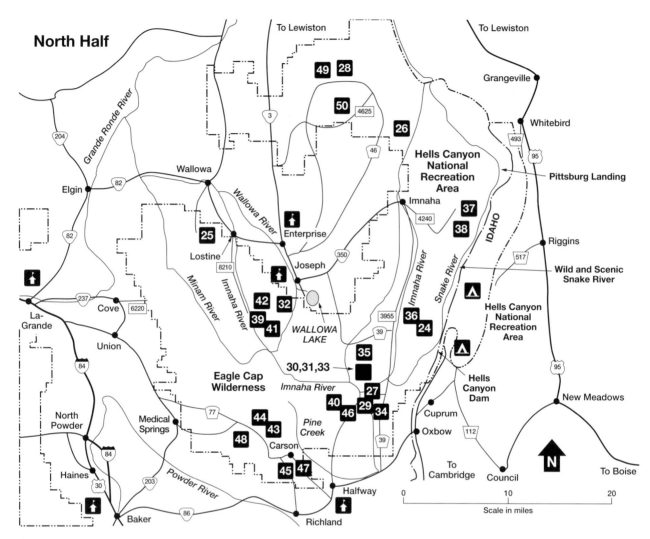

North Half

Grande Ronde River

To Lewiston

To Lewiston

Grangeville

Whitebird

Pittsburg Landing

Hells Canyon National Recreation Area

Imnaha

Wild and Scenic Snake River

Riggins

IDAHO

Hells Canyon National Recreation Area

Hells Canyon Dam

New Meadows

Cuprum

Oxbow

To Cambridge

Council

To Boise

Wallowa River

Enterprise

Lostine

Joseph

WALLOWA LAKE

Eagle Cap Wilderness

Imnaha River

Minam River

Imnaha River

Elgin

Wallowa

La-Grande

Cove

Union

North Powder

Medical Springs

Carson

Pine Creek

Halfway

Richland

Haines

Baker

Powder River

0   10   20
Scale in miles

See charts on pages 117–119 for descriptions of numbered campgrounds.

For Information

Eagle Cap Ranger District and
Hells Canyon National Recreation Area
88401 Hwy. 82
Enterprise, OR 97828
(503) 426-4978

Campground Locations/Activities

(√) = Located in Hells Canyon National Recreation Area

24. **Blackhorse** (√)**:** 42 mi. SE of Enterprise via Hwy. 82, S.R. 350, and F.R. 39. *Activities:* Hiking and fishing.

25. **Boundary:** 25 mi. NW of Enterprise via S.R. 82, F.R. 8250 and 8250040; last 7 mi. gravel. *Activities:* Hiking (trailhead) and fishing.

26. **Buckhorn** (√)**:** 43 mi. NE of Enterprise via S.R. 82, Zumwalt Rd., F.R. 400788; last 41 mi. gravel. *Activities:* Berry picking, horseback riding (ramp), and scenic view.

27. **Coverdale** (√)**:** 47 mi. SE of Enterprise via S.R. 350, F.R. 39 and 3960; last 5 mi. gravel. *Activities:* Hiking and fishing.

28. **Dougherty Springs** (√)**:** 45 mi. NE of Enterprise via S.R. 3, F.R. 46; last 30 mi. gravel. *Activities:* Berry picking.

Eagle Cap Ranger District and
Hells Canyon National Recreation Area *(continued)*

Campground (see map on facing page)	Elevation (feet)	Tent Sites	Tent/Trailer Sites	Fees	Drinking Water	Service Level
24. Blackhorse √	4,000		16	•	•	(c)
25. Boundary	3,600	8				(a)
26. Buckhorn √	5,200	6				(b)
27. Coverdale √	4,300	9	2	•	•	(c)
28. Dougherty Springs √	5,100	8	4			(b)
29. Duck Lake √	5,200	2				(b)
30. Evergreen √	4,500	*	No units designated			(a)
31. Hidden √	4,400	10	3	•	•	(c)
32. Hurricane Creek	5,000	5	3			(b)
33. Indian Crossing √	4,500		14	•	•	(c)
34. Lake Fork √	3,200		10	•	•	(c)
35. Lick Creek √	5,400	7	5		•	(c)
36. Ollokot √	4,000		12	•	•	(c)
37. Sacajawea √	6,982	3				(b)
38. Saddle Creek √	6,800	7(W)				(b)
39. Shady	5,400	4	8			(b)
40. Twin Lakes √	6,500	6				(b)
41. Two Pan	5,600	6	2			(b)
42. Williamson	4,900	5	4			(b)

√Located within Hells Canyon National Recreation Area.
*Group area.
(W) Walk-in tent campsites.
(a) Very primitive, low use, no fee, no water, electricity, sewer or showers.
(b) Primitive, moderate use, no fee, no water, electricity, sewer or showers.
(c) Primitive, moderate use, fee, water, no electricity, sewer or showers.

29. **Duck Lake** (√): 30 mi. NE of Halfway via C.R. 1009, F.R. 66; gravel. *Activities:* Hiking and fishing.
30. **Evergreen** (√): 50 mi. SE of Enterprise via S.R. 350, F.R. 39 and 3960; last 8 mi. gravel. *Activities:* Hiking and fishing.
31. **Hidden** (√): 49 mi. SE of Enterprise via S.R. 350, F.R. 39 and 3960; last 9 mi. gravel. *Activities:* Hiking and fishing.
32. **Hurricane Creek** (no RVs recommended): 6 mi. S of Enterprise via S.R. 82, F.R. 8205; last 2 mi. gravel. *Activities:* Hiking (trailhead) and fishing.
33. **Indian Crossing** (√): 51 mi. SE of Enterprise via S.R. 350, F.R. 39 and 3960; last 10 mi. gravel. *Activities:* Hiking, fishing, and horseback riding (ramp and trailhead).
34. **Lake Fork** (√): 18 mi. NE of Halfway via S.R. 86 and F.R. 39. *Activities:* Hiking (trailhead) and fishing.
35. **Lick Creek** (√): 29 mi. SE of Enterprise via S.R. 82, Hwy. 350 and F.R. 39. *Activities:* Hiking and fishing.
36. **Ollokot** (√): 43 mi. SE of Enterprise via S.R. 350 and F.R. 39. *Activities:* Berry picking and fishing.
37. **Sacajawea** (√) (steep, not recommended for trailers): 63 mi. NE of Enterprise via S.R. 82, Hwy. 350, F.R. 4240 and 4240315; 24 mi. of gravel. *Activities:* Hiking and scenery.
38. **Saddle Creek** (√) (steep, not recommended for trailers): 56 mi. NE of Enterprise via S.R. 82, Hwy. 350 and F.R. 4240; 19 mi. gravel. *Activities:* Hiking and scenery.
39. **Shady:** 26 mi. NW, then SW of Enterprise via S.R. 82, F.R. 8210; last 9 mi. gravel. *Activities:* Hiking (trailhead) and fishing.
40. **Twin Lakes** (√): 35 mi. N of Halfway via C.R. 1009 and F.R. 66; gravel. *Activities:* Hiking and fishing.
41. **Two Pan:** 27 mi. NW, then SW of Enterprise via S.R. 82, F.R. 8210; last 10 mi. gravel. *Activities:* Hiking (trailhead) and fishing.
42. **Williamson:** 20 mi. NW, then SW of Enterprise via S.R. 82, F.R. 8210; last 3 mi. gravel. *Activities:* Hiking and fishing.

Idaho boastfully shares the awesome sites of Hells Canyon with Oregon. Elevation and scenery changes are dramatic in North America's deepest gorge.

REGION 2

La Grande Ranger District

For Information

La Grande Ranger District
Box 3502, Highway 30
La Grande, OR 97850
(503) 963-7186

Campground Locations/Activities

43. **Boulder Park:** 52 mi. SE of La Grande via S.R. 203, F.R. 67, 77, and 7755; last 14 mi. gravel. *Activities:* Hiking (trailhead), fishing, and horseback riding (horse ramp and corrals).
44. **Two Color:** 49 mi. SE of La Grande via S.R. 203 and F.R. 76, 77 and 7755; last 11 mi. gravel. *Activities:* Hiking and fishing.

Campground (see map on page 116)	Elevation (feet)	Tent Sites	Tent/Trailer Sites	Fees	Drinking Water	Service Level
43. Boulder Park	4,900	6				(a)
44. Two Color	4,800	14			•	(b)

Note: Other campgrounds (9-14) in La Grande Ranger District are depicted in the South Map descriptions of Wallowa-Whitman National Forest, page 113 .

(a) Primitive, moderate use, no fee, no water, electricity, sewer or showers.

(b) Primitive, moderate use, fee, water, no electricity, sewer, or showers.

Pine Ranger District

For Information

Pine Ranger District
General Delivery
Halfway, OR 97834
(503) 742-7511

Campground Locations/Activities

45. **Eagle Forks:** 10 mi. NW of Richland via F.R. 7735; gravel road. *Activities:* Fishing, hiking (trailhead), and gold panning.
46. **Fish Lake:** 29 mi. N of Halfway via C.R. 1009 and F.R. 66; gravel. *Activities:* Hiking (trailhead), fishing, boating (launch), and swimming.
47. **McBride:** 10 mi. W of Halfway via C.R. 413 and F.R. 7710 and 77; gravel road. *Activities:* Hiking and fishing.
48. **Tamarack:** 36 mi. NW of Richland via F.R. 7735 and 77; gravel. *Activities:* Hiking and fishing.

Campground (see map on page 116)	Elevation (feet)	Tent Sites	Tent/Trailer Sites	Fees	Drinking Water	Service Level
45. Eagle Forks*	3,000	7	5		•	3
46. Fish Lake	6,600	10	5			2
47. McBride	4,800	11	8		•	2
48. Tamarack	4,600	12	12		•	3

*Picnic sites available.

(a) Primitive, moderate use, no fee, no water, electricity, sewer or showers.

(b) Primitive, moderate use, fee, water, no electricity, sewer or showers.

With all its recreational opportunities, the Wallowa-Whitman National Forest also encompasses Hells Canyon National Recreation Area and some of the best fishing in the state.

Wallowa Valley Ranger District

For Information

Wallowa Valley Ranger District
88401 Hwy. 82
Enterprise, OR 97828
(503) 426-4978

Campground Locations/Activities

49. **Coyote:** 40 mi. NE of Enterprise via S.R. 3 and F.R. 46; last 26 mi. gravel. *Activities:* Hiking.
50. **Vigne:** 35 mi. NE of Enterprise via S.R. 3 and F.R. 46 and 4625; last 21 mi. gravel. *Activities:* Hiking and fishing.

Campground (see map on page 116)	Elevation (feet)	Tent Sites	Tent/Trailer Sites	Fees	Drinking Water	Service Level
49. Coyote*	4,800	21	8			(a)
50. Vigne	3,500		7		•	(a)

*Picnic sites available.
(a) Primitive, moderate use, no fee, no water, electricity, sewer or showers.

The 10,000-foot peaks and wilderness terrain of the Wallowa Mountains and Eagle Cap Wilderness are often called the "Switzerland of America." Wallow Lake is one of the busiest recreation destinations in the summer.

Region 3

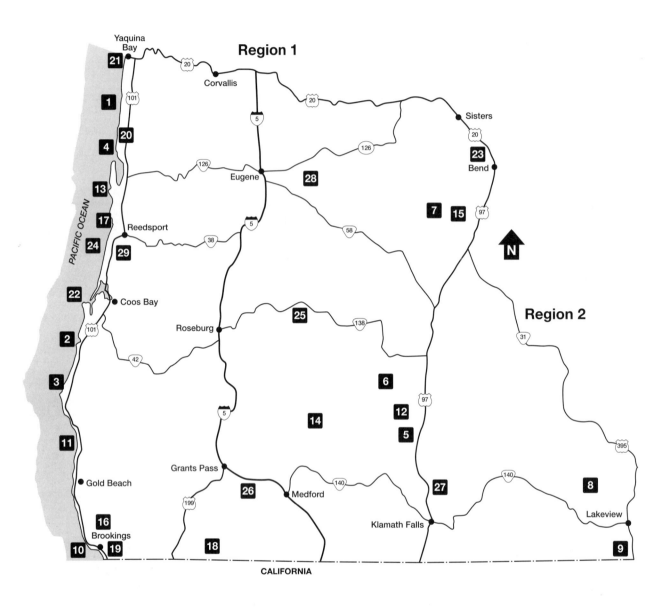

*Recreation sites are scattered throughout region. See BLM map on page 133 for site locations.

Oregon is renowned for its stunning coastal vistas. Region 3 includes exquisite landscapes inland and along the coast from the California border north to Highway 20 at Newport.

REGION 3

Beachside State Park

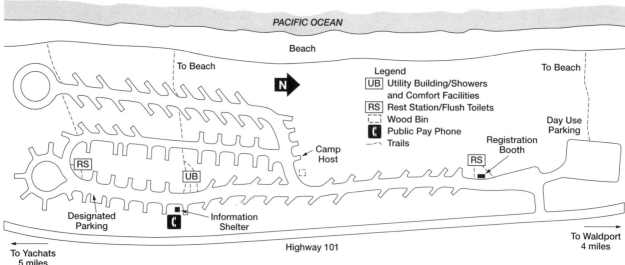

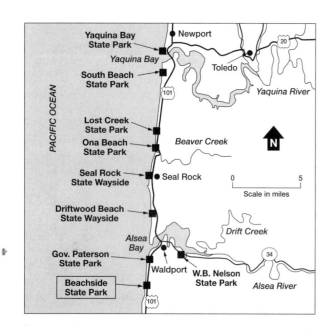

For Information

Beachside State Park
c/o South Beach State Park
5580 South Coast Highway
South Beach, OR 97366
(503) 867-7451
FAX—867-3254

Location

Beachside State Park is located on U.S. 101, 4 miles south of Waldport. With the campground adja-cent to the beach, the small park encompasses 17 acres that includes a dense forest of native shore pine. Alsea Bay, located 4 miles north of the park, offers a variety of activities including fishing, clam-ming, and crabbing. Excellent opportunities are found along the Alsea River for steelhead, blue-back, Chinook, and silver salmon. Dungeness and rock crabs can be caught off nearby piers or by boat in the bay. Boat and equipment rentals are readily available along with launching and moorage facilities in Waldport. The scenic Yachats River, 4 miles south of the park, also offers good blueback and trout fishing. The park is convenient to several miles of broad ocean beaches and a variety of coastal recreation attractions.

Facilities and Activities

The campground is open year-round. Reserva-tions are accepted from Memorial Day weekend through Labor Day.
32 RV campsites w/electric & water hookups (30′ maximum length)
   showers/drinking water
   flush toilets
   tables
49 tent campsites
hiker/biker camp
6 picnic sites
swimming/beachcombing/fishing
sightseeing/kite flying
accessible campsites/restrooms/showers for peo-ple with disabilities

Kip Anderson

Trails lead to impressive views of North America's deepest gorge in Hells Canyon National Recreation Area.

Lillian Morava

Windsurfing at its best can be found from the Pacific Coast to the windswept Columbia River Gorge.

Eric Kessler

Mickey Little

Oregon's largest land mammal, the Roosevelt Elk, roams freely on a wildlife preserve just east of Reedsport.

Some climbs at Smith Rock State Park are rated among the most difficult in the world.

America's largest sea cave, Sea Lion Cave, provides fascinating views of barking Stellar sea lions with their pups.

Mt. Jefferson's reflection hints of the breathtaking scenery amid Oregon's 13 national forests.

Stretching 47 miles along the Pacific Coast, Oregon Dunes National Recreation Area is a year-round playground of shifting sand that forms some of the continent's highest sand dunes.

Wallowa Lake exemplifies northeast Oregon's reputation as a "land of superlatives." Bounded by glacial lateral moraines, the lake is the hub of summer activities.

Once the home of saber-toothed tigers, giant pigs, and three-toed horses, John Day Fossil Beds National Monument is a colorful geological showcase of age-old sediments.

Spectacular waterfalls, such as Latourell at Talbot State Park, make a trip through the Columbia River Gorge National Scenic Area a must.

Umpqua National Forest boasts steelhead runs, white-water rafting thrills, backcountry trekking, and camping to suit any outdoor pursuit. ▶

From sun-up to sun-down, Oregon's landscapes romance the spirit of adventurers. This is Bullard's Beach State Park.

Over 70 state parks and waysides provide amenities along Oregon's coast. Swimmers at Honeyman State Park can vouch for the fun-filled attractions.

From the Deschutes to the Rogue and Umpqua Rivers, white-water thrills await paddlers.

Trails throughout the Columbia River Gorge lead to botanical areas and spectacular sites such as Multnomah Falls, second highest in the country (620 ft).

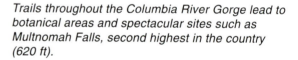

Embraced in Oregon's only national park, Crater Lake is the deepest lake in the U.S. (1,932 ft).

Pioneers traveled over 2,000 miles along the Oregon Trail in search of a new life. Campers can find exhibits along roadside and state parks, such as this one at Emigrant Springs.

Lillian Morava

Lillian Morava

Vista House on Crown Point was built in 1918 as a cliff-top memorial to the pioneers who braved the Columbia River rapids on their westward journey.

Kip Anderson

Open beaches along the north coast offer an array of activities and beautiful settings for family vacations.

Oregon Tourism Division

Hat Rock is a large monolith on the banks of the Columbia River just east of Umatilla. Like many day-use parks, Hat Rock offers picnicking, fishing, swimming, and hiking.

Some of the most rugged and magnificent seascapes on the U.S. mainland can be found along Oregon's 360 miles of coastline.

The longest continuous section of the Oregon Coast Trail stretches for 64 miles from the Columbia River to Tillamook Bay.

A year-round recreational haven, Mt. Hood features five ski areas, three with night skiing. There's even mid-summer snowboarding and skiing on the glacier above Timberline Lodge.

Silver Falls State Park features 10 waterfalls in a lush, narrow canyon.

Oregon Parks and Recreation Department

Where trails meet, so do outdoor-lovers who seek their own form of recreation, and transportation!

Mickey Little

Lillian Morava

Mt. Hood's beauty dominates every vista for a 100 miles in any direction—a perfect backdrop for Trillium Lake.

Lillian Morava

Oregon's excellent state park system makes camping an enjoyable way to experience Oregon's natural beauty.

Known as the "white-water capital of Oregon," the wild and scenic Rogue River is also legendary for its steelhead and salmon fishing.

Kip Anderson

Stunning vistas and historic lighthouses keep shutterbugs merrily traveling the coastline year-round.

Lillian Morava

Inland or off-shore, cast your luck for world-class fishing!

Oregon Tourism Division

Just steps off the beaten path lie tranquil settings.

"The lightning rod of the Cascades!" At 9,182 feet, Mt. Thielsen looms over its own wilderness area of high alpine forests and open meadows.

Lillian Morava

Bullards Beach State Park

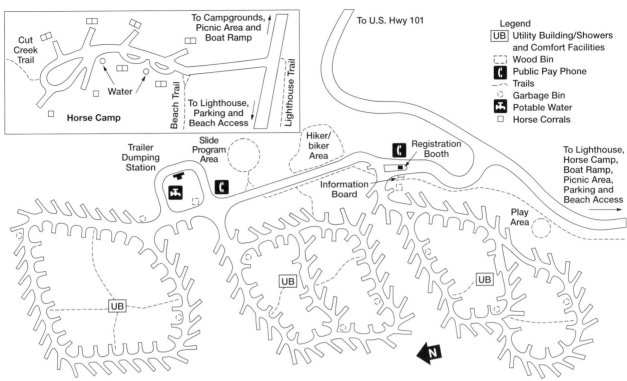

For Information

Bullards Beach State Park
P.O. Box 25
Bandon, OR 97411
(503) 347-2209

Location

Bullards Beach State Park is located on U.S. 101, 2 miles north of Bandon at the mouth of the Coquille River. A 1-mile trail accesses visitors to the park's 1,226 acres and 4 miles of sandy ocean beaches. A horse camp located near the beach with several small corrals provides great access to the 7-mile horse trails. Fishing, boating, and beachcombing are the main attractions at the park. A boat ramp is located near the picnic area for launching into the Coquille River. Historic Coquille Lighthouse, built in 1896, is located at the end of the road leading through the picnic area. Excellent fishing is found in the Coquille River as well as the ocean. In early November and late March, steelhead run up the river. Silver and Chinook salmon can be caught in the river and the ocean. Crabs are found in the lower tidal section of the

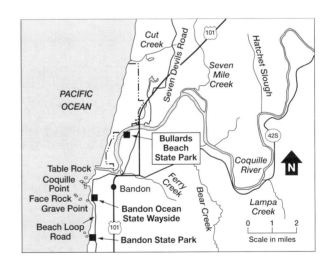

river, while clams can be found in nearby tidal flats. Charter boats are available in several nearby towns for ocean fishing. Bandon and other nearby towns in the vicinity offer a variety of interesting attractions that include a lumber mill, cheese factory, and fish hatchery. Brandon is often called "The Cranberry Capitol" of Oregon. Large cranberry bogs can be seen throughout the area. Other outstanding recreational areas nearby include Face Rock Viewpoint,

REGION 3

Bullards Beach State Park *(continued)*

Sunset Bay State Park, Shore Acres State Park, and Cape Arago.

The campground is open year-round on a first-come, first-served basis. Reservations are available for the horse camp.

Facilities and Activities

92 RV campsites w/full hookups (55′ maximum length)
   showers/drinking water
flush toilets
tables
trailer dump station
100 RV campsites w/electricity & water
8 horse camps
100 picnic sites
beachcombing/sightseeing
boat ramp/boating/fishing
lighthouse/history
accessible campsites/restrooms/showers/telephone for people with disabilities

Around every bend lies another stunning view of Oregon's spectacular coastline. This is just north of Bullards Beach State Park at Sunset Bay State Park.

Bureau of Land Management Recreation Sites

For Information

Bureau of Land Management
Oregon State Office
P.O. Box 2965
1300 N. E. 44th Avenue
Portland, Oregon 97208
(503) 280-7001

Site Descriptions/Activities

1. **Cavitt Creek Falls Recreation Site:** In a dense forest setting off the beaten path, Cavitt Creek Falls is a favorite place for locals to relax. It is best known for its swimming hole at the base of a 10-foot waterfall. The small campground is also nice for picnics. *Activities:* Swimming.

2. **Gerber Recreation Site:** Experience the wildlife and wetlands found at this recreation area. Relax while bass fishing or camping. Watch for eagles, nesting geese, deer, and antelope. *Activities:* Boating/rafting, fishing, hunting, wildlife viewing, and hiking.

3. **Hyatt Lake:** This outstanding high Cascade Mountain landscape encompasses several reservoirs with scenic vistas of Mt. Loughlin. Hyatt Lake provides opportunities for year-round recreation. The fee campground also has showers and a dump station. *Activities:* Boating/rafting, fishing, hunting, wildlife viewing, hiking, mountain biking, swimming, and winter sports.

4. **Klamath River:** From viewing wildlife to paddling your way through thundering whitewater rapids, the Klamath River offers visitors spectacular camera shots, fly fishing, and mountain biking. *Activities:* Boating/rafting, fishing, hunting, wildlife viewing, exploring historical sites, hiking, and mountain biking.

5. **Lake Creek Falls:** Just south of Triangle Lake along S.R. 36, visitors will find scenic waterfalls and popular natural water slides and trails. Visit the Watchable Wildlife site at the fish ladder where, at times, you can see hundreds of migrating salmon on their way to spawning grounds upstream. *Activities:* Fishing, wildlife viewing, hiking, and swimming.

6. **Loon Lake Recreation Site:** Located 20 miles southeast of Reedsport along C.R. 3, this area boasts one of the coast's finest campgrounds and a warm, sandy beach. Campsites are available for tents and motor homes. The lake is popular for swimming, fishing, and water ski-ing. *Activities:* Boating/rafting, wildlife viewing, mountain biking, and swimming.

7. **McKenzie River:** Just 30 minutes east of Springfield on Highway 126, this site offers easy access to world class salmon and steelhead fishing among some of Oregon's finest scenery. The river is also one of the region's most popular whitewater and float boating streams. Wildlife includes osprey, bald eagles, and blue herons. There is a Watchable Wildlife site at Silver Creek near Vida. *Activities:* Boating/rafting, fishing, hunting, wildlife viewing, hiking, and swimming.

8. **Millpond/Rock Creek Recreation Sites:** Located close to one another, these recreation sites are popular for picnicking and camping. Millpond caters to large groups with its baseball field, pavilion, playground, and small swimming hole. *Activities:* Swimming.

9. **North Umpqua Wild and Scenic River:** Anglers nationwide are lured to this river by its steelhead, Chinook and coho salmon. Its emerald green waters and the whitewater rapids attract both rafters and kayakers. The North Umpqua Scenic Byway (S.R. 138) parallels the river offering numerous turnouts and magnificent viewpoints for photos. Swiftwater Day-Use Area is a popular destination for fishing and riverside relaxation. Salmon migrate upstream here to Deadline Falls. A nearby interpretive site also provides a good viewing area for osprey as

Public lands administered by the BLM offer countless recreational opportunities in areas that host plenty of wildlife with sensational scenery.

REGION 3

Bureau of Land Management Recreation Sites *(continued)*

Bureau of Land Management Recreation Sites *(continued)*

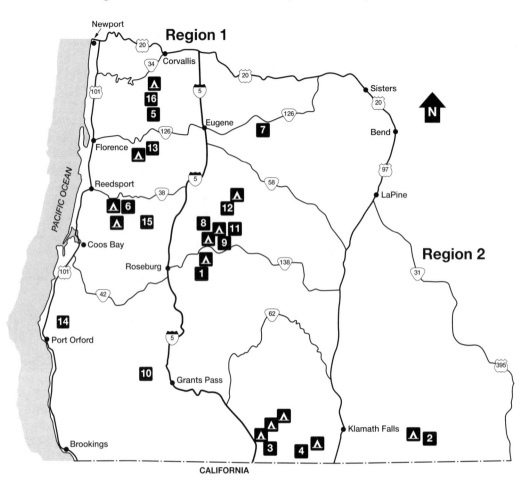

they hunt over the river. Several miles upriver, the Susan Creek Recreation Area (day-use only) provides a beautiful hike to a 50-foot waterfall. Across Swiftwater Bridge, photographers, wildlife watchers, hikers, and mountain bikers can begin the 77-mile North Umpqua Trail, which ultimately connects with the Pacific Crest National Scenic Trail high in the Cascades near the headwaters of the North Umpqua. *Activities:* Boating/rafting, fishing, wildlife viewing, geological and botanical sightseeing, hiking, biking, and swimming.

10. **Rogue Wild and Scenic River:** The Rogue River is an internationally renowned recreation area, unique for its whitewater, salmon and steelhead fishing, scenic beauty, watchable wildlife, and cultural resources. From May through September, the Rand Visitor Center (3 miles west of Galice) provides information on both the "wild" and "recreational" sections of the Rogue River. Floating the "wild" section of the river requires permits from June 1 to September 15. The Rogue River National Recreation

Site	Campsites	Picnic Sites	Trails	Drinking Water	Toilets
1. Cavitt Creek Falls	•	•		•	•
2. Gerber*	•	•	•	•	•
3. Hyatt Lake*	•	•	•	•	•
4. Klamath River*	•			•	•
5. Lake Creek Falls	•		•		
6. Loon Lake*	•	•		•	•
7. McKenzie River*	•	•	•		•
8. Millpond/Rock Creek	•	•		•	•
9. North Umpqua*	•	•	•	•	•
10. Rogue River	•	•	•	•	•
11. Scaredman	•	•		•	•
12. Sharps Creek	•	•	•	•	•
13. Siuslaw River*	•	•	•	•	•
14. Sixes River	•	•			•
15. Tyee*	•	•		•	•
16. Upper Lake Creek*	•		•		

*Barrier free access.

Trail and the Rainie Falls Trail provide hiking access into the "wild" section of the river. The Grave Creek to Marial Back Country Byway, along with the Galice-Hellgate Back Country Byway, provide motorists with panoramic vistas and interpretive waysides depicting the natural history of the Rogue River Canyon. *Activities:* Boating/rafting, fishing, hunting, wildlife viewing, geological and botanical sightseeing, exploring historical sites, hiking, mineral collecting, and swimming.

11. **Scaredman Recreation Site:** A little more primitive than others in the area, this no-fee campground is the perfect destination for the harried city dweller wanting to get away from it all. It is adjacent to Canton Creek, a picturesque tributary of the North Umpqua River. A popular swimming hole is located about one-quarter of a mile away. There is world-class fishing on the North Umpqua just a few minutes away in the Steamboat area. *Activities:* Hunting, wildlife viewing, and geological sightseeing.

12. **Sharps Creek:** Twenty-four miles southeast of Cottage Grove, this area is great for camping, swimming, hiking, and gold panning. The nearby proposed Calapooya Divide Back Country Byway will take motorists past active small gold mining claims to scenic vistas where magnificent landscapes quilted with old and new forests are spread out below. *Activities:* Fishing, hunting, botanical sightseeing, hiking, mountain biking, mineral collecting, and swimming.

13. **Siuslaw River:** Forty minutes southwest of Eugene, visitors can enjoy camping and recreational activities while visiting Whittaker Creek and the Old Growth Trail. This challenging 1.25-mile trail climbs to the rewarding vistas of the coast range. Up river, along the proposed Siuslaw River Back Country Byway, discover numerous boat launches and fishing access sites among the many side roads available for sightseeing. *Activities:* Boating/rafting, fishing, hunting, wildlife viewing, geological and botanical sightseeing, hiking, mountain biking, and swimming.

14. **Sixes River:** This gold mining hot-spot of 1856 still draws recreational gold miners. This rustic camping site is very popular in the summer months. *Activities:* Mountain biking and mineral collecting.

15. **Tyee Recreation Site:** North of Roseburg on the main stem of the Umpqua River, this popular bass fishing site draws fishermen back year after year. Tyee Campground, popular for river activities, includes a covered pavilion that accommodates groups. Birdwatchers will find osprey in the area. *Activities:* Boating/rafting and fishing.

16. **Upper Lake Creek:** Picnic or camp near Hult Reservoir. Try a little canoeing, warm water fishing, or explore the many miles of roads and trails. Some routes can even be followed over the surrounding mountains to the Alsea Recreation Area and Back Country Byway. *Activities:* Boating/rafting, fishing, hunting, ORV playing, hiking, mountain biking, and swimming.

What better way to share time with family and friends. BLM lands in Region 3 offer world-class salmon and steelhead fishing, fantastic rockhounding, sensational hiking, and limitless watersports.

REGION 3

Cape Blanco State Park

For Information

Cape Blanco State Park
P.O. Box 1345
Port Orford, OR 97465
(503) 332-6774

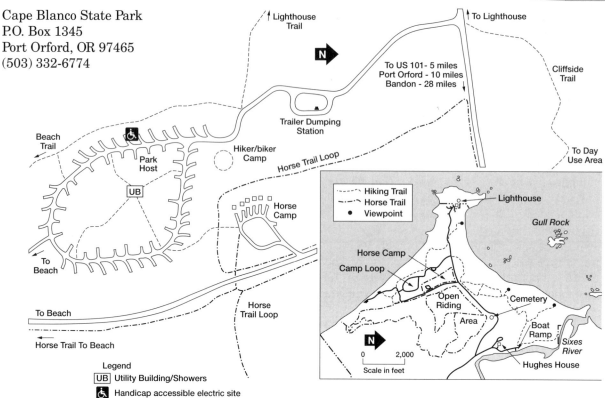

Legend
UB Utility Building/Showers
Handicap accessible electric site

Location

Cape Blanco State Park is located 5 miles north and 5 miles west off U.S. 101, and 9 miles north of Port Orford. It is adjacent to the historic 1870 Cape Blanco Lighthouse, the most westerly lighthouse in the contiguous 48 states. It is also Oregon's oldest continuously operated lighthouse. A hiker/biker camp and horse camp with corrals are available for campers who can choose from a variety of activities in and near this 1,880-acre park. A special attraction at Cape Blanco is the historic Hughes House, which was constructed in 1898. Between the Cape Blanco overnight camp and the day-use area are the remnants of a cemetery and former church site, "Mary, Star of the Sea," used by the Hughes family and other settlers of the area. There are several other historical areas in the vicinity including Battle Rock Park. Beachcombers and rockhounds can find agates and other stones, driftwood, seashells, and occasionally even Japanese glass floats. There are numerous trails available for the ambitious hiker.

Excellent fishing is possible for cod, halibut, sole, salmon, smelt, trout, and steelhead.

Facilities and Activities

The campground is open mid-April through late October on a first-come, first-served basis. Reservations are available for the horse camp.

58 RV/tent campsites w/electric & water hookups (40′ maximum length)
hiker/biker camp
horse camp
   showers
   drinking water
   flush toilets
   tables
   trailer dump station
1 picnic site
swimming/fishing
beachcombing/rockhounding
hiking/trails
sightseeing/history
accessible campsites/restrooms for people with
   disabilities

Cape Blanco State Park *(continued)*

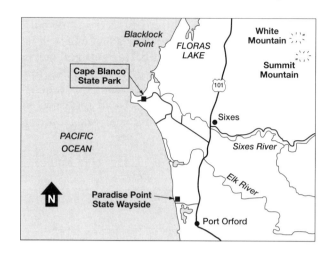

Exquisite beach settings are accessible from many state parks. This is Harris Beach State Park, south of Cape Blanco and north of Brookings.

Carl Washburne State Park

For Information

Carl Washburne State Park
c/o J.M. Honeyman State Park
84505 Hwy. 101S
Florence, OR 97439
(503) 997-3851
FAX—997-4425

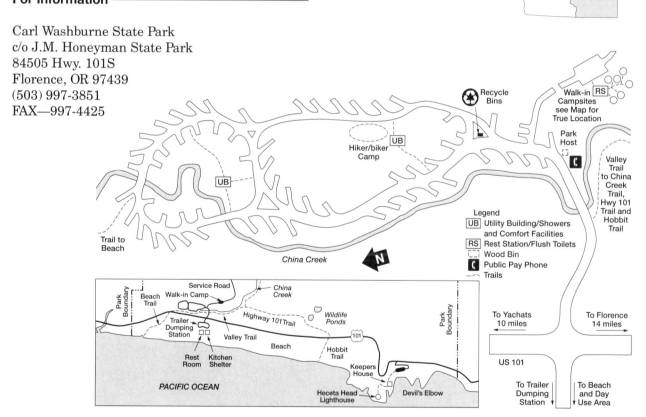

Location

Carl Washburne State Park, 1,089 acres in size, is located on U.S. 101, 14 miles north of Florence. The large rolling hills, west of The Coast Highway (U.S. 101), are actually sand dunes that have been stabilized and covered by a variety of plants. Some of these plants include shore pine, Sitka spruce, small fir, cedar, and hemlock; with an understory of evergreen huckleberry, rhododendron, salal, and manzanita. Fishing, hiking, and nature study are some of the attractions of the park. Beachcombers

Carl Washburne State Park *(continued)*

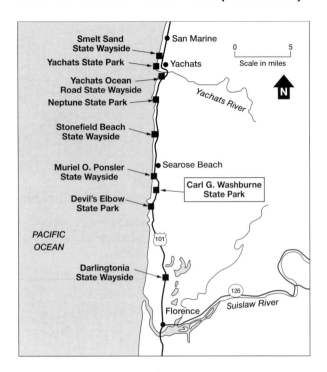

Trail, which follows China Creek (runs through the campground) to the valley meadow, offers sightings of resident Roosevelt Elk. Recreational opportunities are available in nearby state parks that include Darlingtonia (botanical area of Cobra lilies), Devil's Elbow (view of Heceta Head Lighthouse), Muriel O. Ponsler, Stonefield Beach, and Neptune.

Facilities and Activities

The campground is open year-round on a first-come, first-served basis.

58 RV campsites w/full hookups (50' maximum
   length)
2 tent campsites
6 walk-in tent campsites
hiker/biker camp area
   laundry
   showers
   drinking water
   flush toilets
   wood
   tables
9 picnic sites
beachcombing/swimming/fishing
hiking/trails/sightseeing/wildlife viewing

make many interesting finds including marine life living in tide pools formed in the rocky cliffs. Fishing and clamming are favorite activities at the park. Ocean fishing along the Central Oregon Coast is good at almost any time of the year. The Valley

Magnificent views of Haceta Head Lighthouse stop many photographers along Highway 101 just south of Washburne State Park.

Collier Memorial State Park

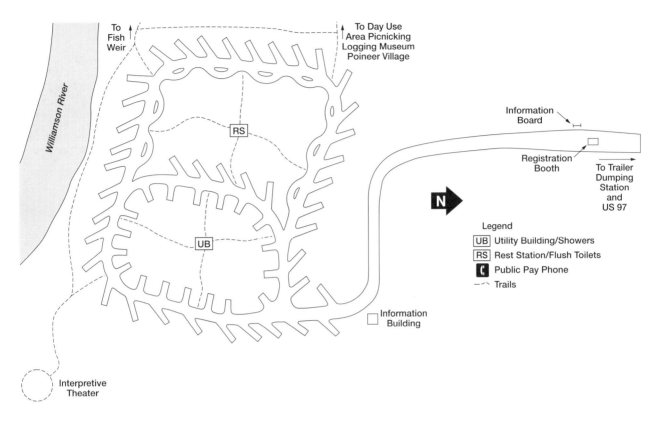

Legend
UB	Utility Building/Showers
RS	Rest Station/Flush Toilets
₵	Public Pay Phone
---	Trails

For Information

Collier Memorial State Park
46000 Highway 97N
Chiloquin, OR 97624
(503) 783-2471

Location

Located on U.S. 97, 30 miles north of Klamath
Falls, Collier Memorial State Park features a
campground, picnic area, a pioneer village, and a
unique museum of early logging equipment. This
655-acre park, elevation 4,200 feet, is located at
the confluence of Spring Creek and the Williamson
River, both highly regarded for fly fishing. There
are two day-use picnic areas. The larger, set at the
confluence of the creek and river, offers modern
restrooms, picnic tables with fire rings, a kitchen
shelter with stove and a children's play area. A
nature trail follows the river and creek, past the

*One of your first stops in any park should be an
information center for local activities and special events.*

Collier Memorial State Park *(continued)*

Pioneer Village, .5 mile to the other picnic area set along the west bank of Spring Creek. The museum is recognized as having one of the finest collections of logging equipment in the country. The pioneer village contains authentic cabins relocated here and filled with artifacts. The park is dominated by large, mature ponderosa pine trees.

Facilities and Activities

The campground is open mid-April through late October on a first-come, first-served basis. The museum is open year-round.

50 RV campsites w/full hookups (60′ maximum length)
18 tent campsites
 pull-through sites
 showers/drinking water
 flush toilets
 wood & electric stoves
 tables
81 picnic sites
 kitchen shelter w/electric stove
play area/fishing/sightseeing
hiking/trails/nature study
logging museum/slide program
history/pioneer village/gift shop

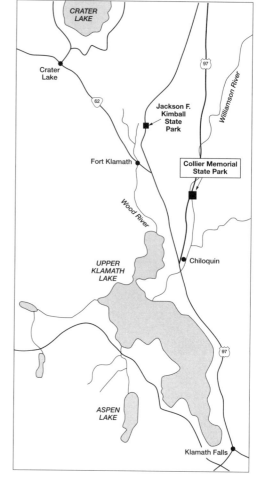

Just northwest of Collier Memorial State Park lies Oregon's only national park, Crater Lake. This is the deepest lake in the U.S.!

Crater Lake National Park

For Information

Crater Lake National Park
P.O. Box 7
Crater Lake, Oregon 97604
(503) 594-2211

Wizard Island and Merriam cones are really volcanoes within a volcano!

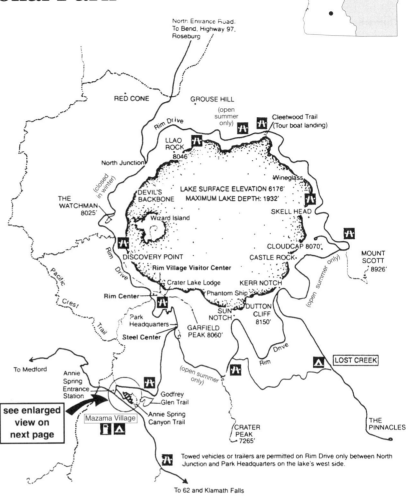

Location

Crater Lake National Park is located in southern Oregon on the crest of the Cascade Mountains. The park's most remarkable feature is a magnificent blue lake within the caldera of Mount Mazama, a collapsed volcano. Rolling mountains, volcanic peaks, and evergreen forests surround this enormous scenic wonder that is America's deepest lake. To witness the lake's indescribable blue water and the park's total beauty, visitors traveling from the west and south can follow Hwy. 62 into the park's south entrance. The north entrance is accessed via Hwy. 97 southbound from Bend to Highway 138. Weather permitting, Crater Lake can be viewed year round via the access road from Hwy. 62 and the south entrance. The north entrance is open from mid-June to mid-October. Crater Lake National Park, established in 1902, covers 183,180 acres and has the distinction of being the sixth oldest national park in the U.S.

Points of Interest

▲ Reaching a depth of 1,932 feet, the lake is the deepest in the U.S., the second deepest in the Western Hemisphere (Great Slave Lake in Canada is 83 feet deeper) and the seventh deepest in the world.

▲ Its maximum width is 6 miles with a surface elevation of 6,176 feet and an average depth of 1,500 feet.

▲ Walls of the caldera tower 500 to 2,000 feet above the water's surface.

▲ Approximately 60 kinds of animals are found in the park.

▲ About 33 miles of the Pacific Crest Trail pass through the park at elevations varying between 5,450 feet to 7,500 feet.

▲ Only two seasons dominate Crater Lake's weather, winter and summer!

REGION 3

Crater Lake National Park (continued)

Facilities and Activities

214 RV and tent campsites
backcountry campsites
drinking water
flush toilets
sanitary dump (Mazama only)
showers and laundry (Mazama Village)
picnicking
boat tours
fishing
hiking/backpacking
100 miles of maintained trails/elevations
  6,000'–9,000'
33 miles of Pacific Crest Trail
bicycling *
horseback riding*
snowmobiling (only on north entrance road)
cross-country skiing*
2 visitor centers
museum and exhibits
guided walks and tours
cabin-like motel at Mazama Village
restaurant, snacks, gifts, souvenirs
camping supplies, groceries, ice
pay showers and laundry
gasoline, auto needs (May to mid-October)
post office
*Only on designated roads and trails; check for
  regulations

General Information

▲ Fees are charged to enter and camp in the park.
▲ Towed vehicles or trailers are permitted on Rim Drive only between North Junction and park headquarters on the lake's west side.
▲ The visitor centers at Rim Village and Steel Center are open daily during summer. Services include displays, a movie, activity schedules, map and publications sales, and first aid.
▲ A museum and geological talks are provided at Sinnott Memorial Overlook.
▲ Guided walks and campfire programs are provided. Get details from visitor centers.
▲ A Junior Ranger Program is provided for children between 6 and 12 years old at Mazama campground amphitheater.
▲ Mazama and Lost Creek Campgrounds operate on first-come, first-served basis. No reservations are taken and campgrounds are closed in winter. Lost Creek is open to tent camping only. There is a 14-day limit of stay. Drinking water and flush toilets are available when weather permits.

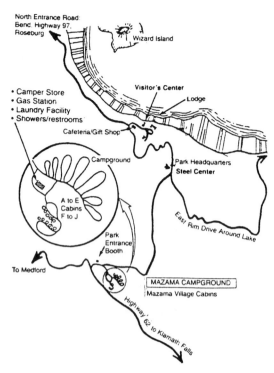

▲ Campsites are limited to 6 people or one family unit; no more than 2 vehicles in one site are permitted.
▲ No RV hook-ups are available. The sanitary dump station is at Mazama.
▲ The campgrounds sometimes fill up in the summer; campers should arrive by early afternoon to get a site.
▲ Showers and laundry are available at Mazama Village Camper Store.
▲ Free backcountry permits are required for all backcountry overnight stays. Topo maps and permits are available at the Steel Center or Rim Village Visitor Centers. There is a 14-day limit of stay.
▲ Backcountry camping is allowed all year.
▲ Pacific Crest Trail hikers can self-register as they enter the park.
▲ Travel below the Crater Lake rim is forbidden except on the Cleetwood Cover Trail.
▲ Wheelchair access is available at most viewpoints, the visitor centers at Rim Village and Steel Center, Mazama Campground Amphitheater, restrooms, and camper store.
▲ Mountain bikers are welcome on all paved roads and the Grayback Nature Trail. They are not allowed on other trails or anywhere in the backcountry.
▲ Horses, mules, and llamas can only be used on the Pacific Crest Trail, Bybee Trail, and Bald Crater Loop. Regulations strictly enforced.
▲ Interdenominational services are provided in the park. Check bulletin boards for information.
▲ There are limited activities in the winter.

Deschutes National Forest

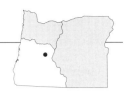

For Information

Deschutes National Forest
1645 Hwy. 20E
Bend, OR 97701
(503) 388-2715

Location

Extending about 100 miles along the east side of the Cascade Mountains Crest, the Deschutes National Forest encompasses more than 1.6 million acres of beautiful central Oregon. U.S. 97 is the main access to the forest. U.S. 20 provides the east and west accesses to the forest.

Points of Interest

▲ The forest contains many alpine meadows, lakes, unique volcanic features, dense evergreen forests, and desert areas. Summer days are moderate with cool nights. Winter weather produces excellent snow for skiing and snowmobiling at the higher elevations. The Deschutes National Forest is a true four-seasons vacationland and offers a wide range of recreational opportunities.

▲ The forest contains more than 100 campgrounds and picnic areas. Most campsites are provided on a first-come, first-served basis. A reservation system is offered for some concessionaire-operated campgrounds as well as some of the horse camps and group sites. Peak season for camping runs from Memorial Day through Labor Day.

▲ Hikers can use more than 700 miles of trails of varying length and difficulty. Most are located in upper elevation forest and alpine areas. Nearly half are within the three wilderness areas, including a portion of the Pacific Crest National Scenic Trail.

▲ Several campgrounds are designed for horse users and provide horse facilities such as ramps and corrals. These campsites are located near horse trails. See the campground charts for details.

▲ A variety of fishing experiences, including fly angling only or catch-and-release, are found for such cold water game fish such as rainbow, brown, brook, and Mackinaw trout. Fishing is also possible for Atlantic salmon, kokanee, and mountain whitefish.

▲ During the fall, mule and black-tailed deer, Roosevelt elk, black bear, pronghorn antelope, blue and ruffed grouse, and several species of waterfowl are hunted within the forest. Oregon State licenses are required to hunt, fish, or trap in the forest.

▲ One of the nation's largest nesting populations of osprey, as well as numerous bald eagles, is located within the Deschutes. Crane Prairie and Wickiup reservoirs, as well as Davis Lake, are especially noted for the numerous shorebirds that migrate through or breed at these bodies of water.

▲ The many lakes and rivers on the Deschutes National Forest offer opportunities for canoeing, sailing, wind-surfing, white-water rafting, swimming, diving, and water-skiing. Most of the Deschutes River is especially suited for canoeing and floating. There are hazardous falls and cascades along the Deschutes River; visitors planning to canoe or float should get details on these hazards from the Bend Ranger District—(503) 388-5664.

▲ Ninety-five percent of all known volcanic features can be found on the Deschutes, more than anywhere else in the U.S. A good place to start exploring this extraordinary volcanic landscape is at the Lava Lands Visitor Center, 11 miles south of Bend on U.S. 97. This Forest Service Visitor Center features displays and interpretive trails that present some of central Oregon's geologic history. For information call: (503) 593-2421.

▲ **Newberry National Volcanic Monument** encompasses the largest ice-age volcano in Oregon. This 5-mile wide caldera was created by several enormous violent eruptions; it contains East and Paulina Lakes, which are renowned for excellent trout fishing, a lava flow of black glass called obsidian, Paulina Falls, and Paulina Peak. The monument is 25 miles south of Bend via U.S. 97, then east on C.R 21. In winter the roads into this area are only plowed for the first 10 miles to the Sno-Park (permits required). See details on Newberry National Volcanic Monument in Region 2 under its own heading.

Other special places to visit include Lava Butte, Lava River Cave, Benham Falls, Lava Cast Forest Geologic Site, Odell and Crescent lakes, and the Upper Deschutes Recreation and Scenic River. The forest is also home to the Bend Pine Nursery (503-388-5640) and Redmond Air Center (503-548-5071). Call for tours.

Deschutes National Forest *(continued)*

Wilderness Areas

Permits are required for entry into wilderness areas from Memorial Day weekend through October 30th (these dates may vary). Permits for day hikes in the wilderness may be completed at the trailheads. For overnight trips, permits must be obtained at a local Forest Service office or through selected commercial outlets.

Diamond Peak Wilderness encompasses a total of 52,377 acres. Shared with Willamette National Forest, there are 32,567 acres located in the Deschutes National Forest. Elevations range from 4,787 feet to 8,744 feet at Diamond Peak. Great glaciers carved this large volcanic peak. When they receded, the carved bulk of the mountain remained, with snowfields near the summit, and dozens of small lakes surrounding Diamond Peak near the perimeter of the Wilderness. Many of these lakes, 1 to 28 acres in size, fill depressions gouged out by the movement of glaciers. The lower slopes are primarily forested with lodgepole pine grading into mountain hemlock and true firs at higher elevations. Approximately 14 miles of the Pacific Crest National Scenic Trail pass through this wilderness. Another 38 miles of trail, including the 10-mile Diamond Peak Trail, stretch the length of the west side of the peak. For information contact: Crescent Ranger District—(503) 433-2234 and Rigdon Ranger District—(503) 782-2283.

Mt. Jefferson Wilderness contains the second highest peak in Oregon, Mt. Jefferson (10,497′—a dormant volcano). Although nearly 3,000 feet smaller, Three-Fingered Jack (7,841′—an extinct volcano) is also a spectacular site for hikers and horseback riders in the area. The wilderness area contains 111,177 acres that is 62% timber. Within the boundaries there are 150 lakes with about 60 of these lakes providing habitat for Eastern brook and/or rainbow trout. There are nearly 194 miles of trails. Key access points are located on all sides of the wilderness, some beginning in the Deschutes National Forest, others in the Willamette National Forest, and one in the Mt. Hood National Forest. Approximately 36 miles of the Pacific Crest National Scenic Trail run through the Mt. Jefferson Wilderness (accessed from Highway 20 in the south and from Breitenbush Lake in the north). The hiking season usually extends from July 1 to October 1; trails can be blocked with snow banks throughout June and early July. Animals in the wilderness include deer, elk, black bear, and coyotes. For more information contact: Sisters Ranger District—(503) 549-2111 or Detroit Ranger District—(503) 854-3366.

Mt. Washington Wilderness contains 52,559 acres filled with inactive volcanoes, cinder cones, lava fields, and Mt. Washington (7,794′). Evidence of a long history of human use of this area includes a trail made by Native Americans that crosses south of the present McKenzie Pass. Today, many hunters, hikers, and mountain climbers make the Mt. Washington Wilderness their destination. Forty miles of hiking trails wind through the wilderness. With the exception of the Pacific Crest Trail, all the trails are short enough to allow for an easy, one-day trip. The primary trailheads are located in the Willamette National Forest. The primary trail in the Mt. Washington Wilderness, the Pacific Crest National Scenic Trail, extends for over 17 miles, several of them through lava fields. Regularly maintained, the Pacific Crest Trail is easy to follow with the Dee Wright Observatory in the south providing an entrance and Big Lake in the north providing an exit. Several of the 28 lakes are stocked with Eastern brook and/or rainbow trout. The hiking season usually extends from July 1 to October 1. For more information contact: Sisters Ranger District—(503) 549-2111 or McKenzie Ranger District—(503) 822-3381.

Three Sisters Wilderness covers some 285,001 acres that are dominated by the Three Sisters and Broken Top Mountains. A popular destination for mountain climbers, the mountains offer a variety of difficulty levels. Hikers and horseback riders can choose from approximately 433 miles of trials. Trailheads are located on all sides of the wilderness in both the Deschutes and Willamette National Forests. Over 42 miles of the Pacific Crest National Scenic Trail extend through the Three Sisters Wilderness. The Pacific Crest Trail enters the wilderness in the south at Irish and Taylor Lakes and exits the area in the north near Dee Wright Observatory. The trail is easy to follow and regularly maintained during hiking season, which usually runs from July 1 to October 1. Most of the 100 lakes are stocked with Eastern brook and rainbow trout. In the summer months, black-tailed deer, mule deer, and Roosevelt elk roam the wilderness. For more information contact: Bend Ranger District—(503) 388-5664 or Sisters Ranger District—(503) 549-2111.

Deschutes National Forest *(continued)*

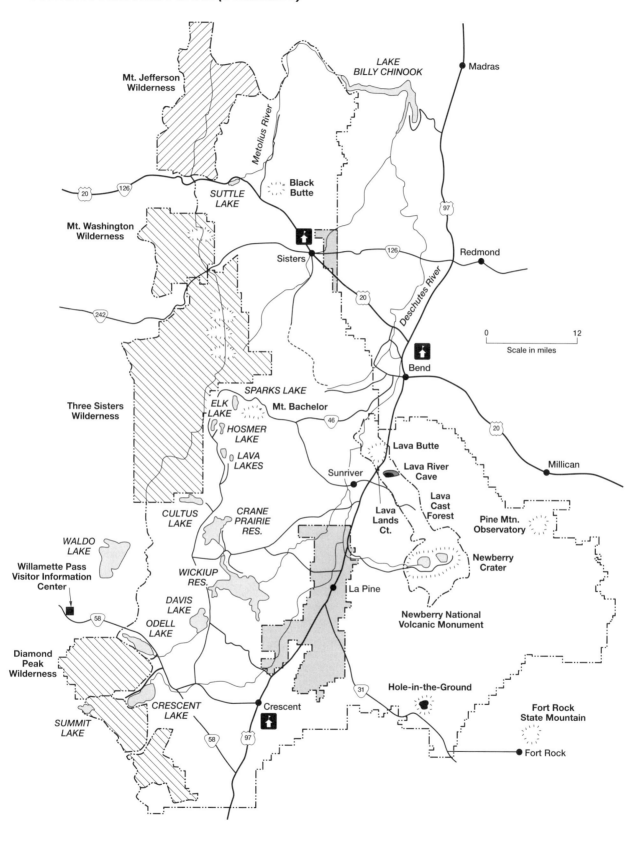

REGION 3

Bend Ranger District

Campground (see map on facing page)	Elevation (feet)	Tent Sites	Tent/Trailer Sites	Drinking Water	Fees
1. Bessen Camp*			5		
2. Big River	4,200	4	9		
3. Bull Bend			6		
4. Cow Meadow†	4,400	4	16		
5. Crane Prairie†	4,400	6	141	•	•
6. Cultus Corral**	4,700	non-designated sites			
7. Cultus Lake*†	4,700		54		•
8. Deschutes Bridge	4,600		15		
9. Devils Lake	5,500	6			
10. Dillon Falls	4,000		7		
11. Elk Lake†	4,900		22		•
12. Fall River*	4,300		12		
13. Gull Point†*	4,300		80		•
14. Lava Lake*	4,800		45	•	•
15. Little Cultus Lake	4,800		12		
16. Little Fawn†*	4,800	4	29	•	•
17. Little Fawn Group Camp†	4,800	reservation group site		•	•
18. Little Lava Lake†	4,800		14		
19. Mallard Marsh	4,900		15		
20. Mile	4,600		8		
21. North Davis Creek*	4,400		17		•
22. North Twin	4,300		10		
23. Point†	4,900		9	•	•
24. Pringle Falls	4,300		7		
25. Quinn Meadow Horse Camp†**	4,400		23 (R)	•	•
26. Quinn River†*	4,400		41	•	•
27. Reservoir	4,400		24		
28. Rock Creek†*	4,400		32	•	•
29. Sheep Bridge†	4,400		17		
30. Slough Camp			4		
31. Soda Creek		4	8		
32. South	4,900		23		
33. South Twin†*	4,800		21	•	•
34. Todd Lake*	6,200	4 (W)			
35. Tumalo Falls*	5,000	4			
36. West Cultus†	4,700	15 (B)			•
37. West South Twin†	4,000		24	•	•
38. Wickiup Butte	4,400		5		
39. Wyeth			3		

*Picnic sites available.
**Horse camp.
†Concessionaire operated.
(B) Boat-in only.
(W) Walk-in campsites only.
(R) Reservations required.

For Information

Bend Ranger District
1645 Hwy. 20E
Bend, OR 97701
(503) 388-5664

Campground Locations/Activities

1. **Bessen Camp:** On Deschutes River; 18 mi. SW of Bend via S.R. 46 and F.R.s 41 and 4140. *Activities:* Boating (launch) and fishing.
2. **Big River:** 22 mi. S of Bend on C.R. 42. *Activities:* Boating (launch) and fishing.
3. **Bull Bend:** 11 mi. NW of La Pine via U.S. 97 and F.R. 43 and 4370. *Activities:* Boating (launch) and fishing.
4. **Cow Meadow:** 46 mi. SW of Bend via S.R. 46 and F.R. 620. *Activities:* Boating and fishing.
5. **Crane Prairie:** 55 mi. SW of Bend via S.R. 46 and F.R. 4270. *Activities:* Boating (launch) and fishing.
6. **Cultus Corral:** Approximately 55 mi. SW of Bend via S.R. 46 and F.R. 4635. *Activities:* Horseback riding (horse facilities).
7. **Cultus Lake:** 55 mi. SW of Bend via S.R. 46 and F.R. 4635. *Activities:* Hiking, boating (launch), swimming, and fishing.
8. **Deschutes Bridge:** 41 mi. SW of Bend via S.R. 46. *Activities:* Fishing.
9. **Devils Lake:** 28 mi. SW of Bend via S.R. 46. *Activities:* Fishing, hiking, and horseback riding.
10. **Dillon Falls:** 11 mi. SW of Bend via S.R. 46 and F.R. 41. *Activities:* Boating (launch) and fishing.
11. **Elk Lake:** 33 mi. SW of Bend via S.R. 46. *Activities:* Boating (launch), sailing, swimming, fishing, and hiking (trails).
12. **Fall River:** 30 mi. S of Bend via U.S. 97 and C.R. 42. *Activities:* Fly fishing and hiking (trails).
13. **Gull Point:** 39.5 mi. SW of Bend via U.S. 97, C.R. 42, and F.R. 42 and 4260. *Activities:* Boating (launch), fishing, swimming, and waterskiing.
14. **Lava Lake:** 38 mi. SW of Bend via S.R. 46 and F.R. 4600-500. *Activities:* Boating (launch), fishing, and hiking (trails).
15. **Little Cultus Lake:** 50 mi. SW of Bend via S.R. 46 and F.R. 4630. *Activities:* Boating, fishing, swimming, and hiking (trails).
16. **Little Fawn:** 38 mi. SW of Bend via S.R. 46 and F.R. 4625. *Activities:* Boating (launch), fishing, and swimming.
17. **Little Fawn Group Camp:** 38 mi. SW of Bend via S.R. 46 and F.R. 4625. *Activities:* Boating (launch), fishing, and swimming.

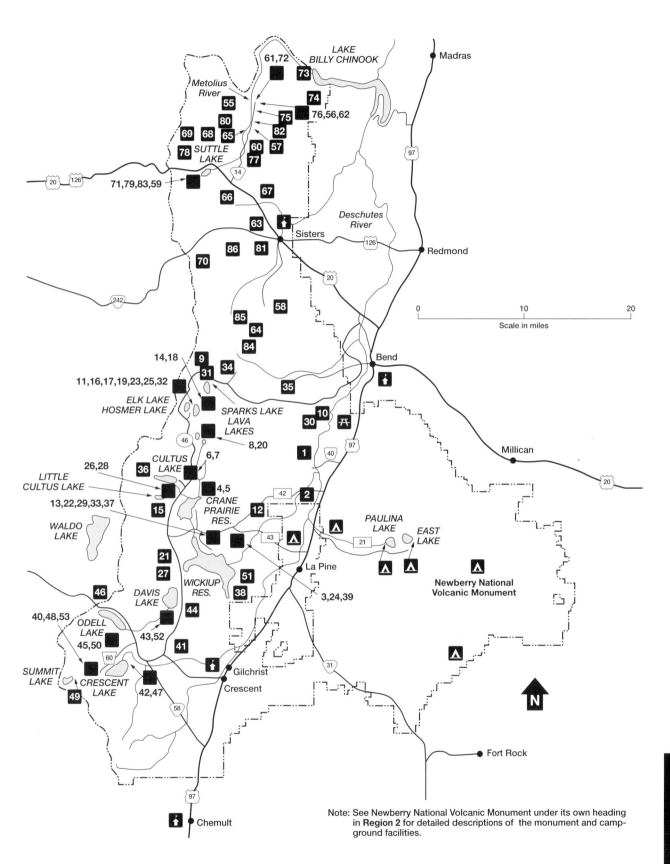

LAKE
BILLY CHINOOK

Madras

61,72
73

Metolius
River

55

74
75
76,56,62

80
69 68 65
78 SUTTLE
LAKE

82

60
57
77

97

71,79,83,59

66
67

Deschutes
River

Redmond

63
Sisters

126

86 81

70

20

58

85

64

84

Bend

14,18
9
31
34

11,16,17,19,23,25,32

35

ELK LAKE
HOSMER LAKE

SPARKS LAKE
LAVA
LAKES

30 10

Millican

20

8,20

1
40
97

6,7

26,28
36
CULTUS
LAKE

4,5

2

42

Paulina
LAKE

EAST
LAKE

LITTLE
CULTUS LAKE

CRANE
PRAIRIE
RES.

13,22,29,33,37

15

12

43
21

Newberry National
Volcanic Monument

WALDO
LAKE

21

La Pine

27

3,24,39

46

WICKIUP
RES.

51

38

DAVIS
LAKE

44

40,48,53
ODELL
LAKE

43,52

45,50

41

60

SUMMIT
LAKE

CRESCENT
LAKE

42,47

Gilchrist

Crescent

31

49

58

Fort Rock

97

Note: See Newberry National Volcanic Monument under its own heading
in **Region 2** for detailed descriptions of the monument and campground facilities.

Chemult

N

18. **Little Lava Lake:** 38 mi. SW of Bend via S.R. 46 and F.R. 4600-500. *Activities:* Boating (launch), fishing, and swimming.
19. **Mallard Marsh:** On Hosmer Lake, 34 mi. SW of Bend via S.R. 46 and F.R. 4625. *Activities:* Boating, fishing, and canoeing.
20. **Mile:** 40 mi. SW of Bend via S.R. 46, 1 mi. before Deschutes Bridge. *Activities:* Fishing on Deschutes River.
21. **North Davis Creek:** At W end of Wickiup Reservoir; 26 mi. W of La Pine via S.R. 46 out of Bend. *Activities:* Boating and fishing.
22. **North Twin:** 38 mi. SW of Bend via U.S. 97, C.R. 42, and F.R. 42. *Activities:* Boating (launch), fishing and swimming.
23. **Point:** On Elk Lake; 34 mi. SW of Bend via S.R. 46. *Activities:* Boating (launch), sailing, fishing, swimming, and hiking (trails).
24. **Pringle Falls:** 9 mi. NW of La Pine via U.S. 97 and just off F.R. 43. *Activities:* Fishing and canoeing.
25. **Quinn Meadow Horse Camp:** 34 mi. W of Bend via S.R. 46 and F.R. 450. *Activities:* Horseback riding (horse facilities), hiking and fishing.
26. **Quinn River:** On W side of Crane Prairie Reservoir; 50 mi. SW of Bend via S.R. 46. *Activities:* Boating (launch) and fishing.
27. **Reservoir:** 27 mi. W of La Pine on Wickiup Reservoir via S.R. 46 and F.R. 44 from Bend. *Activities:* Boating (launch) and fishing.
28. **Rock Creek:** On W side of Crane Prairie Reservoir; 51 mi. SW of Bend via S.R. 46. *Activities:* Boating (launch) and fishing.
29. **Sheep Bridge:** On Wickiup Reservoir; 19 mi. W of La Pine via U.S. 97 N, C.R. 43, and F.R. 42. *Activities:* Fishing.
30. **Slough Camp:** 12 mi. SW of Bend via S.R. 46 and F.R. 41. *Activities:* Boating (launch) and fishing.
31. **Soda Creek:** On Sparks Lake; 26 mi. W of Bend via S.R. 46. *Activities:* Boating, fishing, canoeing, and hiking (trails).
32. **South:** On Hosmer Lake; 34 mi. SW of Bend via S.R. 46 and F.R. 4625. *Activities:* Boating (launch), fishing, and canoeing.
33. **South Twin:** 19 mi. SW of La Pine via U.S. 97N, C.R. 43, and F.R. 42 and 4260. *Activities:* Boating (launch), fishing, and swimming.
34. **Todd Lake:** 24 mi. W of Bend 1 mi. N of S.R. 46. *Activities:* Hiking and fishing.
35. **Tumalo Falls:** 16 mi. W of Bend via S.R. 46 and F.R. 4601 and 4603. *Activities:* Fishing and hiking (trails).
36. **West Cultus** (Boat-in only): Access 48.6 mi. SW of Bend via S.R. 46 and F.R. 4635. *Activities:* Boating, fishing, swimming, and water-skiing.
37. **West South Twin:** 20 mi. W of La Pine via U.S. 97N and F.R. 43, 42, and 4260. *Activities:* Boating, swimming, and fishing.
38. **Wickiup Butte:** East shore of Wickiup Reservoir; 18.3 mi. W of La Pine via C.R. 43 and F.R. 44 and 4260. *Activities:* Boating (launch) and fishing.
39. **Wyeth:** 10 mi. NW of La Pine via U.S. 97 and F.R. 43 and 4370. *Activities:* Boating (launch) and fishing.

Scenery in the Deschutes is as wonderful and diverse as the activities that can be enjoyed. Don't miss the Lava Lands Visitor Center just south of Bend for unique views of Mt. Bachelor.

Crescent Ranger District

Campground (see map on page 147)	Elevation (feet)	Tent Sites	Tent/Trailer Sites	Drinking Water	Fees
40. Contorta Point	4,800		12		
41. Crescent Creek	4,500		10	•	•
42. Crescent Lake*	4,800		46	•	•
43. East Davis Lake	4,400		33	•	•
44. Lava Flow	4,400		12		
45. Odell Creek†	4,800		22	•	•
46. Princess Creek†*	4,800		46	•	•
47. Simax Group Site*	4,800		(G)	•	•
48. Spring*	4,800		68	•	•
49. Summit Lake	5,600		3		
50. Sunset Cove*†	4,800		26	•	•
51. Trapper Creek†	4,800		32	•	•
52. West Davis Lake	4,400		25	•	•
53. Whitefish Horse Camp	4,800		19		•
54. Windy Group Site			(G)	•	•

*Picnic sites available.
†Concessionaire operated.
(G) Group site; reservations required.

For Information

Crescent Ranger District
P.O. Box 208
Crescent, OR 97733
(503) 433-2234

Campground Locations/Activities

40. **Contorta Point:** At S end of Crescent Lake; 8 mi. SW of S.R. 58 and F.R. 60 junction via F.R. 60. *Activities:* Boating, fishing, swimming, and waterskiing.
41. **Crescent Creek:** 9 mi. NW of Crescent on C.R. 61. *Activities:* Fishing.
42. **Crescent Lake:** 3 mi. SW of Crescent Lake Junction with S.R. 58 on F.R. 60. *Activities:* Boating (launch), fishing, swimming, windsurfing, waterskiing, and hiking (trails).
43. **East Davis Lake:** On Davis Lake; 11 mi. NW of S.R. 58 and 61 Junction via S.R. 46. *Activities:* Boating and fishing (fly only).
44. **Lava Flow:** 14 mi. NW of S.R. 58 and 61 Junction via S.R. 46. *Activities:* Boating (launch), fishing, duck hunting, and fly fishing.
45. **Odell Creek:** Just off S.R. 58 at SE end of Odell Lake. *Activities:* Boating, fishing, and hiking (trails).

46. **Princess Creek:** On N side of Odell Lake; 2 mi. E of Willamette Pass on S.R. 58. *Activities:* Boating (launch) fishing, and waterskiing.
47. **Simax Group Site:** At NE end of Crescent Lake; 4 mi. SW of S.R. 58 and F.R. 60 Junction via F.R. 60 and 110. *Activities:* Boating, waterskiing, swimming, and windsurfing.
48. **Spring:** On Crescent Lake; 6.5 mi. SW of Crescent Lake Junction with S.R. 58 on F.R. 60. *Activities:* Boating (launch), fishing, swimming, waterskiing, windsurfing, and hiking (trails).
49. **Summit Lake** (primitive road): 12 mi. SW of Crescent Lake Junction with S.R. 58 via F.R. 60 and 6010. *Activities:* Hiking (trails), canoeing (launch), and fishing.
50. **Sunset Cove:** On N side of Odell Lake via S.R. 58, 5 mi. E of Willamette Pass. *Activities:* Boating (launch), fishing, and windsurfing.
51. **Trapper Creek:** Near Willamette Pass via S.R. 58 and F.R. 5810. *Activities:* Boating (launch), fishing, and hiking (trails).
52. **West Davis Lake:** On S end of Davis Lake; 13 mi. NW of S.R.s 58 and 61 Junction via S.R. 46. *Activities:* Boating and fly fishing.
53. **Whitefish Horse Camp:** 7 mi. SW of S.R. 58 and F.R. 60 Junction, on F.R. 60. *Activities:* Horseback riding (trails), fishing and hiking; boating nearby.
54. **Windy Group Site:** Contact Ranger Station for location and reservations.

A trip down the Deschutes River makes obvious the literal translation of its French name, "Riviere des Chutes" or "river of falls."

Fort Rock Ranger District

For Information

Fort Rock Ranger District
1645 Hwy. 20E
Bend, OR 97701
(503) 388-5664

Campground Facilities

Newberry National Volcanic Monument is managed by the Fort Rock Ranger District. Because Newberry National Volcanic Monument has such unique features and is designated a national monument, the campground facilities and activities are described under their own heading in Region 2. There are over 50,000 acres within the monument that contain approximately 95% of known volcanological features. Do not miss the Lava Lands Visitor Center and many interpretive trails within the monument. Summer and winter recreational opportunities are available.

Interpretive trails within lava flows help visitors understand the geologic wonders left here by volcanic eruptions thousands of years ago.

Sisters Ranger District

For Information

Sisters Ranger District
P.O. Box 249
Sisters, OR 97759
(503) 549-2111

Campground Locations/Activities

55. **Abbot Creek:** N of Sisters via U.S. 20, C.R. 14, then F.R. 1420, 12, and 1280. *Activities:* Hiking.
56. **Allen Springs:** On the Metolius River; N of Sisters via U.S. 20, C.R. 14, then 5 mi. N of Camp Sherman Store. *Activities:* Fishing and hiking (trails).
57. **Allingham:** On the Metolius River; N of Sisters via U.S. 20, C.R. 14, then 1 mi. N of Camp Sherman Store. *Activities:* Fishing and hiking (trails).
58. **Black Pine Springs:** 8 mi. S of Sisters on F.R. 16. *Activities:* Camping/lightly improved.
59. **Blue Bay:** 14 mi. NW of Sisters on Suttle Lake via U.S. 20 and F.R. 2070. *Activities:* Boating (launch), fishing, waterskiing, and hiking (trails).
60. **Camp Sherman:** On the Metolius River; N of Sisters via U.S. 20, C.R. 14, then .5 mi. N of Camp Sherman Store. *Activities:* Fishing and hiking (trails).
61. **Candle Creek:** N of Sisters via U.S. 20, C.R. 14, then 10 mi. N of Camp Sherman Store on the Metolius River. *Activities:* Fishing.
62. **Canyon Creek:** Check with Ranger Station for location and activities.
63. **Cold Spring:** 5 mi. W of sisters via S.R. 242. *Activities:* Camping.
64. **Driftwood** (RVs under 16′): 18 mi. S of Sisters on F.R. 16. *Activities:* Fishing and hiking (trails).
65. **Gorge:** On the Metolius River; N of Sisters via U.S. 20, C.R. 14, then 2 mi. N of Camp Sherman Store. *Activities:* Fishing and hiking (trails).
66. **Graham Corral:** 9 mi. NW of Sisters via U.S. 20, F.R. 1012, 1012-300, and 342. *Activities:* Horseback riding (corral and Metolius-Windigo Horse Trail).
67. **Indian Ford:** 5 mi. NW of Sisters on U.S. 20. *Activities:* Fishing.
68. **Jack Creek:** N of Sisters via U.S. 20 and F.R. 12 and 1230. *Activities:* Fishing and hiking (trails).
69. **Jack Lake:** N of Sisters via U.S. 20 and F.R. 12, 1230, and 1234. *Activities:* Fishing, hiking, and horseback riding.

70. **Lava Camp Lake:** 12 mi. W of Sisters at McKenzie Pass via S.R. 242. *Activities:* Fishing and hiking (trails).
71. **Link Creek:** 15 mi. NW of Sisters via U.S. 20 at W end of Suttle Lake. *Activities:* Boating (launch), fishing, swimming, waterskiing, and hiking (trails).

Campground (see map on page 147)	Elevation (feet)	Tent Sites	Tent/Trailer Sites	Drinking Water	Fees
55. Abbot Creek	2,800	4			
56. Allen Springs	2,800	4	13	•	•
57. Allingham	2,900		10	•	•
58. Black Pine Springs	4,400	7			
59. Blue Bay	3,400		25	•	•
60. Camp Sherman*	3,000		15	•	•
61. Candle Creek			4		
62. Canyon Creek			4		
63. Cold Spring*	3,400		23	•	•
64. Driftwood	6,400		14		
65. Gorge	2,900		18	•	•
66. Graham Corral**	3,400		10	(L)	
67. Indian Ford*	3,200		25	•	•
68. Jack Creek	3,100		9		
69. Jack Lake	3,400	2			
70. Lava Camp Lake	5,200	2	10		
71. Link Creek	3,400		33	•	•
72. Lower Bridge*	2,800		12	•	•
73. Monty	2,100		45	•	
74. Perry South*	2,000	4	62	•	•
75. Pine Rest	2,900	8		•	•
76. Pioneer Ford*	2,800	2	18	•	•
77. Riverside	3,000		22	•	
78. Round Lake	3,400	4			
79. Scout Lake*	3,700		(G)		•
80. Sheep Spring**	3,200		10(R)	•	•
81. Sisters Cow Camp**	open campsites			(L)	
82. Smiling River	2,900		37	•	•
83. South Shore*	3,400		38	•	•
84. Three Creek Lake	6,400		10		
85. Three Creek Meadow**	6,300		19	(L)	
86. Whispering Pine**	4,400		7	(L)	

*Picnic sites available.
**Horse camp.
(L) Water for livestock only; no potable water.
(G) Group reservations required.
(R) Reservations required.

72. **Lower Bridge:** N of Sisters via U.S. 20, C.R. 14, then 9 mi. N of Camp Sherman Store on the Metolius River. *Activities:* Fishing and hiking (trails).
73. **Monty:** 30 mi. NW of Culver via Cove State Park on Lower Metolius River. *Activities:* Fishing and hiking (trails).
74. **Perry South:** 25 mi. NW of Culver via Cove State Park near Lake Billy Chinook. *Activities:* Boating (launch), fishing, and swimming.
75. **Pine Rest:** N of Sisters via U.S. 20, C.R. 14, then 1.5 mi. N of Camp Sherman Store on the Metolius River. *Activities:* Fishing and hiking (trails).
76. **Pioneer Ford:** N of Sisters via U.S. 20, C.R. 14, then 6.5 mi. N of Camp Sherman Store on the Metolius River. *Activities:* Fishing and hiking (trails).
77. **Riverside:** N of Sisters via U.S. 20, C.R. 14, then 2 mi. S of Camp Sherman Store on Metolius River. *Activities:* Fishing.
78. **Round Lake:** 17 mi. NW of Sisters via U.S. 20 and F.R. 12 and 1210. *Activities:* Fishing and hiking (trails).
79. **Scout Lake** (Group area only): 14 mi. NW of Sisters via U.S. 20 and F.R. 2070 and 2066 just S of Suttle Lake. *Activities:* Swimming and hiking (trails).
80. **Sheep Spring** (Reservations required): 22 mi. NW of Sisters via U.S. 20 and F.R. 12 and 1230 just off F.R. 1230. *Activities:* Horseback riding (box stalls and access to Metolius-Windigo Horse Trail).
81. **Sisters Cow Camp:** 4 mi. W of Sisters via S.R. 242 and F.R. 15 and 1514. *Activities:* Horseback riding (corral).
82. **Smiling River:** N of Sisters via U.S. 20, C.R. 14, then 1 mi. N of Camp Sherman Store on the Metolius River. *Activities:* Fishing and hiking (trails).
83. **South Shore:** 14 mi. NW of Sisters via U.S. 20 and F.R. 2070 on Suttle Lake. *Activities:* Boating (launch), swimming, fishing, and hiking.
84. **Three Creek Lake** (RVs to 16'): 18 mi. S of Sisters on F.R. 16. *Activities:* Fishing and hiking (trails).
85. **Three Creek Meadow:** 16 mi. S of Sisters on F.R. 16. *Activities:* Horseback riding (4 box stalls per campsite and access to Metolius-Windigo Horse Trail).
86. **Whispering Pine:** 11 mi. SW of Sisters via S.R. 242 and F.R. 1018. *Activities:* Horseback riding (four box stalls per campsite).

REGION 3

Fremont National Forest

For Information

Fremont National Forest
524 North G. Street
Lakeview, OR 97630
(503) 947-2151

Location

The Fremont National Forest is located in south-central Oregon on the east side of the Cascade Mountains. Many are drawn to this land because of its unrestrained openness, clear skies and distant views, scabrock flats, rock outcroppings, and dramatic cliffs such as Abert and Winter Rim. The Warner Mountain Range is an attraction as well. State Route 140 runs east to west through the forest. State Route 31 and U.S. 395 provide access from north to south.

Points of Interest

▲ The forest includes over one million acres of public land rich in recreational opportunities. Camping, hiking, hunting, and fishing are popular activities. Where campgrounds and picnic areas are provided, they operate on a first-come, first-served basis. Campgrounds do not provide electrical, water or sewer hookups for travel trailers. Campgrounds are generally open from May through October. A few campgrounds may not open until June or July, depending on winter weather.

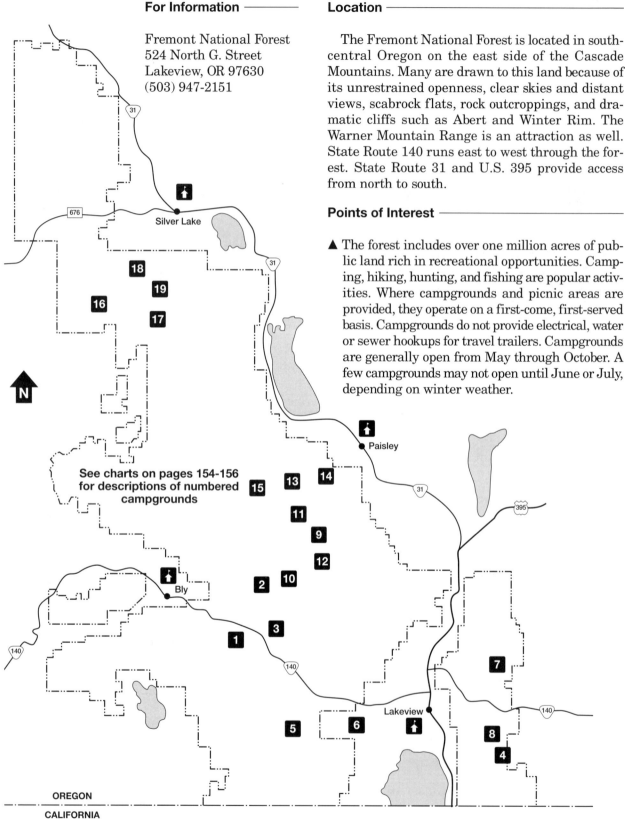

See charts on pages 154-156 for descriptions of numbered campgrounds

Fremont National Forest *(continued)*

▲ Winter recreation activities, such as downhill skiing, cross-country skiing, snowmobiling, snowshoeing, and ice-fishing occur in the forest. The entire forest is open for winter recreation activities with the exception of the Gearhart Mountain Wilderness, which is closed to snowmobiling.

▲ Hiking and backpacking are not particularly difficult in terms of the terrain or in terms of finding one's way. Elevation changes are relatively gradual, considering that it is mountainous country. One of the more popular trails in the forest is the Blue Lake/Palisade Rocks Trail, which runs through the Gearhart Mountain Wilderness. National Recreation Trails (NRT) in the forest include Crane Mountain NRT and Fremont NRT. The forest is in the process of constructing a trail that will be the Desert Trail/Cascade Crest Trail Intertie. It is approximately half completed and is currently well marked for use. Construction of the remainder of the trail is underway.

▲ Most of the trails in the forest are open for a variety of uses, such as equestrian, motor bikes, mountain bikes, and hiking. Trails in the wilderness are closed to motor bikes and mountain bikes. The Crane Mountain NRT encourages only foot and horse travel. Most trails in the forest are free from snow and mud by May through October. The entire forest is essentially open for off-road vehicle use with the exception of the wilderness, semi-primitive/non-motorized, or wildlife-sensitive areas.

▲ Slide Mountain lies at the southeastern end of Winter Rim and is the remnant of a dome-shaped volcano. Several thousand years ago, the volcano experienced a massive slide of the entire north face, exposing its interior structure. The enormous debris slope faces north, providing southbound travelers on S.R. 31 with an excellent view of this geologic phenomenon. Slide Mountain summit offers an excellent scenic overview of lakes, the debris slope, Winter Rim, Summer Lake, and the Diablo Mountains. The summit is an undeveloped site that can be hazardous.

▲ Abert Rim Viewpoint, a scenic overlook, provides a striking contrast between steep-faced Abert Rim and the Chewaucan Valley floor. This is the largest and most definite exposed geologic fault in North America. The viewpoint is nearly 2,500 feet above Abert Lake with a 640-foot vertical cliff. The road is hard surfaced.

▲ Portions of the North Fork of the Sprague River (15 miles) and the Sycan River (59 miles) in the Fremont have been designated as Wild and Scenic Rivers. Yamsay Mountain, Antler, Brattain Butte and Drake/McDowell provide recreationists with moderate opportunities for solitude and isolation because they are "designated" semi-primitive/non-motorized areas.

▲ Crane Mountain, Brattain Butte North and South, Mount Bidwell and Winter Rim provide recreationists with semi-primitive/motorized areas. Trails or primitive roads are designated to accommodate motorized use such as high-clearance 4-wheel drive vehicles, but not too developed

With winter comes an array of new activities to satisfy the snow-lovers.

REGION 3

to discourage 2-wheel drive and other low-clearance vehicles.

▲ Because the Fremont is a wonderful mixture of meadows, conifer and aspen forests, rock cliff faces and sagebrush openings, more than 340 species of wildlife find food and shelter here. Mule deer and Rocky Mountain elk are prevalent, while the lucky viewer may see California bighorn sheep, mountain lion, and bear. Birding is quite good in the area, especially near Abert Lake. Besides a great assortment of waterfowl, golden eagles, owls, and other raptors find nesting habitat here. Raptor viewing opportunities are numerous along the main roads of the forest.

▲ With over 600 miles of streams and many small lakes and reservoirs scattered across the forest, the Fremont has a rich diversity of fish species and habitat types. Largemouth bass, yellow perch, black and white crappie and bullhead are the warm-water game fish found in the forest. Rainbow, red band and brown trout are found in the larger low-elevation streams. Brook and bull trout inhabit the cooler water of the small headwater streams. There is a generous stocking of fingerling rainbow trout, brook trout, and kokanee in several of the lakes and reservoirs.

▲ Hunting opportunities center on big game mammals with mule deer, Rocky Mountain elk, and pronghorn antelope being the major species hunted. Smaller mammals, grouse, and waterfowl are also available to a limited extent. Hunting is strictly regulated by the Oregon Department of Fish and Wildlife.

Wilderness Areas

Gearhart Mountain Wilderness lies deep in the Fremont National Forest. The most prominent feature is Gearhart Mountain and its 8,354-foot summit. On a clear day the mountain provides viewpoints of the distant Steens Mountain to the east and the Cascade Peaks from Mt. Lassen in California to the Three Sisters in central Oregon. Blue Lake, the only lake in the wilderness, lies to the northeast of Gearhart Summit. The wilderness covers over 22,823 acres with elevation ranges between 5,800 to 8,354 feet. There are over 15 miles of trails. For more information contact: Bly Ranger District—(503) 353-2427.

Bly Ranger District

For Information

Bly Ranger District
P.O. Box 25
Bly, OR 97622
(503) 353-2427

Campground (see map on page 152)	Elevation (feet)	Tent/Trailer Sites	Drinking Water	Vault Toilets	Picnic Area
1. Loften Reservoir	6,200	13	•	•	
2. Corral Creek	6,000	5		•	•

Campground Locations/Activities

1. **Loften Reservoir:** 21 mi. SE of Bly on F.R. 3715013 off S.R. 140. *Activities:* Hiking, fishing and boating (launch).
2. **Corral Creek:** Located 19 mi. E of Bly via S.R. 140 and F.R. 34 and 012. *Activities:* Lightly improved, wilderness access, hunting, fishing, and wildlife viewing.

Outstanding national recreation trails lace the Fremont. Backcountry venturers may be fortunate enough to catch a glimpse of Rocky Mountain elk, California bighorn sheep, or maybe the elusive mountain lion!

Lakeview Ranger District

For Information

Lakeview Ranger District
HC 64, Box 60
Lakeview OR 97630
(503) 947-3334

Campground (see map on page 152)	Elevation (feet)	Tent/Trailer Sites	Drinking Water	Vault Toilets	Picnic Area
3. Cottonwood Meadows	6,100	26	•	•	•
4. Deep Creek	5,600	6		•	
5. Dog Lake	5,100	11		•	
6. Drews Creek	4,900	5	•	•	•
7. Mud Creek	6,600	6	•	•	
8. Willow Creek	5,800	11	•	•	

Campground Locations/Activities

3. **Cottonwood Meadows** (RVs under 16′): 25 mi. NW of Lakeview on F.R. 3870 off S.R. 140. *Activities:* Hiking, picnicking, boating, fishing, swimming, and hunting.
4. **Deep Creek:** 28 mi. SE of Lakeview on F.R. 4015 off S.R. 395. *Activities:* Fishing and hunting.
5. **Dog Lake** (RVs under 16′): 25 mi. SW of Lakeview on F.R. 4017 off S.R. 140. *Activities:* Picnicking, fishing, boating, and hunting.
6. **Drews Creek** (RVs under 16′): 13.7 mi. SW of Lakeview on F.R. 4017 off S.R. 140. *Activities:* Boating, water skiing, swimming, fishing, and hunting.
7. **Mud Creek** (RVs under 16′): 18 mi. NE of Lakeview on F.R. 3615 off S.R. 140. *Activities:* Fishing and hunting.
8. **Willow Creek:** 22 mi. SE of Lakeview on F.R. 4011 off S.R. 395. *Activities:* Fishing and hunting.

Check with park officials for facility accessibility to the physically challenged.

Paisley Ranger District

For Information

Paisley Ranger District
P.O. Box 67
Paisley, OR 97636
(503) 943-3114

Campground (see map on page 152)	Elevation (feet)	Tent/Trailer Sites	Drinking Water	Vault Toilets	Picnic Area
9. Campbell Lake	7,200	15	•	•	•
10. Dairy Point	5,200	4	•	•	•
11. Deadhorse Lake	7,300	21	•	•	•
12. Happy Camp	5,200	9	•	•	
13. Lee Thomas	6,100	7	•	•	
14. Marster Spring	4,800	10	•	•	
15. Sandhill Crossing	6,100	5	•	•	

Campground Locations/Activities

9. **Campbell Lake:** 25.4 mi. SW of Paisley on F.R. 2800033 off S.R. 31. *Activities:* Picnicking, boating (launch/no motors), fishing, and swimming.
10. **Dairy Point:** 21.2 mi. SW of Paisley on F.R. 28 off S.R. 130. *Activities:* Fishing and hunting.
11. **Deadhorse Lake:** 26.4 mi. SW of Paisley on F.R. 2800033 off S.R. 31. *Activities:* Picnicking, boating (launch) fishing, swimming and hiking.
12. **Happy Camp:** 23.3 mi. SW of Paisley on F.R. 2800047 off S.R. 31. *Activities:* Fishing and hunting.
13. **Lee Thomas:** 26.5 mi. SW of Paisley on F.R. 3411 off S.R. 31. *Activities:* Hiking, fishing, and hunting.
14. **Marster Spring:** 7.4 mi. S. of Paisley on F.R. 33 off S.R. 31. *Activities:* Fishing and hunting.
15. **Sandhill Crossing:** 28.8 mi. SW of Paisley on F.R. 3411 off S.R. 31. *Activities:* Hiking and fishing.

Silver Lake Ranger District

For Information

Silver Lake Ranger District
P.O. Box 129
Silver Lake, OR 97638
(503) 576-2107

Campground Locations/Activities

16. **Antler Trailhead:** Located 22 mi. SW of Silver Lake via C.R. 4-10 and F.R. 2804, 7645, 036, and 038. *Activities:* Hiking, hunting, equestrian activities, snowshoeing, and cross-country skiing.
17. **East Bay:** 12.8 mi SW of Silver Lake on F.R. 28 off S.R. 31. **Activities:** Boating (launch), swimming, fishing and hunting.
18. **Silver Creek Marsh:** 9.6 mi. SW of Silver Lake on F.R. 27 off S.R. 31. *Activities:* Fishing and hunting.

Campground (see map on page 152)	Elevation (feet)	Tent/Trailer Sites	Drinking Water	Vault Toilets	Picnic Area
16. Antler Trailhead	6,400	7	•	•	•
17. East Bay	5,000	10	•	•	•
18. Silver Creek Marsh	5,000	6	•	•	
19. Thompson Reservoir	5,000	19	•	•	•

19. **Thompson Reservoir:** 11.9 mi. SW of Silver Lake on F.R. 27 off S.R. 31. *Activities:* Boating (launch), swimming, fishing, and hunting.

There is a generous stocking of fingerling rainbow trout, brook trout, and kokanee in several of the lakes and reservoirs in the forest.

Goose Lake State Park

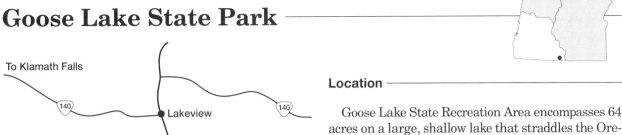

To Klamath Falls

Lakeview

Goose Lake

OREGON
CALIFORNIA

GOOSE
LAKE

New Pine Creek

N

Location

Goose Lake State Recreation Area encompasses 64 acres on a large, shallow lake that straddles the Oregon-California border. At an elevation of 4,740 feet, the park is located off U.S. 395, 15 miles south of Lakeview. Visited by migratory waterfowl in spring and summer, the park makes a great birdwatching destination for campers. The lake water is 2.5 to 3 feet deep as far as 100 feet into the lake, which makes it a popular place to swim and windsurf. There are opportunities for hang gliding nearby.

Facilities and Activities

The campground is open mid-April through late October on a first-come, first-served basis.

48 RV campsites w/ electric & water only (50′ maximum length)
   showers/drinking water
   flush toilets
   stoves
   tables
   trailer dump station
24 picnic sites
boating/windsurfing/swimming
sightseeing/birdwatching
hang gliding nearby

For Information

Goose Lake State Recreation Area
c/o Collier State Park
46000 Hwy. 97N
Chiloquin, OR 97624
(503) 783-2471

Birdwatchers will find a variety of birds for their checklists. Even though this owl may not give a hoot, Goose Lake is known for its migratory waterfowl.

REGION 3

Harris Beach State Park

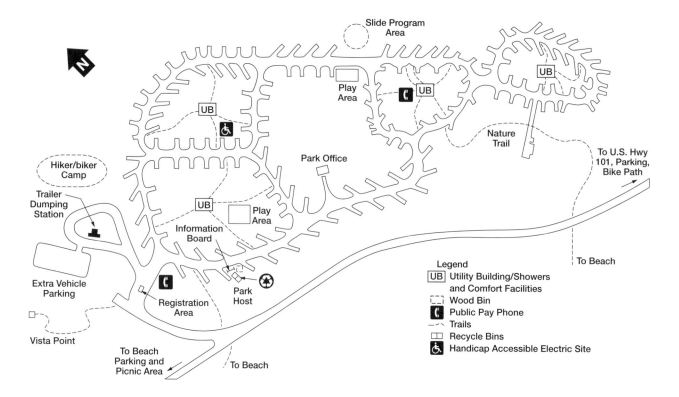

Legend
- **UB** Utility Building/Showers and Comfort Facilities
- **[ ]** Wood Bin
- **C** Public Pay Phone
- **- - -** Trails
- **[ ]** Recycle Bins
- **♿** Handicap Accessible Electric Site

For Information

Harris Beach State Park
1655 Highway 101
Brookings, OR 97415
(503) 469-0224
FAX—469-9539

Location

Located on U.S. 101, north end of Brookings' city limits, Harris Beach State Park features a secluded sandy beach, spectacular views of the rugged coastline and offshore rocks, and a colorful variety of native plants. Beachcombing, surf bathing, rock and surf fishing, and the enjoyment of natural beauty are the major park attractions. The Southern Oregon Coast is a beachcomber's paradise, with a variety of bottles, boxes, kegs, lumber, and an occasional Japanese glass float deposited along the beaches. Rock hunting is also productive, with a variety of precious and semi-precious gemstones found. Near Harris Beach are several state parks that provide additional recreation opportunities and outstanding coastal scenery. To the north the U.S. Forest Service also maintains a number of small campgrounds in the mountains east of U.S. 101. The district ranger stations at Brookings and Gold Beach have additional information. The Brookings area produces about 75% of the Easter lilies grown in the U.S., and vast fields of these beautiful white flowers can be seen in early July. Daffodils are also raised commercially in this area. The Rogue River at Gold Beach, 30 miles north of Brookings, is a great favorite with boaters and fishermen. The Rogue is famous for its excellent salmon, steelhead, and trout fishing from bank or boat. A ride in the mail boat up the Rogue River, lasting from two

Harris Beach State Park *(continued)*

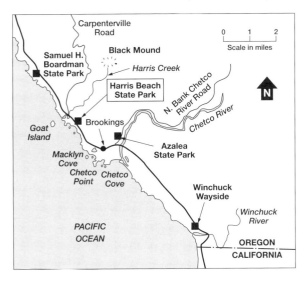

Facilities and Activities

The campground is open year-round. Reservations are accepted from Memorial Day weekend through Labor Day.

34 RV campsites w/full hookups (50' maximum length)
53 RV campsites w/electricity & water
69 tent campsites
hiker/biker camp
club camping
   showers/drinking water
   flush toilets
   tables
   trailer dump station
17 picnic sites
play area/swimming
beachcombing/rockhounding
boating/fishing/sightseeing
accessible campsite/day-use restrooms for people with disabilities

to seven hours, is also an exciting experience. Excellent fishing is available along the coastline, in the Chetco and Winchuck Rivers and smaller streams, and in deep water offshore.

The southern Oregon coast is a beachcomber's paradise with a variety of bottles, boxes, kegs, lumber, and an occasional Japanese glass float deposited along the water's edge!

Humbug Mountain State Park

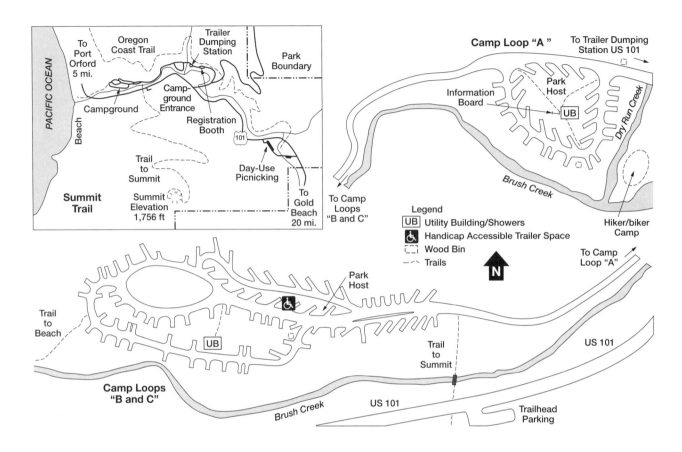

Legend
UB	Utility Building/Showers
♿	Handicap Accessible Trailer Space
⬚	Wood Bin
- - -	Trails

For Information

Humbug Mountain State Park
c/o Cape Blanco State Park
P.O. Box 1345
Port Orford, OR 97465
(503) 332-6774

Location

Located at the base of a towering coastal headland rising 1,756 feet above the sea, Humbug Mountain State Park can be accessed from U.S. 101, 6 miles south of Port Orford. This 1,828-acre park has a scenic three-mile trail that winds its way out of Brush Creek Canyon to the summit of Humbug Mountain for a panoramic view of the area. The 360-mile Oregon Coast Trail goes through Humbug Mountain State Park. Where Brush Creek empties into the Pacific Ocean, surf fishing provides the

Just south of Humbug Mountain, the windswept waters of the Pacific at Cape Sebastian State Park are a haven for windsurfers.

Humbug Mountain State Park *(cibtinued)*

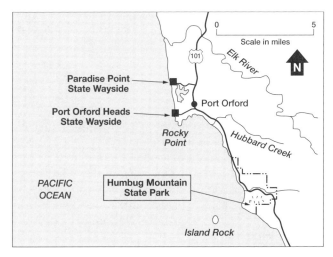

angler with some nice perch. Brush Creek and other nearby streams offer the angler a chance to catch trout. The area offers anglers opportunities to catch cod, halibut, sole, salmon, smelt, trout and steelhead.

Historic sites in the vicinity include Battle Rock Park and Cape Blanco State Park.

Facilities and Activities

The campground is open from mid-April through late October on a first-come, first-served basis.

30 RV campsites w/full hookups (45′ maximum length)
78 tent campsites
hiker/biker camp
    showers/drinking water
    flush toilets
    tables
    trailer dump station
37 picnic sites
beachcombing/rockhounding/geology
hiking/3-mile trail to summit
fishing/sightseeing
accessible campsites/restrooms for people with disabilities

Arch Rock typifies the beauty of Oregon's southern coast. Parks dot the coast and inland terrain for perfect camping destinations.

Jackson Kimball State Park

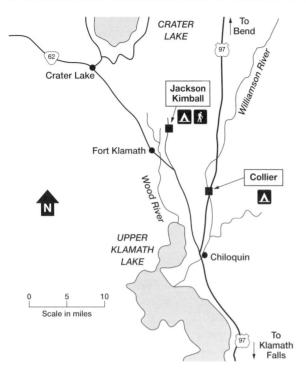

Location

Jackson F. Kimball State Park is located on S.R. 232, 3 miles north of Fort Klamath. This 19-acre, primitive-site campground is in a pine and fir forest. Short trails in the park lead to the headwaters of the Wood River. At an elevation of 4,170 feet, the park is a nice base to explore other nearby points of interest such as Crater Lake National Park, about 20 miles to the northwest.

Facilities and Activities

The campground is open mid-April through late October on a first-come, first-served basis.

10 primitive campsites (30′ maximum trailer length)
   pit toilets
   spring water
   tables
8 picnic sites
hiking/trails to headwaters of Wood River
sightseeing

For Information

Jackson Kimball State Park
c/o Collier Memorial State Park
46000 Highway 97N
Chiloquin, OR 97624
(503) 783-2471

Don't forget your camera for a shot of the locals!

Jessie Honeyman State Park

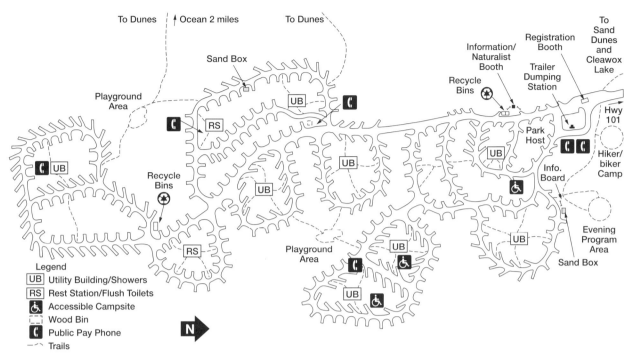

Legend

UB	Utility Building/Showers
RS	Rest Station/Flush Toilets
♿	Accessible Campsite
⬚	Wood Bin
C	Public Pay Phone
---	Trails

N

For Information

Jessie Honeyman State Park
84505 Highway 101S
Florence, OR 97439
(503) 997-3851
FAX—997-4425

Location

Located in the central Oregon coast dunes area, Jessie Honeyman State Park is adjacent to the north boundary of Oregon Dunes National Recreation Area. It is easily accessed from U.S. 101, 3 miles south of Florence. The park, 522 acres in size, is noted for its high sand dunes and spring rhododendron blooms. Two fresh lakes—all of Cleawox Lake on the ocean side of the highway and portions of Woahink Lake on the east side—provide campers with an array of water recreation activities. Swimming, fishing, boating, waterskiing, hiking, and nature study are favorite activities of visitors. The day-use areas at both lakes provide boat launching ramps and swimming beaches. A pleasant trail along Cleawox Lake connects the campground with the picnic areas and includes a loop trail around picturesque Lily Lake. Other scenic state parks nearby are Neptune, Ponsler, Washburne, Devil's Elbow

Intriguing creatures of the coast, seals can be seen up and down the shoreline.

Jessie Honeyman State Park (continued)

(view of Heceta Head Lighthouse), Darlingtonia (botanical area of Cobra lilies), Umpqua Lighthouse, and Tugman. The coastline offers many interesting attractions such as the town of Florence, fishing for steelhead and salmon in the Siuslaw River, and deep sea fishing. This area has spectacular sand dunes, some of which are nearly 500 feet high. Access to the dunes and the beach can be gained by South Jetty Road (Sand Dunes Drive) just 2.5 miles south of the park. Vehicles on the beach in this area are prohibited during certain periods of the year. Information on vehicle restrictions can be obtained at the park headquarters or the campground registration booth.

Facilities and Activities

The campground is open year-round. Reservations are accepted from Memorial Day weekend through Labor Day.

68 RV campsites w/full hookups (55' maximum length)
75 RV campsites w/electricity & water
238 tent campsites
6 group tent areas
hiker/biker camp
    showers/drinking water
    flush toilets
    tables
    trailer dump station
144 picnic sites
2 group reservation picnic areas
swim area/beachcombing
boat ramp/boating/fishing
waterskiing/swimming
hiking/trails
sightseeing/geology
concession restaurant and store
accessible campsites/restrooms for people with disabilities

Adjacent to the north boundary of Oregon Dunes National Recreation Area, Honeyman State Park boasts freshwater lakes and plenty of sand dunes for playing.

Joseph Stewart State Park

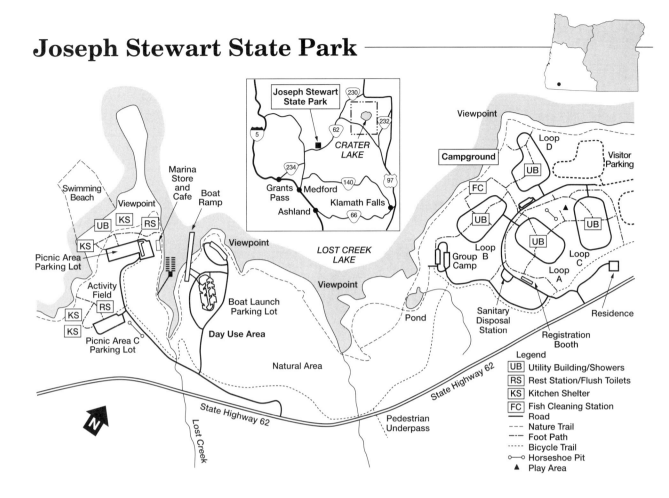

For Information

Joseph Stewart State Park
c/o Valley of the Rogue State Park
3792 North River Road
Gold Hill, OR 97525
(503) 582-1118
FAX—582-1312

Location

Joseph Stewart State Park can be accessed from S.R. 62, 34 miles northeast of Medford. Located on the south shore of the Lost Creek Reservoir, which was formed by waters of the Upper Rogue River, the park offers a variety of recreational opportunities. Boating and waterskiing are very popular at the park. Stocked with trout and bass, Lost Creek Reservoir provides excellent fishing year-round. Fish cleaning facilities are located near the boat launch area. There are 3 miles of paved hiking trails and 5 miles of paved bicycle trails within the park's 910 acres. Trails connect the day-use area to the overnight campground and extend outside the park boundaries to connect to other major trails within the Oregon Recreation Trail System. The Upper Rogue River hiking trail also leads through the park. Crater Lake National Park, 35 miles northeast of Joseph Stewart, is one of Oregon's most scenic attractions.

Facilities and Activities

The campground is open mid-April through late October on a first-come, first-served basis.

151 RV campsites w/electricity & water (80′ maximum length)
50 tent campsites
2 group tent areas
   showers/drinking water
   flush toilets
   wood stoves
   tables
   trailer dump station
2 large picnic areas w/multiple BBQ stands/tables
electric kitchen shelters
play area/fish cleaning facilities
boat ramp/boating/fishing
waterskiing/swimming
hiking/5.5 miles of trails
bicycling/6 miles of trails
sightseeing
concession restaurant and store
accessible restrooms for people with disabilities

La Pine State Recreation Area

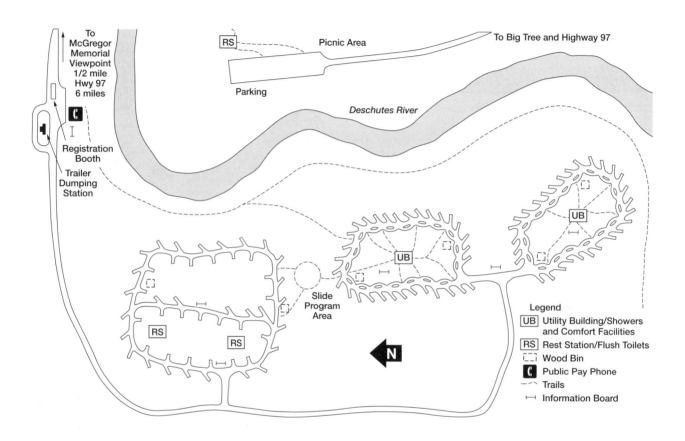

To McGregor Memorial Viewpoint 1/2 mile Hwy 97 6 miles

Registration Booth

Trailer Dumping Station

RS

Picnic Area

Parking

To Big Tree and Highway 97

Deschutes River

UB

UB

Slide Program Area

RS

RS

N

Legend

| UB | Utility Building/Showers and Comfort Facilities |
| RS | Rest Station/Flush Toilets |
| Wood Bin |
| Public Pay Phone |
| Trails |
| Information Board |

For Information

La Pine State Recreation Area
c/o Tumalo State Park
62976 O. B. Riley Road
Bend, OR 97701
(503) 388-6055

Location

Set among ponderosa pine trees, La Pine State Recreation Area is an ideal place to serve as a base camp while exploring Oregon's famous lava lands and the wilderness areas of the nearby Cascade Mountains. Covering 2,333 acres, La Pine State Recreation Area can be accessed from U.S. 97, 27 miles southwest of Bend. The park has 4 miles of frontage on the Deschutes River and 3 miles on the Fall River. This provides access to excellent boating and fly fishing. The Riverside campground is located in a pine forest that features the largest ponderosa pine tree in Oregon. "Big Tree" has a circumference of 326 inches and a total height of 191 feet. La Pine offers the nearest RV hookup campsites to Newberry National Volcanic Monument, approximately 20 miles east of the park. Other nearby attractions include: Century Drive, a 100-mile loop; The Lava Lands Visitors Center; Lava River Caves; Newberry Crater; Paulina and East Lakes; and the High Desert Museum.

Facilities and Activities

The campground is open mid-April through late October on a first-come, first-served basis.

La Pine State Recreation Area *(continued)*

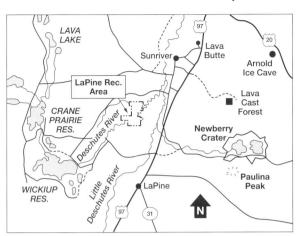

95 RV campsites w/full hookups (40' maximum
   length)
50 RV/tent campsites w/electricity & water
   pull-through sites
   showers/drinking water
   flush toilets
   tables
   trailer dump station
34 picnic sites
play area/waterfalls
rafting/canoeing/fishing
hiking/bicycling/forest roads
sightseeing/wildlife viewing
slide program/nature study/geology

La Pine Recreation Area is the perfect base camp for exploring Newberry National Volcanic Monument. Lava Butte is a huge cinder cone that rises to an elevation of 5,020 feet. Drive to the top to view the lava lands for miles around.

REGION 3

Loeb State Park

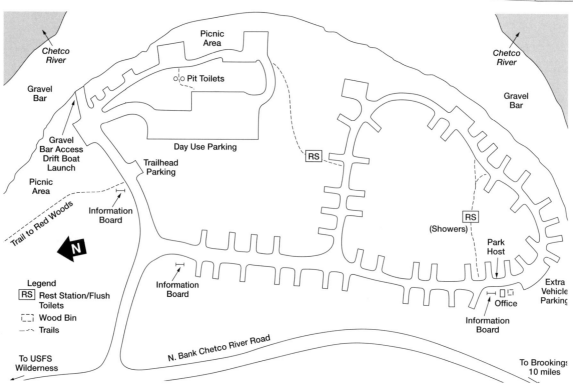

For Information

Loeb State Park
c/o Harris Beach State Park
1655 Highway 101
Brookings, OR 97415
(503) 469-0224
FAX—469-9539

Location

Loeb State Park's 320 acres are set in a beautiful stand of old growth myrtlewood trees on the banks of the Chetco River. Accessed from U.S. 101, 8 miles northeast of Brookings, the state park borders the western boundary of the Siskiyou National Forest. The forest offers access to numerous hiking trails in the area. A trail from Loeb State Park connects with the national forest "Redwood Nature Trail" near the Oregon-California border. The northernmost stand of redwoods in the U.S. is located here.

Facilities and Activities

The campground is open year-round on a first-come, first-served basis.

53 RV/tent sites w/electricity & water (50' maximum length)
   showers
   drinking water
   flush toilets
   tables
24 picnic sites
fishing/swimming
hiking/trails/sightseeing
accessible campsite/day-use restrooms for people with disabilities

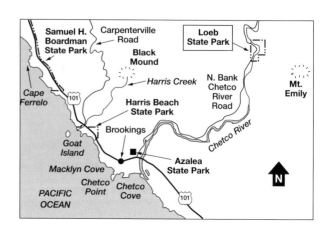

Oregon Dunes National Recreation Area

For Information

Oregon Dunes National Recreation Area
Siuslaw National Forest
855 Highway Avenue P
Reedsport, Oregon 97467
(503) 271-3611

Location

Oregon Dunes National Recreation Area extends 41 miles along the Oregon coast from Florence south to North Bend and Coos Bay. This area fea-

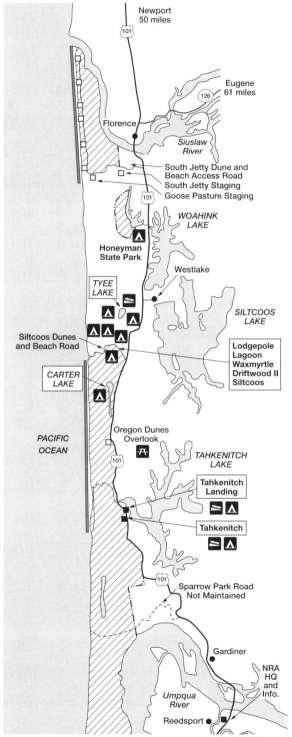

NORTH HALF (FLORENCE TO REEDSPORT)

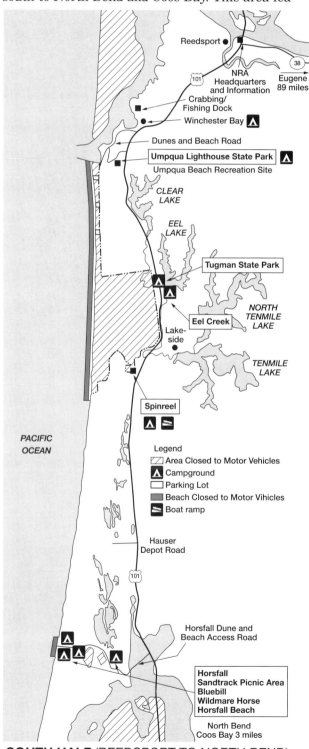

SOUTH HALF (REEDSPORT TO NORTH BEND)

REGION 3

Oregon Dunes National Recreation Area *(continued)*

For those who prefer the "faster outdoor lane," over 7000 acres of dunes are open to off-road vehicles.

Campgrounds	Total Sites	RVs	Tents	Fee	Drinking Water	Toilets Flush/Vault	Hiking Trails	Beach Access	Dune Access	ORV Allowed
North Half Campgrounds (Florence to Reedsport)										
Carter (R)	22	•	•	•	•	F	•		•	
Driftwood II ORV	70	•	•	•	•	F/V	•		•	•
Lagoon	40	•	•	•	•	F/V	•			•
Lodgepole	3	•	•	•	•	F/V				
Siltcoos**	6		•	•	•	V	•	•	•	
Tahkenitch	36	•	•	•	•	F/V	•		•	
Tahkenitch Landing	26	•	•	•		V				
Tyee	14	•	•	•	•	V				
Waxmyrtle (R)	56	•	•	•	•	F/V	•			•
South Half Campgrounds (Reedsport to North Bend)										
Bluebill	19	•	•	•	•	F/V	•			
Eel Creek	52	•	•	•	•	F/V	•		•	
Horsfall Dune & Beach Rd.**	34	•	•	•	•	V	•	•	•	•
Horsfall*/** Staging Area	70	•	•	•	•	V			•	•
Spinreel**	27	•	•	•	•	V			•	•
Wild Mare Horsecamp (R)	12	•	•	•	•	V				
State Parks										
Honeymoon*		66	240	•	•	F	•	•		
Tugman*		115	•	•	•	F				
Umpqua Lighthouse*		22	42	•	•	F	•			

*Showers, full hook-ups, hiker-biker camp (except Umpqua).
**Open to horse staging.
All campgrounds are at approximately 100′ elevation.
(R) Some campsites on reservation system.

Oregon Dunes National Recreation Area *(continued)*

tures 32,000 acres of beaches, dunes, marshes and forest. Administered by the Siuslaw National Forest, the recreation area is easily accessed from U.S. Hwy. 101.

Points of Interest

▲ The recreation area contains the highest beach dunes in the U.S., some 500 feet above sea level.

▲ 7,000 acres of dunes are open to off-road-vehicles.

▲ Beautiful nature trails for hiking lead to stunning scenic areas of the Oregon coast.

▲ 276 bird species, blacktail deer, and hundreds of plant species inhabit the area.

Facilities and Activities

992 RV and tent campsites
hiker-biker camps (Honeymoon and Tugman)
showers (Horsfall, Honeymoon, Tugman, Umpqua)
picnic areas
9 developed hiking trails
boating/ramps
swimming
fishing and surf-fishing
crabbing/clamming
beachcombing
whale watching
dune buggy/ORV riding
10 direct ORV accesses to dunes
horseback riding
11 staging areas
biking
visitor center (Reedsport)
interpretive programs
photographic viewpoints
guide services for fishing, horseback riding
rentals for ORVs, bikes, boats

General Information

▲ Fees are charged to camp in all designated campgrounds. Fees vary according to facilities provided.

▲ A visitor center, located in Reedsport, provides information, maps, displays, and publication sales. It is operated by the Siuslaw National Forest Service.

▲ Campgrounds are open year-round and operate on a first-come, first-served basis. Most sites offer tent pads, picnic tables, fire pits, and parking spaces. State parks offer full hook-ups, showers, and hiker-biker camps (no such camp at

Umpqua). Honeymoon State Park is on a reservation system. Call for information at (503) 997-3641. Peak months are during July and August.

▲ Interpretive programs are offered at Eel and Lagoon campgrounds. Check for posted schedules.

▲ RV hook-ups are available only at Honeymoon, Tugman, and Umpqua Lighthouse State Parks. No hook-ups are available at national forest campgrounds.

▲ Boat ramps are provided at Tyee, Carter Boat Ramp, Tahkenitch Boat Ramp, Tahkenitch Landing Campground, and Spinreel.

▲ ORV and horse access to dunes and beaches are strictly regulated. Check with rangers for closings and restrictions.

▲ Horse camping available at Wildmare Campground only.

▲ Dune buggies, jeeps, and 4 × 4s are required to have ATV-operator permits. ATV permits are valid for two years for residents or 60 days for nonresidents. An operator of a motor vehicle is required to have a valid driver's license. Any unlicensed operator of a 3- or 4-wheeler, if unaccompanied by a licensed driver at least 18 years old, must complete a rider safety course taught by a state certified instructor. Out-of-state enthusiasts must register like residents. Be sure to check with local Motor Vehicles Division office to make sure of proper registration.

▲ Full services for eating, lodging, groceries, supplies and fuel are accessible along Hwy. 101 in nearby communities. A variety of guide services are available for such activities as fishing.

Catch of the day! From ship to shore along Oregon Dunes NRA, the fishing is great fun.

Rogue River National Forest

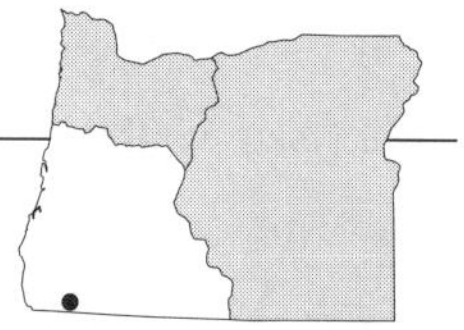

For Information
Rogue River National Forest
P.O. Box 520
333 West Eighth Street
Medford, OR 97501
(503) 776-3600

Location

Rogue River National Forest covers 630,000 acres and surrounds much of the Rogue Valley in southwestern Oregon. The forest, which includes about 53,800 acres in California, is easily reached from Medford, Oregon and nearby communities along I-5. The forest provides a rich diversity of scenery and recreational opportunities.

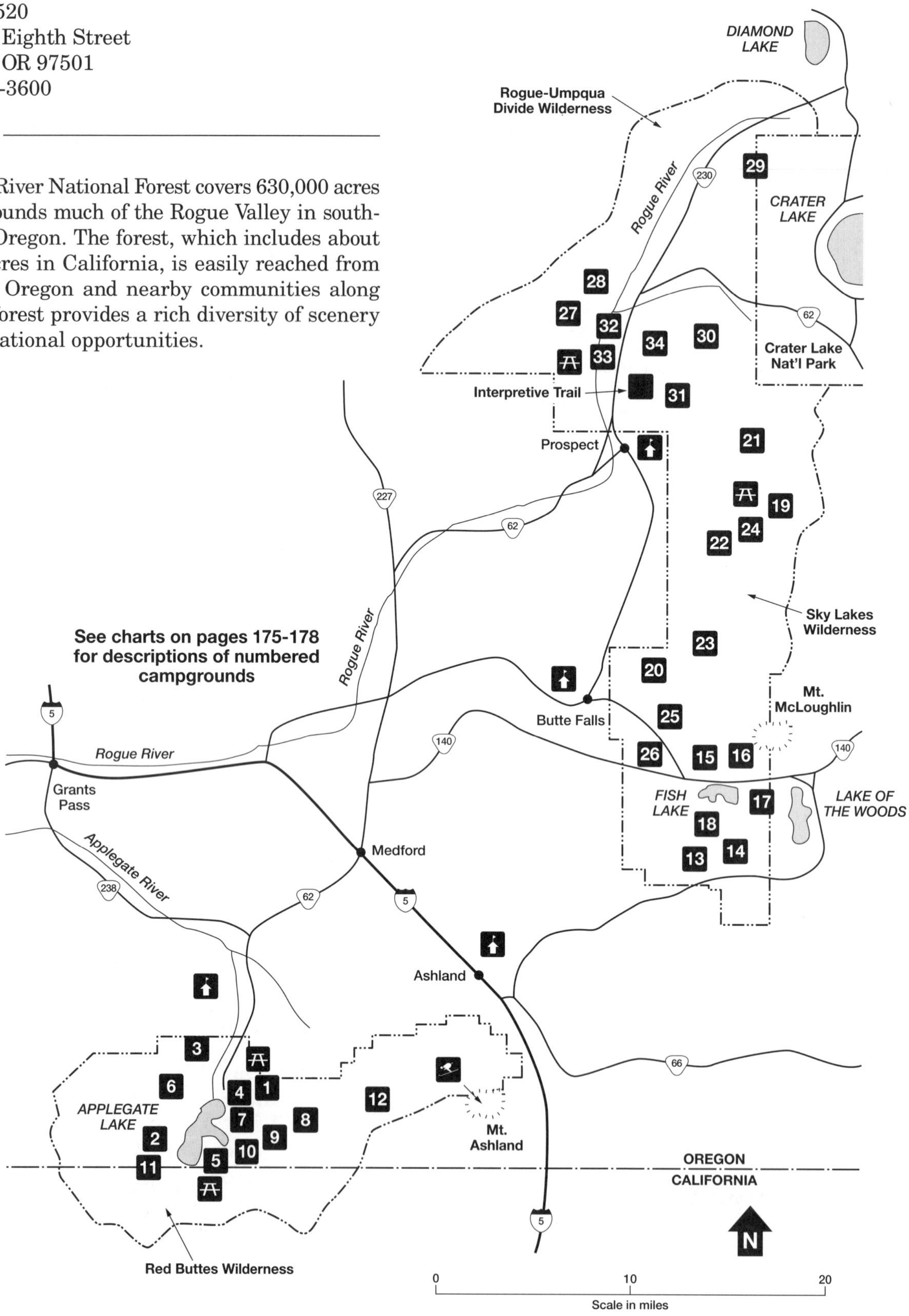

DIAMOND LAKE
Rogue-Umpqua Divide Wilderness
Rogue River
230
29
CRATER LAKE
28
27
32
62
34
30
33
Crater Lake Nat'l Park
Interpretive Trail
31
Prospect
21
227
19
24
62
22
Sky Lakes Wilderness
See charts on pages 175-178 for descriptions of numbered campgrounds
23
Rogue River
20
5
Mt. McLoughlin
25
Butte Falls
140
Rogue River
26
15
16
140
Grants Pass
FISH LAKE
17
LAKE OF THE WOODS
Applegate River
18
Medford
14
13
238
62
5
Ashland
3
66
6
4
1
12
APPLEGATE LAKE
7
8
Mt. Ashland
2
9
10
11
5
OREGON
CALIFORNIA
5
N
Red Buttes Wilderness
0
10
20
Scale in miles

Rogue River National Forest *(continued)*

The beauty of the backcountry can best be seen by trekking any of the 480 miles of trails.

Points of Interest

▲ The Rogue River National Forest is composed of two separate units of land. The western portion includes the headwaters of the Applegate River and lies within the ancient and complex geology of the Siskiyou Mountains. This is a country of narrow canyons and high, steep ridges. Elevations range from 1,600 feet on the Applegate River to 7,533 at the summit of Mount Ashland, the highest point in Oregon west of the Cascades. Environments include open oak woodlands, dense conifer forests, and barren, rocky ridgetops.

▲ The forest's eastern portion contains the upper reaches of the Rogue River located along the slopes of the younger, volcanic Cascade Range. Although the southern Cascades tend to have fairly gentle relief, several deep canyons such as the Middle Fork of the Rogue and the South Fork of Little Butte Creek are located in this part of the forest. The highest point is the top of Mt. McLoughlin (9,495 feet), one of the major volcanic cones in the Oregon Cascades. The area's extensive forest of Douglas-fir, ponderosa pine, and other conifers is enlivened by occasional meadows, lakes, and meandering streams. This part of the forest contains Huckleberry Mountain, the ancestral berry-gathering ground of the Klamath Indians. Historic sites include the route of the old military wagon road across the Cascades to Fort Klamath and the rustic buildings of the Union Creek Historic District.

▲ A wide variety of recreation opportunities is available in the forest including camping, fishing, swimming, hiking, horseback riding, and winter activities such as skiing. There are 35 developed campgrounds (not all may be open each year) and 8 picnic grounds (some combined with campgrounds). Camping is permitted in the three wilderness areas of the forest as well. Other features include 4 viewpoints/points of interest and 5 lookouts that are useable. With over 1,140 miles of stream, 520 miles have fish. There are 30 miles of anadromous stream.

▲ There are approximately 480 miles of trails for hiking and horseback riding. The Pacific Crest National Scenic Trail runs the entire length of the forest through the remote backcountry of the Sky Lakes Wilderness, along the spine of the High Cascades, and extends westward along the crest of the Siskiyou Mountains.

▲ Other remote sections of the forest include the Rogue-Umpqua Divide Wilderness and, to the south in the rugged headwaters of the Applegate River, the Red Buttes Wilderness. Downhill skiing (at Mt. Ashland Ski Area), cross-country skiing, and snowmobiling are popular winter sports in this area.

▲ Northeast of Medford, the scenic route along S.R. 62 and 230 provides access to the spectacular beauty of the Wild and Scenic Upper Rogue River, Crater Lake National Park, and popular recreation developments at Diamond Lake (Umpqua National Forest). Less than a one-hour drive southwest of Medford is Applegate Lake. This 988-acre reservoir offers swimming, hiking, camping, picnicking, fishing, and boating in the dramatic setting of the Siskiyous. The "Siskiyou Loop Discovery Tour" offers a scenic, self-guided driving tour of these mountains.

▲ Other special features of the forest include Rogue River Gorge, Natural Bridge, Upper Rogue National Recreation Trail, Abbott Creek Research Natural Area (2,607 acres), and Ashland Research Natural Area (1,640 acres).

Wilderness Areas

Red Buttes Wilderness, shared with Siskiyou and Klamath National Forests, covers approximately 16,810 acres within the Rogue River National Forest portion. Elevations range from

3,000 to 6,894 feet. The wilderness is situated along the mountainous border between northwestern California and southwestern Oregon. Located near the crest of the rugged Siskiyou Mountains, the wilderness contains the headwaters of the Applegate River, a tributary of the Rogue River, as well as a small portion of the Illinois River drainage. A chain of peaks—Red Buttes, Kangaroo Mountain, Rattlesnake Mountain and others—forms the southern boundary of the area. These peaks comprise the crest of the Siskiyous, and are the watershed divide between the Rogue River to the north and the Klamath River on the south. For information contact: Applegate Ranger District—(503) 899-1812 or Illinois Valley Ranger District—(503) 592-2166.

Rogue-Umpqua Divide Wilderness, shared with Umpqua National Forest, contains 5,877 acres within the Rogue River National Forest portion. This 34,900-acre wilderness is situated in the rugged Western Cascades, along the watershed divide between the Rogue and Umpqua Rivers. By far the largest portion drains into the South Umpqua. The steep terrain supports an extensive forest, interspersed with moist meadows and scenic outcrops of volcanic rocks. For information contact: Prospect Ranger District—(503) 560-3623.

Sky Lakes Wilderness comprises 70,113 acres within the Rogue River National Forest portion. This 113,400-acre wilderness occupies the crest of the High Cascades, extending south from the boundary of Crater Lake National Park to Fourmile Lake. Although steep relief is found in such places as the glacially-carved Middle Fork (Rogue River) Canyon and the slope of Mt. McLoughlin, Sky Lakes Wilderness has generally gentle, densely-forested terrain. The name is derived from the many small lakes, most of them clustered in several glacial basins near the crest of the Cascade Range. For information contact: Butte Falls Ranger District—(503) 865-3581.

A birdseye view depicts some of the rugged terrain along the Rogue River between Agness and Gold Beach. The forest is composed of two separate units of land. The western portion, seen here, lies within the ancient Siskiyou Mountains. This is a country of narrow canyons and high, steep ridges.

Applegate Ranger District

For Information

Applegate Ranger District
Star Ranger Station
6941 Upper Applegate Road
Jacksonville, OR 97530
(503) 899-1812

Campground Locations/Activities

All campgrounds in Applegate Ranger District are accessible off Highway 238.

1. **Beaver-Sulphur:** 5 mi. SE of Star Ranger Station. *Activities:* Camping by stream.
2. **Carberry:** 14 mi. S of Star Ranger Station. *Activities:* Hike-in camping, fishing, and hiking.
3. **Flumet Flat:** 3 mi. S of Star Ranger Station. *Activities:* Historic interpretive trail, group sites and reservations available.
4. **French Gulch:** 10 mi. S of Star Ranger Station. *Activities:* Walk-in camping, hiking, and fishing.
5. **Harr Point:** 12 mi. S of Star Ranger Station. *Activities:* Hike-in/boat-in camping, fishing, hiking, and boating.

The western portion of the Rogue National Forest includes the headwaters of the Applegate River. Applegate Lake, just a one-hour drive southwest of Medford, offers swimming, hiking, fishing, boating, and camping.

Campground (see map on page 172)	Elevation (feet)	Tent Sites	Tent/Trailer Sites	Fees	Water P=Piped; W-Well	Toilets V=Vault; F-Flush
1. Beaver-Sulphur	2,100	10		•	W	V
2. Carberry*	2,000	10 (H)		•	P	V
3. Flumet Flat**	1,700	4	23	•	W	F
4. French Gulch	2,000	9 (W)		•	W	V
5. Harr Point	2,000	5 (H/B)				
6. Hart-Tish Park*	2,000	4		•	P	V
7. Latgawa Cove	2,000	5 (H/B)				
8. Squaw Lakes	3,000	16		•	W	V
9. Stringtown	2,000	7 (W)		•	W	V
10. Tipsu Tyee	2,000	5 (H/B)				
11. Watkins	2,000	14 (W)		•	W	V
12. Wrangle	6,400	5			W	

*Accessible facilities for disabled.
**Group reservations available.
(W) Walk-in camping only.
(H) Hike-in camping only.
(H/B) Hike-in/boat-in camping only.
  Hart-Tish Park: self-contained trailers only.
  Picnic sites for day use available at Hart-Tish Park, Squaw Lakes, and Wrangle.

6. **Hart-Tish Park:** 9 mi. S of Star Ranger Station. *Activities:* Group Sites available. Swimming, boating, picnicking, and hiking.
7. **Latgawa Cove:** 10 mi. S of Star Ranger Station. *Activities:* Hike-in/boat-in camping, fishing, hiking, and boating.
8. **Squaw Lakes:** 17 mi. SE of Star Ranger Station. *Activities:* Group sites available. Swimming, fishing, hiking, picnicking, and walking.
9. **Stringtown:** 12 mi. S of Star Ranger Station. *Activities:* Walk-in camping. Hiking and fishing.
10. **Tipsu Tyee:** 13 mi. S of Star Ranger Station. *Activities:* Hike-in/boat-in camping, fishing, hiking, and boating.
11. **Watkins:** 12 mi. S of Star Ranger Station. *Activities:* Walk-in-camping, fishing, and hiking.
12. **Wrangle:** 20 mi. SE of Star Ranger Station. *Activities:* Hiking and picnicking (community kitchen available).

Ashland Ranger District

For Information

Ashland Ranger District
645 Washington St.
Ashland, OR 97520
(503) 482-3333

Campground (see map on page 172)	Elevation (feet)	Tent Sites	Tent/Trailer Sites	Fees	Water P=Piped; W=Well	Toilets V=Vault; F=Flush
13. Beaver Dam	4,500	3				V
14. Daley Creek	4,500	3				V
15. Doe Point	4,600		25	•	P	F
16. Fish Lake*	4,600		17	•	P	F
17. Fish Lake Resort	4,600		40	•	P	F
18. North Fork	4,500	5	2		W	V

*Accessible facilities for disabled.
Picnic sites for day-use available at Doe Point and Fish Lake.

Campground Locations/Activities

All campgrounds are on S.R. 140 or accessible off S.R. 140.

13. **Beaver Dam:** 22 mi. NE of Ashland off S.R. 140. *Activities:* Fishing, hiking, and biking.
14. **Daley Creek:** 22 mi. NE of Ashland off S.R. 140. *Activities:* Fishing, hiking, and biking.
15. **Doe Point:** 32 mi. NE of Ashland on S.R. 140. *Activities:* Fishing, boating, hiking, picnicking, and swimming.
16. **Fish Lake:** 32 mi. NE of Ashland on S.R. 140. *Activities:* Fishing, boating, hiking, picnicking (shelter), and swimming.
17. **Fish Lake Resort:** 32 mi. NE of Ashland on S.R. 140. *Activities:* Restaurant, cabins, boat rentals, camping, and hiking.
18. **North Fork:** 30 mi. NE of Ashland off S.R. 140. *Activities:* Fishing, hiking, and biking.

The area between Ashland and Medford is steeped in history. Originally home to the Rogue Indians, the forest and river provided them many resources as it does today for recreationists.

Butte Falls Ranger District

For Information

Butte Falls Ranger District
Butte Falls, OR 97522
(503) 865-3581

Campground Locations/Activities

All campgrounds in Butte Falls Ranger District are located off State Highway 62.

19. **Big Ben:** 22 mi. NE of Butte Falls. *Activities:* Fishing and hiking.
20. **Fourbit Ford:** 9 mi. E of Butte Falls. *Activities:* Fishing.
21. **Imnaha:** 24 mi. NE of Butte Falls. *Activities:* Camping by stream.
22. **Parker Meadow:** 17 mi. NE of Butte. *Activities:* Hiking, picnicking, and berry picking.
23. **Snowshoe:** 12 mi. NE of Butte Falls. *Activities:* Camping.
24. **South Fork:** 20 mi. NE of Butte Falls. *Activities:* Fishing and hiking.

25. **Whiskey Springs:** 8 mi. E of Butte Falls. *Activities:* Nature trail and picnicking.
26. **Willow Prairie:** 17 mi. SE of Butte Falls. *Activities:* Horseback riding and horse facilities.

Campground (see map on page 172)	Elevation (feet)	Tent Sites	Tent/Trailer Sites	Fees	Water P=Piped; W=Well	Toilets V=Vault; F=Flush
19. Big Ben	4,000	2				
20. Fourbit Ford	3,200	7		•	W	V
21. Imnaha	3,800	4				
22. Parker Meadow	5,000	3	5	•	W	V
23. Snowshoe	4,000	5				
24. South Fork	4,000	2	4	•	W	V
25. Whiskey Springs	3,200	17	19	•	P	F
26. Willow Prairie	4,400		9	•	W	V

Picnic sites for day use available at Parker Meadows and Whiskey Springs.

Just north of Butte Falls or 34 miles northeast of Medford, Joseph Stewart State Park can be accessed from State Highway 62. Located on the south shore of the Lost Creek Reservoir which was formed by the Upper Rogue River, this beautiful park provides excellent fishing year-round.

Prospect Ranger District

For Information

Prospect Ranger District
Prospect, OR 97536
(503) 560-3623

Campground Locations/Activities

27. **Abbott Creek:** Access off S.R. 62, 10 mi. N of Prospect. *Activities:* Fishing and picnicking.
28. **Farewell Bend:** On S.R. 62, 11 mi. N of Prospect. *Activities:* Fishing, hiking, near Union Creek Resort.
29. **Hamaker:** On S.R. 230, 23 mi. N of Prospect. *Activities:* Fishing and hiking.
30. **Huckleberry Mountain:** Off S.R. 62, 19 mi. NE of Prospect. *Activities:* Hiking and berry picking.
31. **Mill Creek:** Off S.R. 62, 3.5 mi. NE of Prospect. *Activities:* Fishing.
32. **Natural Bridge:** On S.R. 62, 9 mi. N of Prospect. *Activities:* Hiking, geologic point of interest.
33. **River Bridge:** Off S.R. 62, 5.5 mi. N of Prospect. *Activities:* Fishing.
34. **Union Creek:** On S.R. 62, 10 mi. N of Prospect. *Activities:* Fishing, hiking, and picnicking (community kitchen); near Union Creek Resort.

Campground (see map on page 172)	Elevation (feet)	Tent Sites	Tent/Trailer Sites	Fees	Water P=Piped; W=Well	Toilets V=Vault; F=Flush
27. Abbott Creek	3,100		23	•	W	V
28. Farewell Bend	3,400		61	•	P	F
29. Hamaker	4,000		10	•	W	V
30. Huckleberry Mountain	5,400		25		W	V
31. Mill Creek	2,800	8				
32. Natural Bridge*	3,200		16			V
33. River Bridge	2,900	6				V
34. Union Creek	3,200		78	•	P	V

*Accessible facilities for disabled.
Picnic sites for day use only are available at Abbott Creek and Union Creek.

The Rogue River National Forest and campgrounds of the Prospect Ranger District lie adjacent to Crater Lake National Park. The rim of the collapsed caldera stays shrouded with snow through all seasons for a picturesque backdrop to the sapphire blue waters of the lake.

Siskiyou National Forest

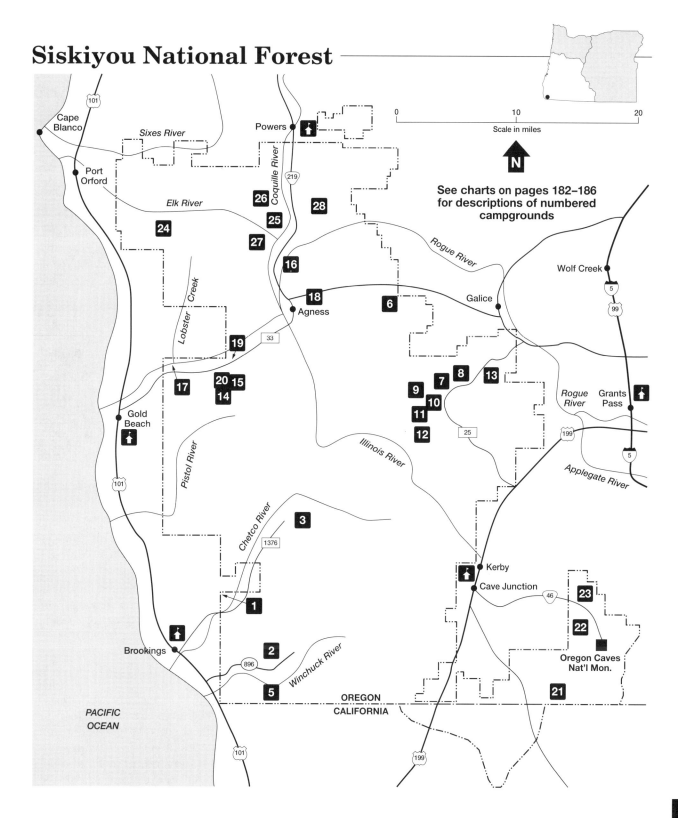

See charts on pages 182–186 for descriptions of numbered campgrounds

REGION 3

For Information

Siskiyou National Forest
200 NE Greenfield Road
P.O. Box 440
Grants Pass, OR 97526
(503) 471-6516

Location

The one-million-acre Siskiyou National Forest is located in the southwest corner of Oregon, with 33,400 acres extending into California. Accessible from both Interstate 5 on the east or U.S. 101 on the west, the lower third of the forest is bisected by

The Siskiyou National Forest covers over a million acres and reaches into the northwest corner of California. With five wilderness areas to choose from, campers will find solitude for hiking and fishing.

U.S. 199 (Redwood Highway), which provides access to the Oregon Caves National Monument and the Redwoods National Park in California.

Points of Interest

▲ Bisected by rivers offering great fishing and spectacular whitewater adventures, the forest provides a great diversity of vegetation and geological formations. The Siskiyou is a botanist's delight. There are more than 1,400 species of herbaceous plants, trees, and shrubs. Many of these are only rarely found elsewhere (Kalmiopsis, Port-Orford-cedar, carnivorous cobra plant, and Brewer weeping spruce).

▲ Campgrounds offer visitors a chance to relax in rustic settings with limited facilities. With a 14-day limit of stay, campsites are offered on a first-come, first-served basis. Most campgrounds have limited services after Labor Day (no water, no garbage pick-up, and no overnight fees). Grayback campground in the Illinois Valley Ranger District offers some campsites for RVs up to 30′ long and reservations through the National Recreation Reservation System. Most campgrounds remain closed during winter and reopen by Memorial Day weekend.

▲ The Elk, Illinois, Rogue, and other rivers contribute to the forest's rich anadromous fisheries resource. Salmon and steelhead attract people from around the world who fish the seasonal migrations.

▲ White-water enthusiasts know the forest for its superb river-running opportunities. Two National Wild and Scenic Rivers—the Rogue and the Illinois—are especially well known. Thousands enjoy the Rogue River each year. The Illinois River is a short-season river, recommended only for the most expert white-water enthusiast. Permits are required for the wild section of each river. Self-issuing permits are required to float the Illinois River during the float season, usually March through May. Permits are required to float the wild section of the Rogue River from approximately June 1 through September 15. Private, professionally guided trips are available.

▲ Winters are usually mild with some snow in the higher elevations. Spring and fall seasons are mild with summers being hot and dry.

Siskiyou National Forest (continued)

Wilderness Areas

The forest contains five wilderness areas. Permits to hike the wilderness areas are not required. Snakebite kits and poison oak first-aid treatment should be carried. During the winter the area usually receives both rain and snow storms. Some trails may contain tree debris.

Grassy Knob encompasses 17,200 acres of steep, rugged terrain. Elevation ranges between 2,000 and 3,000 feet. Thick brush limits access. A short five-mile trail is the only maintained access. The wilderness contains mixed stands of old growth forest that includes the Port-Orford Cedar and some Douglas-fir. The rainforest-covered canyons and ridges offers solitude for hiking, camping, and fishing. For more information contact: Powers Ranger District—(503) 439-3011.

Kalmiopsis is the largest wilderness in the forest with 179,655 acres. It is named for the rare Kalmiopsis leachiana plant that grows here. The wilderness is best characterized as having steep river and creek canyons. Elevation changes, ranging between 2,000 and 4,600 feet, require that all hikers be in good physical condition. There are limited water sources. Some 30 trails are maintained. Most of the western portion is located on the Chetcho Ranger District. The eastern portion is located on the Illinois Valley Ranger District. The northern portion is divided between the Galice and Gold Beach Ranger Districts. Hunting is allowed in this wilderness. For more information contact: Chetco Ranger District—(503) 469-2196 or Illinois Valley Ranger District—(503) 592-2166.

Red Buttes covers approximately 3,414 acres of rocky buttes, forested ridges and meadows in the southeastern part of the forest. This wilderness is shared with the Rogue River and Klamath national forests. Higher elevation hiking trails offer access to remote canyons with steep ridges. On clear days, hikers can see Mt. Shasta to the south in California. There are six maintained trails within this wilderness area. Elevation ranges between 4,000 and 5,600 feet. For more information contact: Illinois Valley Ranger District—(503) 592-2166.

Siskiyou Wilderness is 5,300 acres in size with elevations that range between 4,000 and 7,000 feet. Located in the southwestern Oregon-northern California border area, the wilderness is an older mountain range that contains unique geologic features. Several trails were established by miners and Native Americans in the 19th century as transportation routes. There are 4 to 6 maintained trails on the Siskiyou National Forest portion of this wilderness area. The remaining larger portions of the wilderness are located on the Six Rivers and Klamath national forests in northern California. For more information contact: Illinois Valley Ranger District—(503) 592-2166.

Wild Rogue Wilderness contains 25,658 acres located within the Wild and Scenic Rogue River portion of the Siskiyou National Forest. The Rogue River Trail, located on the north side of the river, is the only trail going through this area. Thick brush on the south side of the river restricts access. Elevation ranges between 800 and 2,800 feet. The area is best known for its river rafting. Lodging is available along the river. The Wild and Scenic River has towering cliffs, canyons, and heavily wooded forest. For more information contact: Gold Beach Ranger District—(503) 247-6651.

Even as far north as Oregon, there are animals to be aware of, including the rattlesnake! When hiking the wilderness areas of the Siskiyou, snakebite kits and poison oak first-aid treatment are recommended.

REGION 3

Chetco Ranger District

For Information

Chetco Ranger District
555 Fifth Street
Brookings, OR 97415
(503) 469-2196

Campground Locations/Activities

1. **Little Redwood** (RVs to 16′): On Wild and Scenic Chetco River. 14 mi. NE of Brookings via C.R. 784 to F.R. 1376 (paved road access). *Activities:* Picnicking, swimming, fishing, and nature trail for hiking.
2. **Ludlum House:** About 16 mi. SE of Brookings via C.R. 896 to F.R. 1107 to 1108. *Activities:* Picnicking, nature viewing, and hiking.
3. **Packers Cabin:** About 19 mi. NE of Brookings via C.R. 784 to F.R. 1376 to F.R. 1917. *Activities:* Picnicking, nature viewing, and hiking.
4. **Snow Camp:** Not depicted on map. Call for reservations and information. *Activities:* Picnicking, nature viewing, hiking, and scenery.

5. **Winchuck** (RVs to 16′): Adjacent to Winchuck River. 14 mi. SE of Brookings via C.R. 896 to F.R. 1107 (paved road access). *Activities:* Picnicking and scenery.

Campground (see map on page 179)	Elevation (feet)	Tent Sites Only	Tent/Trailer Sites	Fee	Drinking Water	Toilets; P=Pit F=Flush; V=Vault;
1. Little Redwood	100	12		•	•	V
2. Ludlum House*(R)		1			•	P
3. Packers Cabin*		1			•	P
4. Snow Camp(R)		1				P
5. Winchuck**	100	5	8	•	•	V

*Primarily for groups.
**Barrier-free restrooms.
(R) Reservations required.
   Picnic sites available at all campgrounds except Snow Camp Lookout.

Sightings of bald eagles are always a treat and a wonderful reminder of the rich natural heritage of this country.

Galice Ranger District

For Information

Galice Ranger District
1465 NE 7th Street
Grants Pass, OR 97526
(503) 476-3830

Campground Locations/Activities

6. **Bearcamp Pasture:** Located at Bear Camp Road Summit (F.R. 23). *Activities:* Picnicking and primitive camping.
7. **Big Pine:** 17.8 mi. NW of Grants Pass. Off I-5, head west on Merlin Galice Road about 12 mi. Turn left onto F.R. 25 and go 12 mi. to the campground. *Activities:* Picnicking, hiking, and rustic camping. Handicapped accessible nature trail and restrooms.
8. **Meyers Camp:** Primitive site. Contact the ranger district office for directions. *Activities:* Hiking and primitive camping.
9. **Sam Brown:** About .5 mi. south of Big Pine Campground via F.R. 25 to F.R. 2512. *Activities:* Group camping, picnicking, fishing, and hiking. Two group covered shelters and solar shower.
10. **Sam Brown Horse Camp:** Just off F.R. 2512 near Sam Brown Campgrounds. *Activities:* Horseback riding and horse corrals.
11. **Secret Creek:** 15.3 mi. SW of Grants Pass. Off I-5 to Merlin-Galice Access Road. Turn left

onto F.R. 25 and travel 16 mi. to campground. *Activities:* Primitive camping.
12. **Spalding Pond:** 21.5 mi. SE of Grants Pass. Off U.S. 199 (Redwood Highway) at Hayes Hill, turn onto F.R. 25. Go about 8 mi. to F.R. 2524. Turn left and go about 5-6 mi. *Activities:* Primitive camping, fishing, and swimming.
13. **Tin Can:** About 3 mi. on F.R. 25 from the Merlin-Galice Road turnoff. *Activities:* Primitive camping/no water.

Campground (see map on page 179)	Elevation (feet)	Tent Sites Only	Tent/Trailer Sites	Fee	Drinking Water	Toilets; P=Pit F=Flush; V=Vault
6. Bearcamp Pasture		1				V
7. Big Pine*	2,300	9	4	•	•	V
8. Meyers Camp		2				P
9. Sam Brown**	2,300	8		•	•	V
10. Sam Brown Horse Camp	2,300	7		•	•	V
11. Secret Creek		2	1		•	P
12. Spalding Pond		1				P
13. Tin Can		2				

*Handicapped accessible restrooms.
**Group shelters and solar shower available.
  Picnic sites available at all campgrounds except Meyers Camp.

Check at ranger stations for information on taking stock into the backcountry.

REGION 3

Siskiyou National Forest   183

Gold Beach Ranger District

For Information

Gold Beach Ranger District and Visitor Center
1225 S. Ellensburg
Box 7
Gold Beach, OR 97444
(503) 247-6651

Campground Locations/Activities

14. **Elko** (snow from Dec.–May): 10.1 mi. SE of Gold Beach off F.R. 1503. *Activities:* Dispersed sites for camping, picnicking, hiking, and nature viewing.
15. **Game Lake** (snow from Dec.–May): Contact Ranger Station for location; sites dispersed accessing nearby trails to Kalmiopsis Wilderness. *Activities:* Picnicking, hiking, and nature viewing.
16. **Illahe** (open April 30–Nov. for fee sites): Located 26 mi NE of Gold Beach via F.R. 33. Turn onto C.R. 375 and drive about 2 mi. *Activities:* Picnicking, hiking, and nature viewing. Boating and fishing available at the Rogue River.
17. **Lobster** (Open all year): Located 9 mi. E of Gold Beach via F.R. 33. *Activities:* Picnicking, hiking, and scenery and nature viewing. Boat ramp, boating, fishing, and swimming available at the Rogue River; Shrader Old Growth Trail nearby.
18. **Oak Flat** (Open all year): NE of Agness 2 mi, off F.R. 23. *Activities:* Picnicking, hiking, and scenery and nature viewing.
19. **Quosatana** (Open April 30–Nov.): 11. 3 mi. NE of Gold Beach on F.R. 33. *Activities:* Boating and fishing available at the Rogue River. Hiking and nature and scenery viewing.
20. **Wildhorse** (snow from Dec.–May): 13.7 mi. NE of Gold Beach off F.R. 3318. *Activities:* Dispersed site accesses Illinois River Trailhead. Horse corral available. Horseback riding, hiking, and scenery and nature viewing.

Campground (see map on page 179)	Elevation (feet)	Tent Sites Only	Tent/Trailer Sites	Fee	Drinking Water	Toilets; P=Pit F=Flush; V=Vault
14. Elko		3				P
15. Game Lake		3				P
16. Illahe	300		20	•	•	V
17. Lobster	100	5		•	•	F
18. Oak Flat		3				P
19. Quosatana*	100		42	•	•	F
20. Wildhorse		3				P

Picnic sites available at all campgrounds except Quosatana.
*Trailer dump station available, but no water during winter months.

What more could you ask for?

Illinois Valley Ranger District

For Information

Illinois Valley Ranger District
26568 Redwood Highway
Cave Junction, OR 97523
(503) 592-2166

Campground Locations/Activities

21. **Bolan Lake:** Located 28.5 mi. SE of Cave Junction. Take U.S. 199 S to O'Brien. Turn E onto C.R. 5560 and 5828. After 6 mi., the road becomes F.R. 48. Go about 7 mi and turn onto F.R. 4812. Go about 4.5 mi. to the lake. *Activities:* Lake stocked with trout. Only non-motorized boats allowed on lake. A hiking trail goes from the lake up to a fire lookout.
22. **Cave Creek:** Located 14 mi. E of Cave Junction along S.R. 46 (Caves Highway). *Activities:* Berry picking, fishing, and closed access to Oregon Caves.
23. **Grayback:** Located 12 mi. E of Cave Junction along S.R. 46 (Caves Highway). *Activities:* Nearby Oregon Caves National Monument offers tours of a unique underground series of caverns. Bring good walking shoes and a jacket since it can get quite chilly inside the caves. An admission fee is charged for this tour. Picnicking, hiking, and nature viewing. Barrier-free nature trail.

Campground (see map on page 179)	Elevation (feet)	Tent Sites Only	Tent/Trailer Sites	Fee	Drinking Water	Toilets; P=Pit F=Flush; V=Vault
21. Bolan Lake	5,400	12				V
22. Cave Creek	2,900	18		•	•	V
23. Grayback*	1,800		39	•	•	F

*On Reservation System 1-800-280-2267.
  Picnic sites available only at Grayback. Picnic shelter available.

Although rarely seen, one of the forest's magnificent residents includes the black bear.

White-water enthusiasts know the forest for its superb river-running opportunities. Two National Wild and Scenic Rivers, the Rogue and Illinois, are especially well known. The Illinois, a short-season river, is recommended only for the most expert white-water runners.

REGION 3

Powers Ranger District

For Information

Powers Ranger District
Powers, OR 97466
(503) 439-3011

Campground Locations/Activities

24. **Butler Bar:** Located 22 mi. E of Port Orford on the Wild and Scenic Elk River. Access via F.R. 5325. *Activities:* Primitive camping. Hiking, picnicking, swimming, and fishing.
25. **Daphne Grove** (up to 30' RVs): Located along the South Fork Coquille River. 15 mi. S of Powers on F.R. 33. *Activities:* Fishing, hunting, swimming, picnicking, and hiking trails.
26. **Myrtle Grove** (Not suitable for trailers): Located 8 mi. S of Powers on F.R. 33. *Activities:* Primitive camping along the South Fork Coquille River. Picnicking and nature viewing.
27. **Rock Creek:** Located 19 mi. S of Powers along F.R. 3347. *Activities:* Picnicking, hiking, fishing, and swimming. Access to Azalea Lake Trail #1262.
28. **Squaw Lake:** Located 21 miles SE of Powers on F.R. 3348-080. *Activities:* Site of annual Fishing Derby each June. Fishing and hiking.

Campground (see map on page 179)	Elevation (feet)	Tent Sites Only	Tent/Trailer Sites	Fee	Drinking Water	Toilets; P=Pit F=Flush; V=Vault
24. Butler Bar	600	4	5			P
25. Daphne Grove*	800	2	12	•	•	V
26. Myrtle Grove	600	5				P
27. Rock Creek	1,200	4	3	•	•	V
28. Squaw Lake	2,200	3	4		•	V

*Group campsite available (accommodates up to 25 people). Barrier-free restrooms and one accessible camping site. Picnic sites available at all campgrounds.

Remember to keep food stored so animals, small or large, are not tempted to join you for a meal!

The Siuslaw National Forest administers Oregon Dunes National Recreation Area. Known as the "Sahara by the Sea," it features a 47-mile stretch of inspiring sand dune formations.

Siuslaw National Forest (South Half)

For Information

Siuslaw National Forest
4077 S.W. Research Way
P.O. Box 1148
Corvallis, OR 97339-1148
(503) 750-7000

Location

For information on the North Half of Siuslaw National Forest and campgrounds in Hebo Ranger District, see Region 1 of this *Camper's Guide*.

The 630,395-acre Siuslaw National Forest is located in the Coast Mountain Range of Oregon and extends from Tillamook to Coos Bay. U.S. 101 pro-

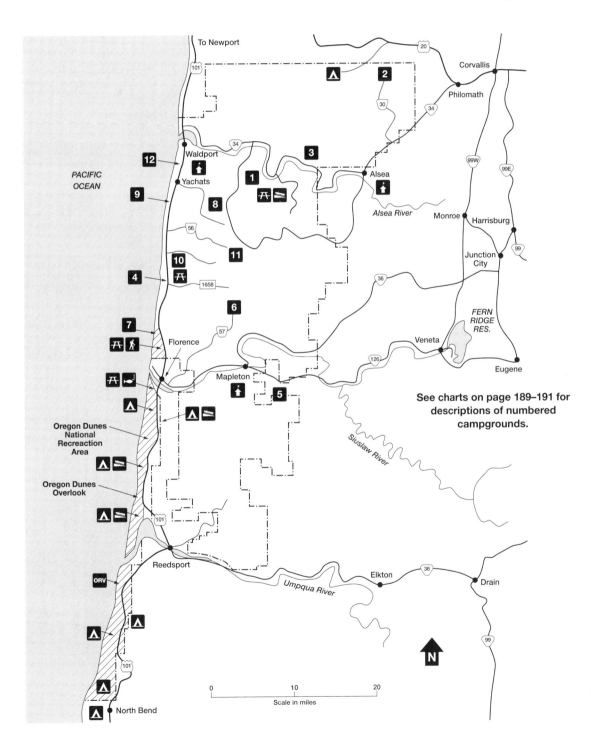

See charts on page 189–191 for descriptions of numbered campgrounds.

vides access to dense Douglas-fir forest that is complemented by lush, green vegetation and miles of sand dunes. The Pacific Ocean creates a moderate climate over the forest and constantly changes its mood. Expect summer fog. Temperatures remain mild year-round. Siuslaw National Forest is located in two separate portions, the North Half and South Half.

Points of Interest

▲ Visitors find a variety of things to do including camping, beachcombing, whale watching, fishing, crabbing, hiking, boating, hunting and sand dune touring. The forest offers a diversity in hiking opportunities ranging from walks on the beach to lengthy wilderness trails. All offices provide information on regulations and activities such as plant gathering, off-road-vehicle use, fire precautions, hunting, and fishing.

▲ The highest point in the forest and in the Coast Range is Marys Peak with an elevation of 4,097 feet. On a clear day the view is spectacular, stretching from the ocean to the Cascade Range. A 9.4-mile auto tour that takes about two hours is available.

▲ Cascade Head Scenic/Research Area, Cape Perpetua, and the Oregon Dunes National Recreation Area are just a few of the main scenic attractions on the coast. Farther inland, the many streams provide for a fisherman's delight. Berry picking is very popular with visitors as well as residents. The Cascade Head Scenic Area was the first Scenic/Research Area designated in the U.S. Comprising 9,670 acres of land in the Hebo Ranger District, it is a fitting designation for an area that is unique in geographic and botanic diversity, animal life, and the activities of man. The landscape at Cascade Head is made up of several environments: the estuary and its associated floodplain, the river system and ocean edge, and the higher elevations, which include the headland and forest. The area is open to the public and there are hiking trails. Camping is also permitted.

▲ Cape Perpetua Scenic Area is located along the Central Oregon Coast, 3 miles south of Yachats. Hiking, camping, beachcombing, wildlife viewing, tidepool exploring and Visitor Center exhibits await visitors. Cape Perpetua Visitor Center is located 3 miles south of Yachats off U.S. Highway 101. Open daily and free to the public, the center offers a movie and dioramas on the geologi-

cal history of the Oregon Coast. Nearby are the Devil's Churn and Cook's Chasm, two ocean spectaculars. Cape Perpetua Overlook, 2 miles off U.S. 101 at Cape Perpetua Campground, offers an excellent view of the coast.

▲ The Oregon Dunes Overlook, located 11 miles south of Florence, is one of the few sites in the Oregon Dunes where motorists can stop and see the dunes without making an extensive side trip. The overlook is constructed in the sand dunes between U.S. 101 and the beach. It features a series of observation platforms from which visitors can view the Oregon dunes and Pacific Ocean. In addition, it is designed barrier-free so that it is fully accessible to the handicapped. Open year-round, the overlook is an unstaffed interpretive site.

▲ The dense forest and ocean shoreline on the Siuslaw provide habitat for some 350 species of wildlife, including black-tailed deer, Roosevelt elk, bear, fox, mountain lion and squirrel. Both migratory and resident bird are found along the coast and in the mountains. Big game hunting is a popular sport in the forest.

▲ Of nearly 10,000 miles of forest streams, 2,000 miles support fish such as salmon, steelhead, and trout. Many visitors enjoy fishing the rivers—the Nestucca, Alsea, Siuslaw and Siletz— as well as the 30 freshwater lakes near the Oregon Dunes National Recreation Area.

▲ Gray whales migrate south from the Bering Sea to Baja California from December through March. They return north from March through May. Visitors can watch them from viewpoints on Umpqua Lighthouse, Heceta Head, Cape Perpetua, Yaquina Head, and Cascade Head.

From December through March, watch gray whales migrate along the coast from strategic places like Umpqua Lighthouse State Park.

Oregon Dunes National Recreation Area

Managed by the Siuslaw National Forest, Oregon Dunes National Recreation Area is a land of magnificent sand dunes, lakes, forested areas, and ocean beaches. It extends 40 miles along the Pacific Ocean, from the Siuslaw River south to the Coos River. At the widest point, the National Recreation Area extends inland approximately 2.5 miles. The sand dunes are one of nature's outstanding phenomena. The National Recreation Area office is located in Reedsport at the junction of U.S. 101 and S.R. 38. Detailed information about camping and recreation opportunities in the Oregon Dunes National Recreation Area is covered separately under its own name in **Region 3** of this *Guide*.

Wilderness Areas

Cummins Creek Wilderness covers approximately 9,173 acres and offers camping, fishing, and hiking. Accessible from U.S. 101, the Wilderness is 11 miles south of Waldport. The wilderness preserves the last remaining virgin stands of Sitka spruce, western hemlock, and Douglas fir in Oregon's coast lands. The Cummins Ridge Trail, 6.2 miles, leads east along Cummins Ridge through dense Sitka spruce and Douglas fir stands. For more information contact: Waldport Ranger District—(503) 563-3211.

Drift Creek Wilderness, about 5,800 acres in size, contains one of the largest stands of old-growth forest in the Coast Range Mountains. Hiking trails provide access to the unique terrain of this wilderness. Horses and pack animals are not allowed within the wilderness due to sensitive soils. For more information contact: Waldport Ranger District—(503) 563-3211.

Rock Creek Wilderness encompasses approximately 7,400 acres of steep and brushy terrain. Hiking trails provide access through the wilderness. For more information contact: Waldport Ranger District—(503) 563-3211.

Alsea Ranger District

For Information

Alsea Ranger District
18591 Alsea Hwy.
Alsea, OR 97324
(503) 487-5811

Campground Locations/Activities

1. **Blackberry:** 18 mi. E of Waldport via S.R. 34. *Activities:* Boat ramp, electricity, fishing. On Alsea River.
2. **Marys Peak:** 20 mi. SW of Philomath via S.R. 34 and Marys Peak Rd. *Activities:* Marys Peak scenic viewpoint and hiking.
3. **Riveredge Group Camp** (capacity for 200 people): 11 mi. W of Alsea via S.R. 34. *Activities:* Picnic shelter, fishing, boating access, field sports, and trails paved for hiking; reservations required for group camp.

Campground (see map on page 187)	Elevation (feet)	Tent/Trailer Sites	Fee	Water	Toilets F=Flush; V=Vault
1. Blackberry	100	32	•	•	F
2. Marys Peak	3,600	6	•	•	V
3. Riveredge Group Camp*	100	1	•	•	F

*Campsites on reservation system: 1-800-280-CAMP.
All campgrounds have picnic sites and are accessible to handicapped.

Just offshore of the Dunes, anglers come from around the world in pursuit of chinook and coho salmon.

Mapleton Ranger District

For Information

Mapleton Ranger District
10692 Highway 126
Mapleton, OR 97453
(503) 268-4473

Campground Locations/Activities

4. **Alder Dune:** 7 mi. N on U.S. 101 from Florence. Access to Alder Lake, Alder Dune Lake and dunes. Access to beach by way of Sutton Trail. *Activities:* Hiking and fishing.
5. **Archie Knowles:** 4 mi. E of Mapleton via S.R. 126. *Activities:* Recreational use of open field area for picnics or game activities.
6. **North Fork:** From Florence go E one mi. on S.R. 126 to North Fork Siuslaw Road, then 12 mi. N to site. *Activities:* Fishing, picnicking, and large field area for activities. Boat launch for drift boats available.
7. **Sutton:** 5 mi. N of Florence on U.S. 101. *Activities:* Hiking, fishing, canoeing, biking, picnicking, amphitheater, group picnic area, and boat ramp. Group camping and picnicking requires reservations and fees are collected.

Campground (see map on page 187)	Elevation (feet)	Tent Sites	Tent/Trailer Sites	Fee	Water	Toilets F=Flush; V=Vault
4. Alder Dune*	100		39	•	•	F
5. Archie Knowles*	200		9	•	•	F
6. North Fork	400	5				V
7. Sutton*	100		79	•	•	F

*Picnic sites available.
North Fork has group sites. Sutton has bike camping. Group camping and picnicking are also available by reservations with fee.

Frolic in the sand . . .

. . . or enjoy a swim in one of the many fresh-water lakes along the coast. This is Lake Marie at Umpqua Lighthouse State Park.

Waldport Ranger District

For Information

Waldport Ranger District
P.O. Box 400
Waldport, OR 97394
(503) 563-3211

Boasting sand dunes that rise more than 500 feet, the Oregon Dunes National Recreation Area is a mecca for ORV recreationists.

Campground Locations/Activities

8. **Canal Creek** (narrow winding access road): 7 mi. SE of Waldport on Hwy. 34, then 4 mi. S on F.R. 3462. *Activities:* Camping, fishing, hunting, picnic shelter, playfield, and beach access.
9. **Cape Perpetua:** 2.7 mi. S of Yachats, E of U.S. 101. *Activities:* Visitor center, Scenic Area, auto tour, Pacific Ocean, fishing, and hiking trails.
10. **Rock Creek:** 10 mi. S of Yachats, E of U.S. 101. *Activities:* Fishing, nearby sandy beach and Rock Creek Wilderness.
11. **Ten Mile:** 12.5 mi S of Yachats on U.S. 101, then 5.6 mi E on F.R. 56. *Activities:* Primitive. Open all year.
12. **Tillicum Beach:** 4.7 mi. S of Waldport on U.S. 101. *Activities:* Ocean view, beach access, hiking and fishing.

Campground (see map on page 187)	Elevation (feet)	Tent/Trailer Sites	Fee	Water	Toilets F=Flush; V=Vault
8. Canal Creek*	200	9	•	•	V
9. Cape Perpetua**	100	37	•	•	F
10. Rock Creek	100	17	•	•	F
11. Ten Mile	400	6			V
12. Tillicum Beach	100	60	•	•	F

*Picnic sites available.
**Accessible to handicapped. Group camping available.

Winchester Bay has a fleet of boats for anglers to go out and "catch a memory for a lifetime!"

REGION 3

South Beach State Park

For Information

South Beach State Park
5580 South Coast Highway
South Beach, OR 97366
(503) 867-7451
FAX—867-3254

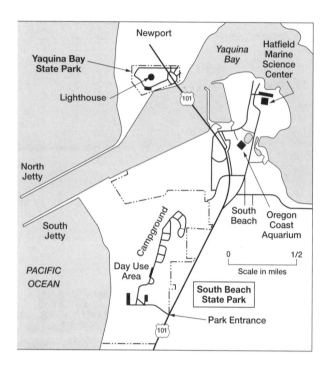

Location

South Beach State Park is located on U.S. 101, 2 miles south of Newport. This 434-acre park provides access to several miles of broad, sandy beach, and jetty fishing just south of Yaquina Bay bridge. The park includes a portion of the bay's south jetty. High sand dune ridges provide views of the busy bay and shelter for the campground. Nearby attractions include Alsea Bay Bridge Interpretive Center in Waldport (11 miles south), the Hatfield Marine Science Center (1 mile north), and the Oregon Coast Aquarium (1 mile north). Yaquina Bay, located just north of the park offers fishing, clamming, and crabbing. Fish caught off the South Yaquina Jetty include ling cod, sea bass, perch, and salmon. Yaquina Bay also has a quantity of Dungeness and rock crab that can be caught off the nearby piers or by boat in the bay. Charter boats, launching, moorage facilities and boat or other equipment rentals are available. Rockhunters find agates, jasper, petrified wood, and other stones near the North Yaquina Jetty. The historic Yaquina Bay Lighthouse, 2 miles north within Yaquina Bay State Park, is open on weekends in the winter and all week during the summer. It is an excellent site for

Broad sandy beaches along South Beach attract more than windersurfers. Rockhunters find agates, jasper, petrified wood, and other stones near the North Yaquina Jetty.

South Beach State Park *(continued)*

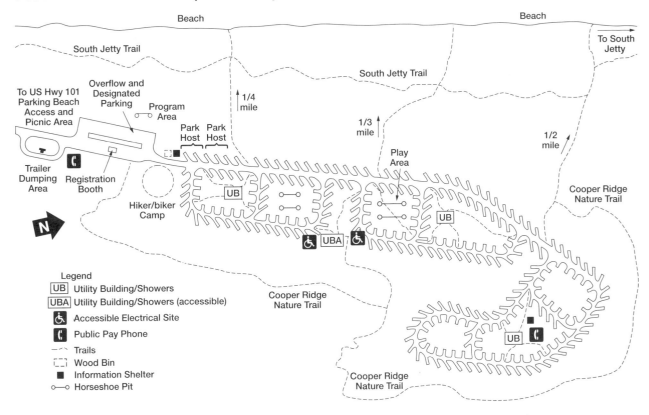

Legend
UB Utility Building/Showers
UBA Utility Building/Showers (accessible)
Accessible Electrical Site
Public Pay Phone
Trails
Wood Bin
Information Shelter
Horseshoe Pit

coastal viewing. Vehicular travel on the ocean beach is prohibited from Neskowin south to the Sea Lion Caves.

Facilities and Activities

The campground is open year-round. Reservations are accepted from Memorial Day weekend through Labor Day.

254 RV/tent campsites w/electricity & water (50'
   maximum length)
hiker/biker camp area
   showers/drinking water
   flush toilets
   tables
   trailer dump station
5 picnic sites
beachcombing/fishing/swimming
accessible campsite/restrooms/showers for people
   with disabilities

Superb beach and wind conditions appeal to windsurfers from around the country.

Sunset Bay State Park

For Information

Sunset Bay State Park
10965 Cape Arago Highway
Coos Bay, OR 97420
(503) 888-3778
FAX—888-5650

Location

Located 12 miles southwest of Coos Bay, Sunset Bay State Park offers a variety of recreational opportunities in a shallow cove sheltered by high sandstone cliffs. Fishing, swimming, skin diving, surfing, and boating make this beautiful park a popular destination. The campground is nestled in a wooded valley near a broad sandy beach. Two scenic, day-use state parks adjacent to Sunset make the park even more appealing. Shore Acres State Park, just south of Sunset Bay, provides a glass-enclosed observation shelter to view 180 degrees of Oregon's spectacular coast. Shore Acres natural scenery is complemented by a unique garden on the park grounds. Bordering the south boundary of Shore Acres is Cape Arago State Park. Because of the park's excellent ocean view, the Coast Guard and U.S. Army used this site as a radio station and lookout during World War II. Simpson Reef Viewpoint is an ideal place to observe seals, sea lions, and other marine life on the offshore rocks.

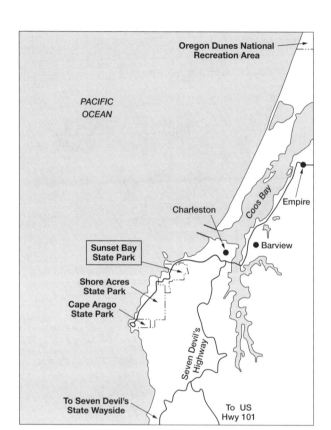

High sandstone cliffs shelter the cove waters of Sunset Bay. This is a favorite destination of divers, anglers, surfers, and photographers.

Sunset Bay State Park *(continued)*

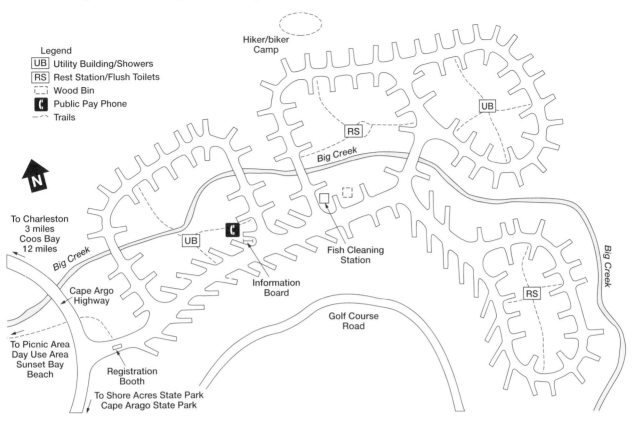

Legend
- **UB** Utility Building/Showers
- **RS** Rest Station/Flush Toilets
- Wood Bin
- **C** Public Pay Phone
- Trails

Hiker/biker Camp

UB

RS

Big Creek

Fish Cleaning Station

Information Board

Big Creek

RS

Big Creek

To Charleston 3 miles Coos Bay 12 miles

Cape Argo Highway

Golf Course Road

To Picnic Area Day Use Area Sunset Bay Beach

Registration Booth

To Shore Acres State Park Cape Arago State Park

Facilities and Activities

The campground is open from mid-April through late October. Reservations are accepted from Memorial Day weekend through Labor Day. Reservations are essential during July and August and for all weekends and holidays.

29 RV campsites w/full hookups (50′ maximum length)
34 RV campsites w/electricity & water
74 tent campsites
10 group tent areas at Norton Gulch/1 at Cape Arago
hiker/biker camp
   showers/tubs
   drinking water
   flush toilets
   camp stoves
   tables
   trailer dump station
60 picnic sites
40 portable tables
2 group picnic areas/reservations only
1 covered kitchen shelter
1 fish cleaning station

swimming/beachcombing/hiking
boat launch area/boating/fishing
sightseeing/birdwatching/wildlife viewing
geology/tide pool observation/ocean wading
accessible campsites/restrooms for people with
   disabilities

Don't miss breathtaking views from two beautiful parks, Shore Acres and Cape Arago, just south of Sunset Bay.

Tumalo State Park

For Information

Tumalo State Park
62976 O.B. Riley Road
Bend, OR 97701
(503) 388-6055

Location

Located along the beautiful Deschutes River, Tumalo State Park can be accessed from U.S. 20, 5 miles northwest of Bend. This 320-acre park is situated in a juniper-forested canyon at an elevation of 3,225 feet high near the town of Tumalo. The basalt canyon cliffs extend down to the stream. Fishing for German brown and rainbow trout is especially good during the spring and late summer. The park is located in the center of a volcanic wonderland. South on U.S. 97 is Newberry National Volcanic Monument, which covers 56,000 acres. The monument connects Newberry Crater to Lava Cast Forest, the Northwest Rift Zone, Lava River Cave and Lava Butte. Other nearby attractions include Smith Rock State Park, Pilot Butte State Park, and La Pine State Recreation Area. There are many U.S. Forest Service campgrounds in the area.

Facilities and Activities

The campground is open mid-April through late October on a first-come, first-served basis except for group activities.

20 RV campsites w/full hookups (35′ maximum length)
68 tent campsites
2 group tent area
hiker/biker camp
    showers/drinking water
    flush toilets
    wood stoves
    tables
95 picnic sites
2 group picnic areas/by reservation
play areas/2 swim areas
hiking/fishing
interpretive center/slide programs

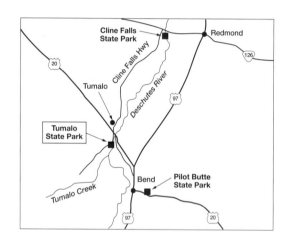

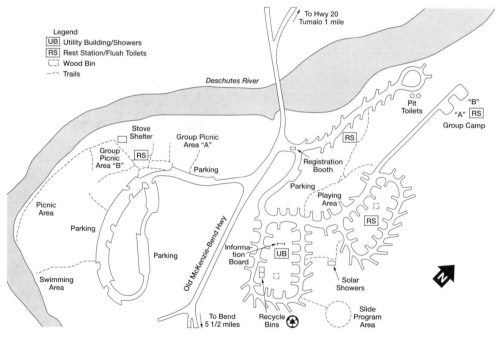

Umpqua Lighthouse State Park

For Information

Umpqua Lighthouse State Park
c/o Sunset Bay State Park
10965 Cape Arago Highway
Coos Bay, OR 97420
(503) 888-3778
FAX—888-5650

Location

Umpqua Lighthouse State Park, 450 acres in size, is nestled in the central Oregon coast dunes area next to the lighthouse that signals the entrance to Umpqua River. Located off U.S. 101, 6 miles south of Reedsport, the park features scenic forest-rimmed freshwater lakes in an area of extensive sand dunes that rise to 500 feet, ocean beaches, and the Umpqua River. Swimming, fishing, and sightseeing are some of the park's popular activities. During spring and early summer, the beauty of the park is highlighted by rhododendrons growing along the lake shore. The jetty at the mouth of Winchester Bay is a popular fishing spot with visitors at Umpqua Lighthouse State Park. A road past the lighthouse takes you to the jetty and on to the ocean beaches. Vehicular travel on the ocean beach in this area is restricted during certain periods of the year. The sand dunes in the area are reputed to be among the highest in the U.S. Nearby state parks of interest include William Tugman, Jessie Honeyman, Umpqua Wayside, Millicoma Myrtle Grove, Golden and Silver Falls, Sunset Bay, Shore Acres, and Cape Arago. Oregon Dunes National Recreation Area encompasses the coastal area just north of the park and Reedsport to 11 miles south of Florence. The area offers a great variety of recreational pursuits and exceptional fishing.

Facilities and Activities

The campground is open mid-April through late October on a first-come, first-served basis.

22 RV campsites w/full hookups (45′ maximum
    length)
    showers/drinking water
    flush toilets
    wood stoves
    tables
41 tent campsites
32 picnic sites
swim area/beachcombing/fishing
hiking/trails/geology
sightseeing/wildlife viewing

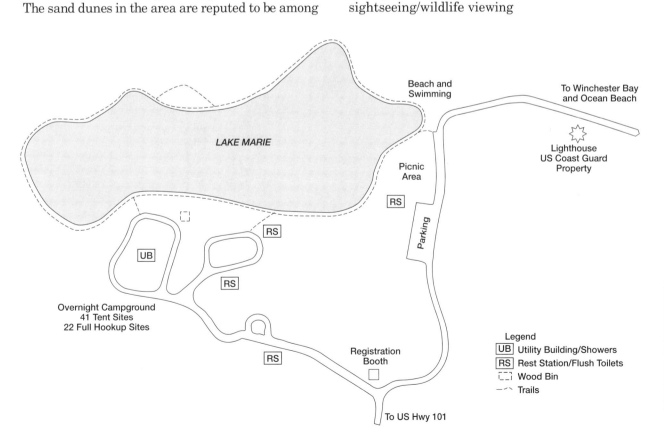

Umpqua National Forest

For Information

Umpqua National Forest
2900 N.W. Stewart Parkway
P.O. Box 1008
Roseburg, OR 97470
(503) 672-6601

Location

Comprising some 984,880 acres in southwestern Oregon, the Umpqua's green, timbered slopes extend from the summit of the Cascade Mountain range westward to the lowland ranches. State Route 138, part of a National Scenic Byway System, provides year-round access to the heart of the forest.

Points of Interest

▲ The Umpqua National Forest is named for the Umpqua Indians who once fished its rivers and roamed its wooded hills. Recreation opportunities vary from major attractions like nearby Crater Lake National Park, the North Umpqua Wild and Scenic River, and Diamond Lake, to secluded waterfalls and quiet retreats like Skookum Lake or Yasko Falls. Around every bend in the road, a new sight, and a new experience awaits you.

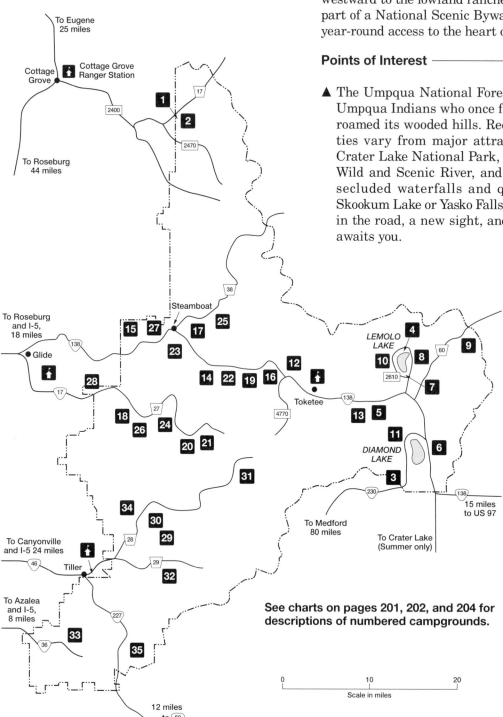

See charts on pages 201, 202, and 204 for descriptions of numbered campgrounds.

Umpqua National Forest *(continued)*

▲ Two beautiful rivers, the North and South Umpqua, have their headwaters within the forest and flow westward. They later join as the Umpqua River below Roseburg on their way to the Pacific Ocean. Both rivers are renowned for fishing, particularly the North Umpqua, which features both summer and winter runs of steelhead trout.

▲ The North Umpqua Trail follows the North Umpqua River for about 77 miles on lands administered by the Umpqua National Forest, Bureau of Land Management, and Douglas County. The trail provides a variety of outstanding recreation opportunities.

▲ Miles of forest roads are available for touring, and if you enjoy hiking, horseback riding, motorcycling, or mountain biking, many trails meander through the forest and provide an opportunity for peace and solitude.

▲ Snow activities can usually be planned from December to March at the higher elevations. Whether your interest is snowmobiling, cross-country skiing, or sliding down a slope on an inner-tube, you will find plenty of room for snow play in the forest.

Miles of trails for hiking, biking, or horseback riding lead to many peaceful settings.

▲ Diamond Lake, a 3,000-acre natural lake, is a summer and winter playground with fishing, boating, camping, hiking, snowmobiling, and cross-country or downhill skiing.

▲ Oregon Cascades Recreation Area encompasses 157,000 acres that include portions of the Umpqua (35,500 acres), Willamette, and Deschutes national forests. It is managed by these forests to provide a wide range of recreational opportunities, including motorized use in some portions.

▲ The forest has 398 miles of maintained trails for hiking, 63.2 miles of designated National Scenic Trail, 66 mammal species, 153 bird species, and 18 fish species.

▲ Other points of interest include Shadow Falls, Incense Cedar Grove, South Umpqua Falls, the world's tallest sugar pine, Cow Horn Arch, and Cow Creek Gorge.

Wilderness Areas

The Forest includes three wildernesses. The Oregon Cascades Recreation Area is adjacent to the Mt. Thielsen Wilderness.

Boulder Creek encompasses 19,500 acres surrounding Boulder Creek, a main drainage into the North Umpqua River. The lower portion of Boulder Creek is a critical spawning stream for anadromous fish. A wide variety of wildlife, geologic formations and plants can be found here, including an impressive stand of old-growth ponderosa pine. For information contact: Diamond Lake Ranger District—(503) 498-2531 or North Umpqua Ranger District—(503) 496-3532.

Mt. Thielsen Wilderness is made up of high alpine forests and open meadows. This 55,100-acre wilderness has elevation ranges from 5,000 to 9,182 feet at Mt. Thielsen, the "lightning rod of the Cascades." The Pacific Crest National Scenic Trail winds through the Mt. Thielsen Wilderness for 26 miles along the summit of the Cascade Range. A trailhead on S.R 138, one mile east of the north entrance to Crater Lake National Park, is the southern entrance point. For information contact: Diamond Lake Ranger District—(503) 498-2531.

Rogue-Umpqua Divide Wilderness is characterized by high forested mountains and ridges separating the Rogue and Umpqua River drainages. This 33,000-acre wilderness has elevation ranges from 3,200 to 6,800 feet. Abundant flora and fauna and geological outcroppings, such as the Devil's Slide and Hole-in-the-Ground, can be found throughout the wilderness. For information contact: Tiller Ranger District—(503) 825-3201.

Cottage Grove Ranger District

For Information

Cottage Grove Ranger Station
78406 Cedar Park Road
Cottage Grove, OR 97424
(503) 942-5591

Campground Locations/Activities

1. **Cedar Creek:** 21 mi. SE of Cottage Grove.
   From Cottage Grove Exit 174 on I-5 take Row
   River Road (F.R. 2400) E 19 mi. to F.R. 17 (2143).
   Turn left (NE) on F.R. 17 and continue for 2 mi.
   Activities: Fishing, mountain biking, and hiking.
2. **Rujada:** 19 mi. SE of Cottage Grove via F.R. 17.
   Activities: Fishing, stream, playfield, and hiking. (Closed to vehicles in winter)

Diamond Lake has exceptional fishing and year-round activities.

Campground (see map on page 198)	Elevation (feet)	Tent Sites	Tent/Trailer Sites	Fees	Drinking Water	Toilets F=Flush; V=Vault
1. Cedar Creek	1,600	1	8			V
2. Rujada	1,200	2	8	•	•	V/F

The Umpqua River, renowned for its steelhead trout runs in summer and winter, flows westward to the Pacific.

Diamond Lake Ranger District

For Information

Diamond Lake Ranger Station
HC 60, Box 101
Idleyld Park, OR 97447
(503) 498-2531

Campground Locations/Activities

3. **Broken Arrow:** 80 mi. E of Roseburg on S.R. 138, turn S onto F.R. 4795 at the north entrance to Diamond Lake Recreation Area. Proceed 3.2 mi. and turn right at the South Shore. Go .5 mi. to the campground entrance on the left. *Activities:* Biking, fishing, and hiking.

4. **Bunker Hill:** Located 72 mi. E of Roseburg on S.R. 138, turn N onto F.R. 2610, the Lemolo Lake Road. Proceed 5.5 mi. crossing the Lemolo Lake Dam. Turn right onto F.R. 2610-999. *Activities:* Hiking, fishing, and boating.

5. **Clearwater Falls:** 47 mi. E of Idleyld Park via S.R. 138. *Activities:* Fishing, hiking, and waterfalls.

6. **Diamond Lake:** 54 mi. E of Idleyld Park, off S.R. 138, F.R. 4795 on the W shore of Diamond Lake. *Activities:* Boat launch, fishing, biking, and hiking.

7. **East Lemolo:** Located 72 mi. E of Roseburg on S.R. 138, turn N onto F.R. 2610, the Lemolo Lake Road. Go 3 mi. and turn right onto F.R. 2610-400. Proceed 2 mi., turn left onto F.R. 2610-430. The campground is at the end of the road, .3 mi. *Activities:* Hiking, fishing, and biking.

8. **Inlet:** 50 mi. E of Idleyld Park, off S.R. 138, on F.R. 2610, on F.R. 400 at Lemolo Lake. *Activities:* Fishing and hiking nearby.

9. **Kelsay Valley:** Located 74 mi. E of Roseburg on S.R. 138, turn N onto F.R. 60, the Windigo Pass Road. Proceed 4.5 mi. and turn right onto F.R. 6000-958, the Kelsay Valley Road. The campground is at the end of the road 1.5 mi. *Activities:* Picnicking and hiking.

10. **Poole Creek:** 50 mi. E of Idleyld Park, off S.R. 138 at Lemolo Lake, via F.R. 2610. *Activities:* Fishing, hiking nearby, boat launch, swimming, and water sports.

11. **Thielsen View:** 54 mi. E of Idleyld Park, off S.R. 138, then F.R. 4795 on the W shore of Diamond Lake. *Activities:* Fishing, hiking, biking, and boat launch.

12. **Toketee Lake:** 36 mi. E of Idleyld Park, via S.R. 138, then F.R. 34. *Activities:* Boat launch, fishing, and hiking.

13. **Whitehorse Falls:** 43 mi. E of Idleyld Park via S.R. 138. *Activities:* Fishing, hiking, and waterfalls.

Campground (see map on page 198)	Elevation (feet)	Tent Sites	Tent/Trailer Sites	Fee	Drinking Water	Toilets F=Flush; V=Vault
3. Broken Arrow*	5,200		148**	•	•	F
4. Bunker Hill			8			V
5. Clearwater Falls	4,200	12				V
6. Diamond Lake*(R)	5,200		238**	•	•	F
7. East Lemolo		no designated sites				V
8. Inlet	4,200		14			V
9. Kelsay Valley		no designated sites				V
10. Poole Creek(R-G)	4,200		59	•	•	V
11. Thielsen View	5,200		60**		•	V
12. Toketee Lake	2,500		33			V
13. Whitehorse Falls	3,800	5				V

*Showers and RV dump station available.
**Sites available for physically challenged.
(R) Reservations available through National Recreation Reservation System (NRRS): 1-800-280-2267.
(R-G) Reservations available for groups through NRRS.

Everyone enjoys a walk through the forest!

North Umpqua Ranger District

For Information

North Umpqua Ranger District
Glide, OR 97443
(503) 496-3532

Campground Locations/Activities

14. **Apple Creek** (trailers up to 24′): From the North Umpqua Ranger Station, take S.R. 138 E 28 mi. to campground (on the right side of the highway). *Activities:* Hiking, fishing, and white-water boating.

15. **Bogus Creek** (trailers up to 35′): From the North Umpqua Ranger Station, take S.R. 138 E 18.6 mi. to campground (left side of the highway). *Activities:* Boating and fishing.

16. **Boulder Flat** (trailers up to 24′): From the North Umpqua Ranger Station, take S.R. 138 E for 36 mi. to campground on left side of highway. *Activities:* Boating and fishing.

17. **Canton Creek** (trailers up to 24′): From the North Umpqua Ranger Station, take S.R. 138 E for 23 mi. to F.R. 38, Steamboat Creek Road. Continue on F.R. 38 approximately ¼ mi. to the campground. *Activities:* Hiking and swimming.

18. **Coolwater** (trailers up to 24′): From the North Umpqua Ranger Station, take S.R. 138 W ¼ mi. to Little River Road (F.R.17). Follow F.R. 17 for 15.5 mi. to campground, on the right side of the road. *Activities:* Picnicking, hiking, fishing, and swimming.

19. **Eagle Rock** (trailers up to 24′): From the North Umpqua Ranger Station, take S.R. 138 E for 35 mi. to Eagle Rock campground, located on the left side of the highway. *Activities:* Hiking, fishing (fly only), and white-water boating.

20. **Hemlock Lake** (trailers up to 35′): From the North Umpqua Ranger Station, take S.R. 138 W ¼ mi. to Little River Road (F.R.17). Follow road for 32 mi. to campground. *Activities:* Hiking, fishing (rainbow trout and kokanee salmon), sightseeing, photography, swimming, and boating.

Campground (see map on page 198)	Elevation (feet)	Tent Sites	Tent/Trailer Sites	Fees	Drinking Water	Toilets F=Flush; V=Vault
14. Apple Creek	1,365	8				V
15. Bogus Creek	1,100	4	11	•	•	F/V
16. Boulder Flat	1,600	1	10			V
17. Canton Creek	1,195	2	3	•	•	F
18. Coolwater	1,300		7		•	V
19. Eagle Rock	1,676	2	23	•	•	V
20. Hemlock Lake	4,400	4	9			V
21. Hemlock Meadows	4,400		1			V
22. Horseshoe Bend*(R)	1,300	2	22	•	•	F
23. Island	1,189		7			V
24. Lake in the Woods	3,200	3	11	•	•	F/V
25. Steamboat Falls	1,400	3	7			V
26. White Creek	1,600	4			•	V
27. Williams Creek	1,100	3				V
28. Wolf Creek(R)	1,100	3	5	•	•	F

*Some campsites accessible to physically challenged.
(R) Reservation site for groups.

Just off the beaten path is a place for rest and reflection.

North Umpqua Ranger District *(continued)*

21. **Hemlock Meadows** (trailers up to 35′): From the North Umpqua Ranger Station, take S.R. 138 W ¼ mi. to Little River Road (F.R.17). Follow road for 32 mi. This site is located .5 mi. from Hemlock Lake Campground around the east arm of the lake. *Activities:* Hiking, picnicking, fishing, sightseeing, photography, swimming, and boating.

22. **Horseshoe Bend** (trailers up to 24′): From the North Umpqua Ranger Station, take S.R. 138 E 30 mi. to F.R. 4750 near Milepost 48. Turn right on F.R. 4750 and right again on F.R. 4750-001. *Activities:* Hiking, fishing (fly only), and white-water boating.

23. **Island** (trailers up to 24′): From the North Umpqua Ranger Station, take S.R. 138 E 24 mi. to campground located on the right side of the highway. *Activities:* Hiking and white-water rafting.

24. **Lake in the Woods** (trailers up to 35′): From the North Umpqua Ranger Station, take S.R. 138 ¼ mi. W to Little River (F.R.17). Follow Little River Road for 20 mi., at which point it becomes F.R. 27 and is gravel. Continue another 7 mi. to the campground. *Activities:* Hiking, fishing, and hunting.

25. **Steamboat Falls** (trailers up to 24′): From the North Umpqua Ranger Station, take S.R. 138 E for 23 mi. to Road 38, Steamboat Creek Road. Continue 6 mi. on Road 38 to F.R. 3810 and turn right. Cross the bridge, stay to the left, and continue on 3810 for 1 mi. to the campground. *Activities:* Hiking and swimming.

26. **White Creek** (walk-in sites; limited parking lot RV space): From the North Umpqua Ranger Station, take S.R. 138 ¼ mi. W to Little River Road #17. Follow Road for 17 mi. to F.R. 2792, Red Butte Road. Continue on F.R. 2792 for ¼ mi to campground on the left side of the road. *Activities:* Hiking, picnicking, swimming, and fishing.

27. **Williams Creek** (*not* recommended for trailers): From the North Umpqua Ranger Station, take S.R. 138 E 21 mi; turn left on F.R. 4710-038. One campsite is located to the E of the foot bridge and two more campsites are to the W of the bridge. *Activities:* Hiking, fishing (fly angling only), swimming, picnicking, and sightseeing.

28. **Wolf Creek** (trailers up to 35′): From the North Umpqua Ranger Station, take S.R. 138 W ¼ mi. to Little River (F.R.17). Follow F.R. 17 for 12 mi. to campground. *Activities:* Picnicking, fishing, swimming, hiking, softball, volleyball, and horseshoes.

For a friendly visit or the best flies for fishing, you've come to the right place!

Tiller Ranger District

For Information

Tiller Ranger District
27812 Tiller-Trail Hwy.
Tiller, OR 97484
(503) 825-3201

Campground Locations/Activities

29. **Boulder Annex** (trailer use *not* recommended): From the Tiller Ranger Station take C.R. 46, which becomes South Umpqua Road (F.R. 28), for 14 mi. to the campground. Entrance on the left side of road just past the main Boulder Creek Campground. *Activities:* Picnicking, trout fishing in creek and river, and hiking.
30. **Boulder Creek** (trailers to 35'): From the Tiller Ranger Station take C.R. 46, which becomes South Umpqua Road (F.R. 28), for 14 mi. to campground; entrance on right side of road. *Activities:* Picnicking, trout fishing in river and creek, and hiking.
31. **Camp Comfort** (trailers to 35'): From the Tiller Ranger Station take C.R. 46, which becomes South Umpqua Road (F.R. 28), for 26 mi. to campground; entrance on right side of road. *Activities:* Picnicking, trout fishing in river, and hiking.
32. **Cover** (trailers to 35'): From the Tiller Ranger Station take C.R. 46 for 5 mi. to Jackson Creek Road (F.R. 29). Travel on F.R. 29 for 13 mi. to camp; entrance on the right side of road. *Activities:* Picnicking, trout fishing in creek, and hiking.

33. **Devil's Flat:** From I-5, 12 mi. S of Canyonville, take the Azalea exit and head E on C.R. 336 for 17 mi to campground. From Tiller Ranger Station, take C.R. 1 S to Callahan Road (F.R. 3230), right onto F.R. 3230 and right onto F.R. 32 to campground (total of 11 mi.) *Activities:* Picnicking, trout fishing in creek, and hiking.
34. **Dumont Creek** (trailers to 35'): From the Tiller Ranger Station take C.R. 46, which becomes South Umpqua Road (F.R. 28), for 11 mi. to campground; entrance on right side of road. *Activities:* Picnicking and trout fishing in river and creek (steelhead and salmon fishing in river downstream from the mouth of Dumont Creek only).
35. **Threehorn** (trailers to 24'): From the Tiller Ranger Station take C.R. 1 S for 13 mi. to campground; entrance on left side of road. *Activities:* Picnicking and hiking.

The North and South Umpqua Rivers flow westward and join into the mighty Umpqua below Roseburg. The river's beauty and recreational opportunities are an outstanding feature of southwestern Oregon.

Campground (see map on page 198)	Elevation (feet)	Tent Sites	Tent/Trailer Sites	Fee	Drinking Water	Toilets V=Vault
29. Boulder Annex	1,400	4				V
30. Boulder Creek	1,400		8		•	V
31. Camp Comfort*	2,000		5		•	V
32. Cover	1,700		7			V
33. Devil's Flat	2,100	3				V
34. Dumont Creek	1,300		5			V
35. Threehorn	2,600		5		•	V

*Shelter available.

Valley of the Rogue State Park

For Information

Valley of the Rogue State Park
3792 North River Road
Gold Hill, OR 97525
(503) 582-1118
FAX—582-1312

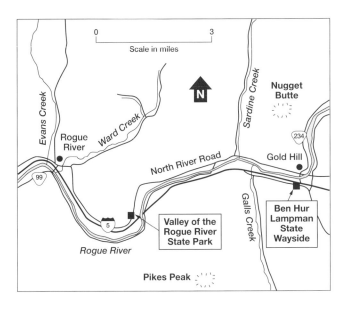

Location

Covering 250 acres at an elevation of 1,010 feet, Valley of the Rogue State Park is located on the banks of the Rogue River, immediately off I-5, 12 miles south of Grants Pass. The park is a major destination for river recreation access. The Rogue River, one of America's great fishing rivers, offers excellent trout, salmon, and steelhead fishing in season. Nearly 3 miles of the Rogue River frontage are available to park visitors for bank angling and boating. Boat trips on the Rogue River are a thrilling experience, whether tahiti rafting in white water, jet-boating from Grants Pass to Hellgate, or sightseeing along Gold Beach on the Pacific Ocean. The park's central location in the picturesque Rogue River Valley makes it an excellent base from which to explore other parks and recreation areas in the vicinity. Nearby state parks include Illinois River, Tou Velle, and Casey day-use areas, and Joseph Stewart campground. The U.S. Forest Service and Bureau of Land Management have developed many

One of America's great fishing rivers, the Rogue is famous for trout, salmon, and steelhead fishing.

Valley of the Rogue State Park *(continued)*

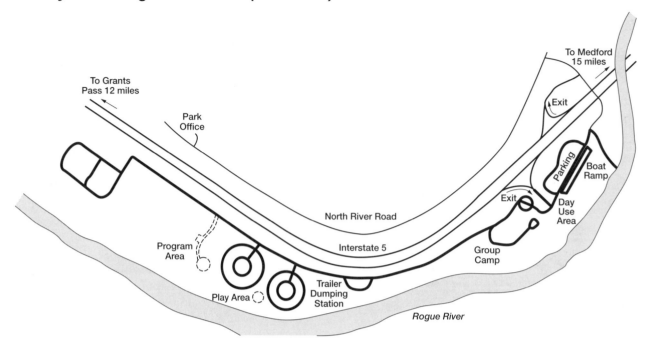

recreation areas in the surrounding mountains. The hills and streams surrounding the Rogue River Valley were once a source of rich gold. A number of nearby museums, historic buildings, and reconstructed "frontier" towns vividly tell the story of the gold mining era and Indian War days.

Facilities and Activities

The campground is open year-round on a first-come, first-served basis.

97 RV campsites w/full hookups (75′ maximum length)
55 RV campsites w/electricity & water
21 tent campsites
3 group tent area
1 group meeting hall
   pull-through sites
   showers/drinking water
   flush toilets
   wood & charcoal stoves
   tables
   trailer dump station
130 picnic sites
3 group picnic areas
boat ramp/boating/fishing/sightseeing
river guides/boats/equipment available in Grants Pass

Thrilling and beautiful are the boat trips whether by jet-boat, raft, or kayak.

Winema National Forest

For Information

Winema National Forest
2819 Dahlia
Klamath Falls, OR 97601
(503) 883-6714
(503) 883-6702 TDD

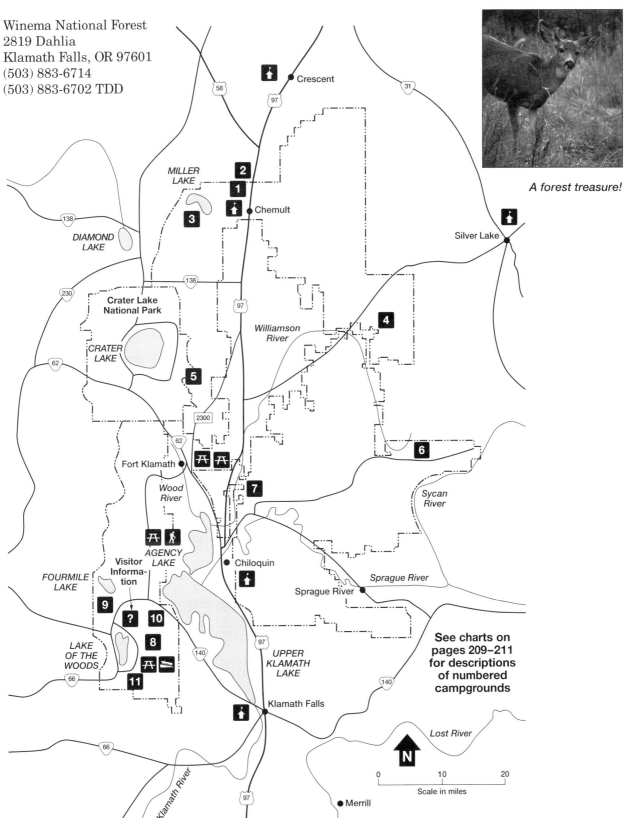

A forest treasure!

See charts on
pages 209–211
for descriptions
of numbered
campgrounds

Scale in miles
0   10   20

REGION 3

Winema National Forest (continued)

Location

The 1.1-million-acre Winema National Forest is located in south central Oregon on the eastern slopes of the Cascade Mountain Range. The forest adjoins Crater Lake National Park near the Cascade crest. The lower slopes border on Upper Klamath Lake, the largest lake in Oregon, and vast marshes, which are protected in National Wildlife Refuges. U.S. 97, running north and south, bisects the forest, which lies between Crescent and Klamath Falls.

Points of Interest

▲ A wide array of recreation opportunities are available, ranging from the solitude of hiking an isolated trail in one of the three wildernesses to family and group activities in developed settings at the Lake of the Woods or Miller Lake. Camping, picnicking, fishing, boating, and hiking opportunities abound. In the winter, snowmobiling, snowplay, and cross-country skiing are popular activities.

▲ Special places of interest include the visitor center at Lake of the Woods, the Pacific Crest National Scenic Trail, the Upper Klamath Canoe Trail, Upper Klamath Lake Loop tour, the Sand Creek Pinnacles, Devils Garden and The Badlands, Mare's Eggs Springs, and Oux Kanee Overlook.

▲ The area is best known for its clear skies, sunshine, and diverse landscape of marshes, lakes, forested slopes, and wide basins. Habitats found in the forest support a variety of fish and wildlife species, from deer and elk to large populations of water-oriented birds, including eagles, osprey, pelicans, and numerous waterfowl.

▲ The forest, which is the newest in Oregon, was created in 1961 from the former Klamath Indian Reservation and portions of adjacent forests. It is rich in heritage with a blending of Native American prehistory and early exploration and settlement. History records a visit to the area by Peter Ogden of the Hudson Bay Company in 1826 and exploration by Lt. John Fremont in 1843. The forest is named for a heroine of the Modoc War of 1872. Wi-Ne-ma, meaning "Woman of a Brave Heart" served as an interpreter and peacemaker between U.S. troops and the Modocs.

Wilderness Areas

Three wilderness areas fall within the boundaries of the forest: Mountain Lakes, Mt. Thielsen (shared with Umpqua and Deschutes National Forests), and Sky Lakes (shared with the Rogue River National Forest).

Mountain Lakes Wilderness encompasses 23,071 acres and shares a similar geologic history with its neighbor to the north, Crater Lake National Park. Mountain Lakes is a large caldera, or broad crater-like basin, formed by the explosion or collapse of a volcanic cone. Once a 12,000-foot peak, the giant volcano collapsed creating the area now known as Mountain Lakes Wilderness. The eight prominent peaks are all that remain of the once surrounding rim. Many small lakes were formed in the area instead of one large lake filling the caldera, as happened at Crater Lake. The wilderness, filled with beautiful alpine lakes, is easily accessible from three directions: the Cover Creek Trail from the south (4 miles long), the Mountain Lakes Trail from the west (6.5 miles), and the Varney Creek Trail from the north (4.5 miles long). These trails are all connected in the wilderness interior by the 10.5 mile Mountain Lakes Look Trail, which climbs from the sparkling blue lakes and winds along the southern caldera rim. Moss Creek Trail and South Pass Trail provide access to the eastern wilderness areas from the Mountain Lakes Loop. For information contact: Klamath Ranger District—(503) 885-3400/885-3408 TDD.

Mt. Thielsen Wilderness is made up of high alpine forests and open meadows. This 55,100-acre wilderness has elevation ranges from 5,000 to 9,182 feet at Mt. Thielsen, the "lightning rod of the Cascades." The Pacific Crest National Scenic Trail winds through the Mt. Thielsen Wilderness for 26 miles along the summit of the Cascade Range. A trailhead on Highway 138, one mile east of the north entrance to Crater Lake National Park, is the southern entrance point. This wilderness is shared with Umpqua National Forest. For information contact: Chemult Ranger District—(503) 365-7001/7010 TDD or Diamond Lake Ranger District in Umpqua National Forest—(503) 498-2531.

Sky Lakes Wilderness comprises 116,300 acres in the crest of the High Cascades, extending south from the boundary of Crater Lake National Park to Fourmile Lake (70,113 acres lie within the Rogue River National Forest). Although steep relief is found in such places as the glacially-carved Middle Fork (Rogue River) Canyon and the slope of Mt. McLouglin, Sky Lakes Wilderness has generally gentle, densely-forested terrain. The name is derived from the many small lakes, most of them clustered in several glacial basins near the crest of the Cascade Range. For information contact: Klamath Ranger District—(503) 885-3400/3408 TDD or Butte Falls Ranger District in the Rogue National Forest—(503) 865-3581.

Chemult Ranger District

For Information

Chemult Ranger District
P.O. Box 150
Chemult, OR 97731
(503) 365-7001
(503) 365-7010 TDD

Campground Locations/Activities

1. **Chemult Recreation Site:** 1 mi. N of Chemult via U.S. 97 and Miller Lake Road. *Activities:* Picnicking, snowmobiling, and cross-country skiing.
2. **Corral Springs:** 4 mi. NW of Chemult via U.S. 97 and F.R. 9774. *Activities:* Picnicking and hunting.
3. **Digit Point:** 12 mi. W of Chemult via U.S. 97 and Miller Lake Road. *Activities:* Hiking, boating, fishing, and swimming.
4. **Jackson Creek:** 25 mi. S of Chemult via U.S. 97, 22 mi. NE on Silver Lake Hwy. (676), 5 mi SE on F.R. 49. *Activities:* Fishing, horseback riding (corral), and hunting.
5. **Scott Creek:** 24 mi. SW of Chemult via U.S. 97; F.R. 66, F.R. 2300, then F.R. 2310. *Activities:* Hunting.

Campground (see map on page 207)	Elevation (feet)	Tent Sites	Tent/Trailer Sites	Fees	Drinking Water	Toilets F=Flush; V=Vault
1. Chemult Recreation Site*	4,800	6**			•	V
2. Corral Springs	4,900	7				V
3. Digit Point*	5,600		64	•	•	F
4. Jackson Creek	4,600		12			V
5. Scott Creek	4,700		6			V

*Picnic sites available.
**Sno-park in winter w/permit; overnight RV use of parking lot/no hookups.

Don't miss Oregon's Wildlife Refuges. They offer special opportunities to observe, learn, and enjoy plants and animals in their natural habitat. What better way to understand the role management plays in the stewardship of America's resources. Beautiful sandhill cranes can be seen in the refuge near the north end of Upper Klamath Lake.

REGION 3

Chiloquin Ranger District

For Information

Chiloquin Ranger District
P.O. Box 357
Chiloquin, OR 97624
(503) 783-4001
(503) 783-4010 TDD

Campground Locations/Activities

6. **Head of the River:** 5 mi. N of Chiloquin via
   U.S. 97, 20 mi. on Williamson River Road, then
   .5 mi. N. *Activities:* Fishing.
7. **Williamson River:** 1 mi. NE of Collier State
   Park via U.S. 97. *Activities:* Fishing and rafting.

Campground (see map on page 207)	Elevation (feet)	Tent Sites	Tent/Trailer Sites	Fees	Drinking Water	Toilets F=Flush; V=Vault
6. Head of the River	4,600		6			V
7. Williamson River*	4,200	3	7	•	•	V

*Picnic sites available.

Special moments to remember come in different ways.

Pack your bags and your road or knobby tires. Nowhere will you find road touring or mountain biking more inspiring.

Klamath Ranger District

For Information

Klamath Ranger District
1936 California Avenue
Klamath Falls, OR 97601
(503) 885-3400
(503) 885-3408 TDD

Adjacent to Winema National Forest lies the Klamath Forest National Wildlife Refuge. From April to August visitors might spot a beautiful "fish hawk" or osprey.

Campground Locations/Activities

8. **Aspen Point:** 35 mi. NW of Klamath Falls via S.R. 140 at Lake of the Woods. *Activities:* Picnicking, boating, swimming, fishing, waterskiing, and hiking; resort nearby, some multiple occupancy campsites.
9. **Fourmile Lake:** 35 mi. NW of Klamath Falls via S.R. 140. 5.5 mi. on F.R. 3661. *Activities:* Hiking, picnicking, boating, swimming, fishing, and horseback riding (horse facilities at trailhead).
10. **Odessa:** 22 mi. NW of Klamath Falls via S.R. 140, 1 mi. on F.R. 3639. *Activities:* Picnicking, fishing, and boating.
11. **Sunset:** 35 mi. NW of Klamath Falls via S.R. 140 and Dead Indian Highway. *Activities:* Picnicking, boating, fishing, swimming, waterskiing, and hiking; resort nearby.

Campground (see map on page 207)	Elevation (feet)	Tent Sites	Tent/Trailer Sites	Fees	Water	Toilets F=Flush; V=Vault
8. Aspen Point*	5,000	6	55	•	•	F
9. Fourmile Lake*	5,800		25	•	•	F
10. Odessa	4,100		5			V
11. Sunset*†	5,000		67	•	•	F

*Picnic sites available. Aspen Point also provides a dump station.
†Accessible to handicapped.

Forest campgrounds typically have a table, fireplace, and a tent or trailer parking place. Hookups are not available in the Willamette, but nearly all campgrounds have water and either pit, vault, or flush toilets.

Willamette National Forest

For Information

Willamette National Forest
211 East 7th Avenue
P. O. Box 10607
Eugene, OR 97440-2607
(503) 465-6521

Location

For information on campgrounds north of U.S. 20 on the Willamette National Forest, see Region 1 of this *Camper's Guide.* Information given here includes that portion of the forest located south of U.S. 20.

East of Eugene, the Willamette National Forest stretches for 110 miles along the western slopes of the Cascades and extends from the Mt. Jefferson area east of Salem to the Calapooya Mountains northeast of Roseburg. The forest is 1,675,407 acres in size or about the size of the state of New Jersey. Access to the forest comes from four major highways, U.S. 20 and S.R. 22, 58, and 242. The nearest entry point to the Willamette National Forest is just 20 miles from the Eugene-Springfield area off S.R. 58.

Points of Interest

▲ Recreation opportunities on the forest are numerous. There are over 80 campgrounds and picnic grounds containing some 1,200 units. Units are composed of a table, fireplace, and a tent site or trailer parking place (hookups are not available). Nearly all campgrounds have water and either pit, vault, or flush toilets. Offered on a first-come, first-served basis, there are occupancy restrictions in most campgrounds ranging from 10–16 days. Some sites have a users fee. Some sites and group areas are the National Recreation Reservation System.

▲ There are over 1,400 miles of trails in the forest for hikers. Many are low-elevation, easy-access trails for year-around hiking pleasure. Three very scenic, low-elevation trails have been designated National Recreation Trails. They are the McKenzie River Trail, Fall Creek Trail, and South Breitenbush Gorge Trail. The Fall Creek and McKenzie River Trails are within 50 miles

of Eugene (bus service is available from Eugene to McKenzie Bridge). The South Breitenbush Gorge Trail is located 60 miles east of Salem.

▲ For the fishing enthusiast, many kinds of trout are found in the forest's lakes and streams including brook, rainbow, brown, cutthroat, and bull trout. Kokanee salmon have been planted in some lakes.

▲ Big game animals include Roosevelt elk, bear, and blacktailed and mule deer. The forest is open to hunting and fishing in regular season established by the Oregon Department of Fish and Wildlife and subject to its regulations.

▲ Two developed ski areas, Hoodoo and Willamette Pass Ski Area, operate under special use permits from the Willamette National Forest. Cross-country skiing is also popular, and many forest roads and trails lend themselves to this activity.

▲ There are two snowmobile areas in the forest. One is located near Willamette Pass on Waldo Lake road, and the other is located near Big Lake just off Santiam Pass on U.S. 20.

▲ Rainfall on the Willamette National Forest varies from 40 to more than 150 inches a year, much of it in snow that covers the higher Cascades each year. The forest is blanketed with Douglas-fir, the most valuable timber species in the U.S. Producing about 8% of all timber cut on National Forest lands, the Willamette National Forest is often the top timber producer among the 159 national forests in the U.S.

▲ Brochures on hiking trails, snowmobile and cross-country ski trails, and maps of the forest and wilderness areas are available through the forest headquarters or ranger district offices.

Three national recreation trails in the forest provide year-around hiking pleasure through an array of scenic settings.

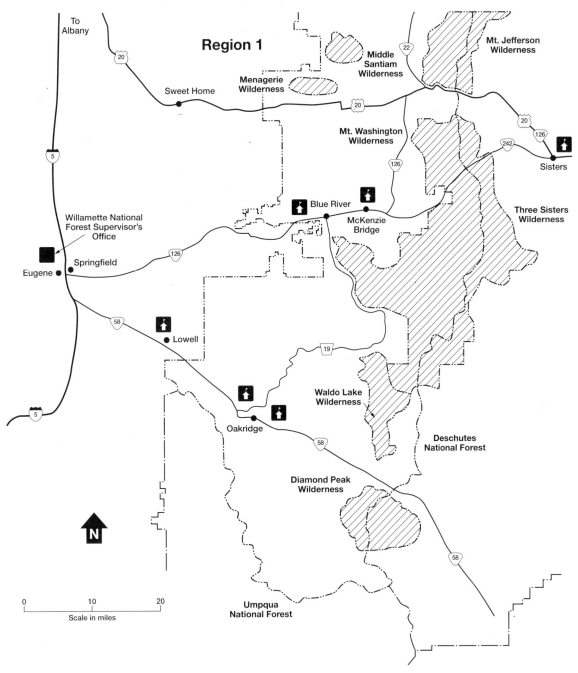

Wilderness Areas

The Willamette has eight wilderness areas totaling 380,805 acres. These areas, which encompass seven major mountain peaks in the Cascades, are popular with hikers, backpackers, and mountain climbers. See the Willamette National Forest in Region 1 for information on four of the eight Wilderness Areas located north of U.S. 20: Bull of the Woods, Menagerie, Middle Santiam, and Mt. Jefferson.

Some wildernesses have special area regulations. Check with the local ranger district office for further information and detailed maps. Descriptions of wilderness areas located on the Willamette south of U.S. 20 are as follows.

Diamond Peak Wilderness encompasses 52,377 acres with elevations between 4,787 and 8,744 feet. Diamond Peak, 8,744 feet, was formed as the entire land mass of the Cascades was undergoing volcanic activity and uplift. Great glaciers carved

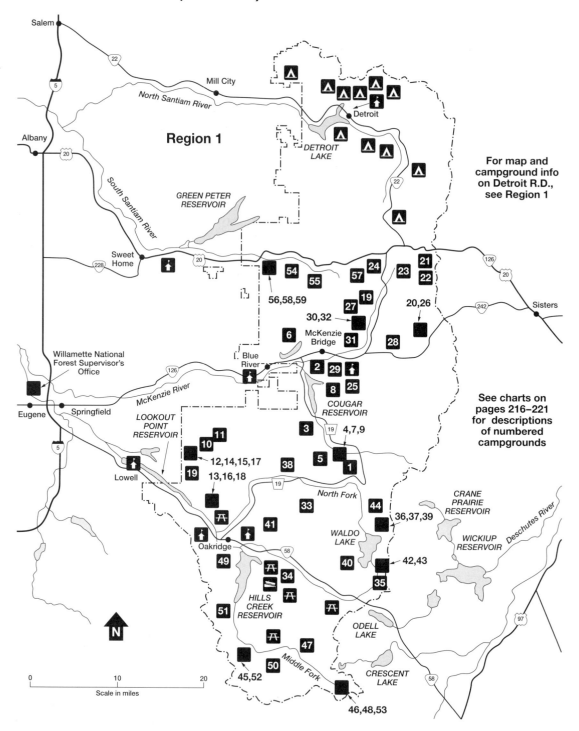

Salem

Mill City

22

5

North Santiam River

Albany

20

Region 1

South Santiam River

Detroit

DETROIT LAKE

For map and campground info on Detroit R.D., see Region 1

GREEN PETER RESERVOIR

22

126

20

Sweet Home

228

20

54

55

56,58,59

57 24

23

21 22

Sisters

242

20

27 19

30,32

20,26

6

McKenzie Bridge

31

28

Willamette National Forest Supervisor's Office

126

Blue River

McKenzie River

2 29

8 25

COUGAR RESERVOIR

See charts on pages 216–221 for descriptions of numbered campgrounds

Eugene   Springfield

LOOKOUT POINT RESERVOIR

3   19   4,7,9

5

38

1

10 11

12,14,15,17

19   13,16,18

Lowell

5

North Fork

33

19

44

36,37,39

CRANE PRAIRIE RESERVOIR

Deschutes River

WICKIUP RESERVOIR

WALDO LAKE

41

Oakridge

58

40

42,43

35

49

34

51

HILLS CREEK RESERVOIR

ODELL LAKE

97

47

45,52   50   *Middle Fork*

46,48,53

CRESCENT LAKE

58

N

0   10   20

Scale in miles

the large volcanic peak. When they receded, the carved bulk of the mountain remained, with snow-fields near the summit, and dozens of small lakes surrounding Diamond Peak near the perimeter of the wilderness. Many of these lakes, 1 to 28 acres in size, fill depressions gouged out by the movement of glaciers. The lower slopes are primarily forested with lodgepole pine grading into mountain hemlock

and true firs at higher elevations. Approximately 14 miles of the Pacific Crest National Scenic Trail pass through this wilderness. Another 38 miles of trail, including the 10-mile Diamond Peak Trail, stretch the length of the west side of the peak. For information contact: Crescent Ranger District— (503) 433-2234 and Rigdon Ranger District—(503) 782-2283.

Willamette National Forest *(continued)*

Mt. Washington Wilderness is often referred to as the "Black Wilderness." With over 52,516 acres, this area is dominated by Mt. Washington, 7,794 feet high. Mt. Washington rises above more than 75 square miles of lava-strewn plains. It is the home for blacktailed and mule deer, as well as black bear and an occasional cougar. Approximately one-half of the 28 lakes are stocked with trout. It is a rugged retreat used primarily by hunters, hikers, and mountain climbers. Mt. Washington, a dissected volcano, is a popular climb. The area includes Belknap Crater, a 6,872-foot cinder and ash cone. Elevations range from 3,000 to 7,794 feet. The Pacific Crest National Scenic Trail extends for 16.6 miles through the wilderness. For information contact: McKenzie Ranger District—(503) 822-3381 or Sisters Ranger District—(503) 549-2111.

Oregon Cascade Recreation Area is a unique land allocation covering 86,200 acres with elevation ranges between 4,300 and 9,182 feet. This area was designated by Congress for management at a near-natural state. The southern portion of the recreation area lies between the heavily used Diamond Lake Developed Recreation Area and Mt. Thielsen Wilderness. It is immediately north of Crater Lake National Park. The rest of the recreation area lies north of the Diamond Lake area and takes in portions of the Willamette and Deschutes national forests. Many lakes, ponds, rivers, and streams offer rich recreational experiences. The headwaters of the Willamette, Deschutes, Klamath, and North Umpqua Rivers can be found here. A 15,770-acre addition to the Diamond Peak Wilderness is included in the total acreage of the recreation area. For more information contact: Diamond Lake Ranger District—(503) 498-2531.

The Oregon Cascade Recreation Area provides a vast assortment of lakes, ponds, rivers, and streams for family activities.

Wildlife viewing is always a thrill.

Three Sisters Wilderness covers 242,400 acres with elevation ranges between 2,000 and 10,358 feet. Heavily forested, there are also alpine meadows, waterfalls, glaciers and glacial lakes, and lava fields. Major peaks include: the North, Middle, and South Sisters (all above 10,000 feet), along with Broken Top, the best example in the Pacific Northwest of the effect of advanced glaciation. Wildlife include blacktailed and mule deer, Roosevelt elk, black bear, bobcat, and coyote. Fish populations include Eastern brook trout and rainbow trout. Collier Glacier, which lies between the North and Middle Sisters, is the largest glacier in Oregon. Other geological features include Rock Mesa, Collier Cone, and Yapoah Crater. There are approximately 260 miles of trails. For more information contact: Blue River Ranger District—(503) 822-3317 or Sisters Ranger District—(503) 549-2111, or McKenzie Ranger District—(503) 822-3381, or Oakridge Ranger District—(503) 782-2291, or Bend Ranger District—(503) 388-5664.

Waldo Lake Wilderness encompasses 37,162 acres of steep to moderate slopes that include many basin areas with lakes, meadows, and rock outcrops. Located in the Western Cascades and High Cascades province, the wilderness has elevations between 2,800 and 7,144 feet. The Western Cascades portion is typified by steep, dissected slopes. The High Cascades are mostly Douglar-fir, Western hemlock, and some true fir. Waldo Lake, one of the purest in the world, is a predominant feature of the High Cascades. Hiking, camping, and fishing are primary uses of the area. There are approximately 84 miles of trails. For information contact: Oakridge Ranger District—(503) 782-2291.

Blue River Ranger District

For Information

Blue River Ranger Station
Blue River, OR 97413
(503) 822-3317

Campground Locations/Activities

1. **Box Canyon Horse Camp:** Access is via S.R. 22. Off F.R. 19 (Aufderheide Drive), 30.5 miles SE of Blue River. *Activities:* Camping, horseback riding, and hiking.
2. **Delta:** Access via S.R. 126. Travel F.R. 400, via F.R. 19 (Aufderheide Drive), 6.5 mi. E of Blue River. *Activities:* Camping, picnicking, fishing, and hiking.
3. **French Pete:** Access via S.R. 126. Travel F.R. 19 (Aufderheide Drive), 20 miles SE of Blue River. *Activities:* Camping, picnicking, fishing, and hiking.
4. **Frissell Crossing:** Access via S.R. 126. Travel F.R. 19 (Aufderheide Drive), 31 mi. SE of Blue River. *Activities:* Camping, picnicking, fishing, and hiking.
5. **Homestead:** Access via S.R. 126. Travel F.R. 19 (Aufderheide Drive), 27 miles SE of Blue River. *Activities:* Camping and fishing.
6. **Mona:** Access via S.R. 126, on F.R. 15, 7 miles NE of Blue River. *Activities:* Camping, picnicking, boating, swimming, fishing, and water skiing.
7. **Roaring River:** Access via S.R. 126. Travel F.R. 19 (Aufderheide Drive), 32 miles SE of Blue River. *Activities:* Camping and fishing.
8. **Slide Creek:** Access via S.R. 126. On Cougar Reservoir, 17 mi. SE of Blue River off F.R. 19 on eastside F.R. 500. *Activities:* Camping, picnicking, boating, swimming, fishing, and water skiing.
9. **Twin Springs:** Access via S.R. 126. Travel F.R. 19 (Aufderheide Drive), 29 mi. SE of Blue River. *Activities:* Camping, picnicking, and fishing.

Campground (see map on page 214)	Elevation (feet)	Tent Sites	Tent/Trailer Sites	Fees	Water	Toilets F=Flush; V=Vault
1. Box Canyon Horse Camp	3,600		14			V
2. Delta**†	1,200		39	•	•	V
3. French Pete	1,800		17	•	•	V
4. Frissell Crossing	2,600		12	•	•	V
5. Homestead	2,200		7			V
6. Mona	1,360		23	•	•	F
7. Roaring River*	2,600		group of 50		•	V
8. Slide Creek**	1,700		16	•	•	V
9. Twin Springs	2,400	3	5			V

*Group areas/reservations required.
*Picnic sites available.
†Accessible to handicapped.

There are 1,400 miles of trails in the forest. The McKenzie River Trail, located just 50 miles from Eugene, is a very scenic low-elevation trail that has been designated as a National Recreation Trail. ▶

Lowell Ranger District

For Information

Lowell Ranger Station
Lowell, OR 97452
(503) 937-2129

Campground Locations/Activities

10. **Clark Creek Camp:** Access via S.R. 58. Travel Fall Creek F.R. 18, 15 mi. E of Lowell. *Activities:* Ballfield, small outdoor chapel, 5 camping shelters, kitchen area, hiking, fishing, swimming, and volleyball posts.
11. **Bedrock:** Access via S.R. 58. Travel Fall Creek F.R. 18, 16 mi. NE of Lowell. *Activities:* Camping, swimming, fishing, and hiking.
12. **Big Pool:** Access via S.R. 58. Travel Fall Creek Road #18, 14 mi. E of Lowell. *Activities:* Camping, swimming, fishing, and hiking.
13. **Black Canyon:** S.R. 58, 6 mi. W of Oakridge. *Activities:* Camping, picnicking, boating, fishing, hiking, water skiing, and swimming.
14. **Broken Bowl:** Access via S.R. 58. Travel Fall Creek Road (F.R. 18), 12 mi. NE of Lowell. *Activities:* Camping, picnicking, fishing, swimming, and hiking. Some group sites available.
15. **Dolly Varden:** Access via S.R. 58. Travel Fall Creek Road (F.R. 18), 12 mi. NE of Lowell. *Activities:* Picnicking, hiking, swimming, fishing, and camping.
16. **Hampton:** Travel S.R. 58, upper end of Lookout Point Reservoir, 9 mi. W of Oakridge. *Activ-ities:* Boating, swimming, fishing, water skiing, and camping.
17. **Puma:** Access via S.R. 58. Travel Fall Creek Road (F.R. 18), 18 mi. NE of Lowell. *Activities:* Camping, swimming, fishing, and hiking.
18. **Shady Dell:** Travel S.R. 58, 5 mi. W of Oakridge. **Activities:** Camping and fishing.
19. **Winberry:** Winberry Road (F.R. 1802), 12 mi. E of Lowell. Access via S.R. 58. *Activities:* Picnicking, fishing, and hiking.

Campground (see map on page 214)	Elevation (feet)	Tent Sites	Tent/Trailer Sites	Fees	Water	Toilets F=Flush; V=Vault
10. Clark Creek Camp*†	1,000	group of 80		•	•	V
11. Bedrock†	1,100	6	14	•	•	V
12. Big Pool	1,000	3	2	•	•	V
13. Black Canyon**†	1,000	13	59	•	•	V
14. Broken Bowl**†	1,000	3	6	•	•	F
15. Dolly Varden	1,000	2	4		V	
16. Hampton	1,000		5	•	•	V
17. Puma†	1,100	1	10	•	•	V
18. Shady Dell	1,000	6	3	•	•	V
19. Winberry	1,900	5	2	•	•	V

*Group areas/reservations required.
**Picnic sites available.
†Accessible to handicapped.

Known for its scenic streams and lakes, the Willamette Forest has a rich natural history to explore. Hundreds of archeological sites show that the Kalapuya, Molala, and Klamath Indians hunted and gathered plants in these mountains for thousands of years.

REGION 3

McKenzie Ranger District

For Information

McKenzie Ranger Station
McKenzie Bridge, OR 97413
(503) 822-3381

Campground Locations/Activities

20. **Alder Springs:** Access via S.R. 242 or McKenzie Hwy., 12 mi. E of McKenzie Bridge. *Activities:* Picnicking, camping, and hiking.
21. **Big Lake:** Access via U.S. 20. 4 mi. south of Santiam Pass (Hwy.20) on Big Lake Road (F.R. 2690), northshore of Big Lake. *Activities:* Camping, fishing, picnicking, water skiing, boating, and swimming.
22. **Big Lake West:** Access via U.S. 20. 4 mi. south of Santiam Pass (Hwy. 20) on Big Lake Road (F.R. 2690), westshore of Big Lake. *Activities:* Camping, boating, hiking, water skiing, and swimming.
23. **Coldwater Cover:** Access via S.R. 126, 18 mi. NE of McKenzie Bridge. *Activities:* Camping, hiking, non-motorized boating, and fishing.

24. **Fish Lake:** Travel via S.R. 126, 22 mi. NE of McKenzie Bridge. *Activities:* Camping, picnicking, interpretive display at guard station (lake dries up in summer).
25. **Horse Creek:** Access via S.R. 126. On Horse Creek Road (F.R. 2638), 1.5 mi. SE of McKenzie Bridge. *Activities:* Camping and fishing.
26. **Ice Cap:** Off S.R. 126 on F.R. 655 via F.R. 2672, 17 mi. NE of McKenzie Bridge. *Activities:* Camping, fishing, and hiking.
27. **Lake's End:** Access via S.R. 126. Boat access on Smith Reservoir, 13 mi. NE of McKenzie Bridge. *Activities:* Camping, picnicking, boating, and fishing.
28. **Limberlost:** Travel McKenzie S.R. 242, 5 mi. E of McKenzie Bridge. *Activities:* Camping, picnicking, and hiking.
29. **McKenzie Bridge:** Off S.R. 126, 1 mi. west of McKenzie Bridge. *Activities:* Camping, picnicking, fishing, and boating.
30. **Olallie:** Off S.R. 126, 11 mi. northeast of McKenzie Bridge. *Activities:* Camping, fishing, and boating.
31. **Paradise:** Off S.R. 126, 4 mi east of McKenzie Bridge. *Activities:* Camping, picnicking, fishing, boating, and hiking.
32. **Trailbridge:** 13 mi. northeast of McKenzie Bridge off S.R. 126 and Trail Bridge Reservoir. *Activities:* Camping, boating, fishing, and hiking.

Campground (see map on page 214)	Elevation (feet)	Tent Sites	Tent/Trailer Sites	Fees	Water	Toilets F=Flush; V=Vault
20. Alder Springs	3,600		7			V
21. Big Lake**	4,650		21	•	•	F
22. Big Lake West	4,650		13			V
23. Coldwater Cove†	3,100		35	•	•	V
24. Fish Lake	3,200		8		•	V
25. Horse Creek*	1,400		group of 100	•	•	V
26. Ice Cap**	3,000	8	14	•	•	F
27. Lake's End	3,000	17				V
28. Limberlost	1,800	4	10			V
29. McKenzie Bridge**	1,400		20	•	•	V
30. Olallie	2,000		17	•	•	V
31. Paradise**	1,400		64	•	•	F
32. Trailbridge	2,000		28	•	•	F

*Group areas/reservations required.
**Picnic sites available.
†Accessible to handicapped.

The forest has many unique areas of ecological, geological, scenic, and historical interest. Check at ranger stations for information on special interest areas.

Oakridge Ranger District

For Information

Oakridge Ranger Station
46375 Highway 58
Westfir, OR 97492
(503) 782-2291

Campground Locations/Activities

33. **Blair Lake:** Access via S.R. 58. Travel on Salmon Creek and Wall Creek Roads, 17 mi. northeast of Oakridge. *Activities:* Camping, picnicking, non-motorized boating, fishing, swimming, and hiking.
34. **Blue Pool:** Travel S.R. 58, 9 mi. east of Oakridge. *Activities:* Camping, picnicking, swimming, and fishing.
35. **Gold Lake:** Travel S.R. 58, then F.R. 500, 28 mi. east of Oakridge. *Activities:* Camping, picnicking, non-motorized boating, fishing, hiking, and swimming.
36. **Harralson Horse Camp:** Access off S.R. 58. On spur F.R. 5898 via Waldo Lake Road (F.R. 5897), 35 mi. NE of Oakridge. *Activities:* Horseback riding and hiking.
37. **Islet:** Access via S.R. 43. 37 mi. E of Oakridge via Waldo Lake Roads (F.R.s 5897 and 5898). *Activities:* Picnicking, fishing, boating, swimming, and hiking.

Old-growth forests are a wondrous hallmark of the Pacific Northwest. While in the Willamette, old-growth areas can be experienced in the Oakridge, Lowell, and Rigdon ranger districts.

38. **Kiahanie:** Access via S.R. 58. Then travel F.R. 19 (Aufderheide Drive), 18 mi. northeast of Westfir. *Activities:* Camping, picnicking, and fishing.
39. **North Waldo:** Off S.R. 58, 36 mi. from Oakridge, via Waldo Lake Roads (F.R. 5897 and 5898A). *Activities:* Picnicking, boating, swimming, fishing, and hiking.
40. **Rhododendron Island:** Access by boat, westside of Waldo Lake, 31 mi. E of Oakridge via Waldo Lake Roads (F.R. 5897 and 5896) to Shadow Bay. *Activities:* Picnicking, boating, swimming, and fishing.
41. **Salmon Creek:** Access via S.R. 58. Travel Salmon Creek Road F.R. 24), 4 mi. east of Oakridge. *Activities:* Camping, picnicking, fishing, swimming, and kayaking.
42/43. **Shadow Bay/Shadow Bay Group:** 31 mi. east of Oakridge via S.R. 58, then Waldo Lake Roads (F.R. 5897 and 5986). *Activities:* Camping, picnicking, non-motorized boating, swimming, fishing, and hiking.
44. **Skookum Creek:** Access via S.R. 58. 31 mi. northeast of Westfir via F.R. 19 (Aufderheide Drive), then southeast on F.R. 1957 for 3.7 mi. *Activities:* Camping, picnicking, hiking, and horse facilities.

Campground (see map on page 214)	Elevation (feet)	Tent Sites	Tent/Trailer Sites	Fees	Water	Toilets F=Flush; V=Vault
33. Blair Lake	4,800	9			•	V
34. Blue Pool**	1,900		25	•	•	V/F
35. Gold Lake**	4,800		25	•	•	V
36. Harralson Horse Camp	5,600		6			V
37. Islet	5,400		55	•	•	F
38. Kiahanie	2,200		21	•	•	V
39. North Waldo	5,400		58	•	•	V
40. Rhododendron Island	5,400	3				V
41. Salmon Creek**	1,500		15	•	•	V
42. Shadow Bay	5,400		92	•	•	V/F
43. Shadow Bay*	5,400		group of 200	•	•	V
44. Skookum Creek	4,500		9		•	V

*Group areas/reservations required.
**Picnic sites available.

Rigdon Ranger District

For Information

Rigdon Ranger Station
49098 Salmon Creek Road
Oakridge, OR 97463
(503) 782-2283

Campground (see map on page 214)	Elevation (feet)	Tent Sites	Tent/Trailer Sites	Fees	Water	Toilets F=Flush; V=Vault
45. Campers Flat	2,000		5		•	V
46. Indigo Lake	5,900	5				V
47. Indigo Springs	2,800	3				V
48. Opal Lake	5,400	1				V
49. Packard Creek*	1,600		33	•	•	V
50. Sacandaga	2,400		17			V
51. Sand Prairie†	1,600		21	•	•	V/F
52. Secret	2,000		6			V
53. Timpanogas Lake	5,200		10		•	V

*Picnic sites available.
†Accessible to handicapped.

With more than 80 campgrounds and picnic sites to choose from, the forest is becoming a popular mountain biking destination.

Large animals such as deer and elk can be seen feeding or resting in clearcut units within Rigdon, Oakridge, and Lowell ranger districts.

Campground Locations/Activities

45. **Campers Flat:** Access via S.R. 58. Travel F.R. 21, 23 mi. south of Oakridge. *Activities:* Camping, fishing, picnicking, and hiking.

46. **Indigo Lake:** Access via S.R. 58 to F.R. 21 and Timpanogas Road (F.R. 2154), 43 mi. southeast of Oakridge, 1.9 mi. hike to lake. *Activities:* Picnicking, camping, hiking, fishing, and swimming.

47. **Indigo Springs:** Access via S.R. 58. On F.R. 21, 31 mi. southeast of Oakridge. *Activities:* Camping, picnicking, hiking, and fishing.

48. **Opal Lake:** Access via S.R. 58. On F.R. 21, Timpanogas Road (F.R. 398), 42 mi. SE of Oakridge. *Activities:* Picnicking, boating, swimming, fishing, and waterskiing.

49. **Packard Creek:** Access via S.R. 58, on Hills Creek Reservoir, 7 mi. southeast of Oakridge on F.R. 21. *Activities:* Camping, picnicking, boating, swimming, fishing, water skiing, and hiking.

50. **Sacandaga:** Access via S.R. 58. On F.R. 21, 26 mi. SE of Oakridge. *Activities:* Fishing, picnicking, and hiking.

51. **Sand Prairie:** Access via S.R. 58. Off Hills Creek Reservoir F.R. 21, 14 mi. south of Oakridge. *Activities:* Camping, fishing, hiking, and group picnic area.

52. **Secret:** Access via S.R. 58. Travel F.R. 21, 21 mi. S of Oakridge. *Activities:* Camping, picnicking, and fishing.

53. **Timpanogas Lake:** Access via S.R. 58, then F.R. 21 and Timpanogas Road (F.R. 2154), 43 mi. SE of Oakridge. *Activities:* Picnicking, non-motorized boating, swimming, fishing, and hiking.

Sweet Home Ranger District

For Information

Sweet Home Ranger Station
3225 Highway 20
Sweet Home, OR 97386
(503) 367-5168

Campground Locations/Activities

54. **Fernview:** Access via U.S. 20, 23 mi. east of Sweet Home. *Activities:* Camping, fishing, hiking, and swimming.
55. **House Rock:** Off U.S. 20, 26 mi. east of Sweet Home. *Activities:* Camping, picnicking, swimming, and fishing.
56. **Longbow Camp:** Access via U.S. 20. On F.R. 2032, south side of U.S. 20, 18 mi. east of Sweet Home Ranger Station. *Activities:* Shelter with kitchen/dining area, amphitheater, 6 sleeping shelters.
57. **Lost Prairie:** Access via U.S. 20, 37 mi. east of Sweet Home. *Activities:* Camping, picnicking, and fishing.
58. **Trout Creek:** Access via U.S. 20, 19 mi. east of Sweet Home. *Activities:* Camping, picnicking, swimming, and fishing.
59. **Yukwah:** Access via U.S. 20, 19 mi. east of Sweet Home. *Activities:* Camping, hiking, swimming, and fishing.

Campground (see map on page 214)	Elevation (feet)	Tent Sites	Tent/Trailer Sites	Fees	Water	Toilets F=Flush; V=Vault
54. Fernview	1,400	9	2	•	•	V
55. House Rock**	1,800	13	4	•	•	V
56. Longbow Camp*†	1,200	group of 50		•	•	V
57. Lost Prairie**†	3,200	2	2	•	•	V
58. Trout Creek†	1,200	4	20	•	•	V
59. Yukwah†	1,300		20	•	•	V

*Group areas/reservations required.
**Picnic sites available.
†Accessible to handicapped.

The Willamette Forest is open to fishing in regular seasons. Brook, rainbow, brown, and cutthroat trout can be found in streams and lakes.

William Tugman State Park

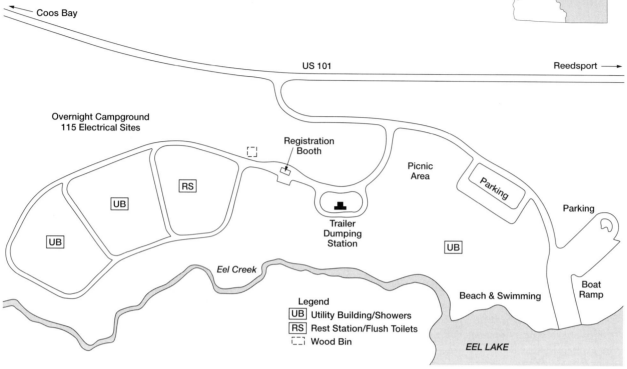

For Information

William Tugman State Park
c/o Sunset Bay State Park
10965 Cape Arago Highway
Coos Bay, OR 97420
(503) 888-3778
FAX—888-5650

Location

William Tugman State Park covers 560 acres around Eel Lake, just off U.S. 101, 8 miles south of Reedsport. Eel Lake is one of several scenic freshwater coastal lakes in this fascinating central Oregon coastal-dunes area. The park's forested beauty is complemented in the spring and early summer by brightly colored rhododendrons growing along the lake shore. Charter boats and fishing tackle are available at Winchester Bay. Some of the fish caught in these waters include chinook and silver salmon, albacore tuna, striped bass, cod, perch, smelt, and various bottom fish. Crabs, clams and oysters are other forms of sea life that are readily taken by sportsmen. Many coastal lakes and streams in the area yield trout, steelhead, salmon, catfish, black bass, and perch. Nearby state parks of interest include Umpqua Lighthouse, Jessie Honeyman, Umpqua Wayside, Millicoma Myrtle Grove, Golden and Silver Falls, Sunset Bay, Shore Acres, and Cape Arago. Oregon Dunes National Recreation Area just north of Reedsport offers many recreational pursuits in a unique coastal setting with some of the highest sand dunes in the U.S.

Facilities and Activities

The campground is open mid April through late October on a first-come, first-served basis.

115 RV/tent campsites w/electricity & water (50′
   maximum length)
hiker/biker camp
   showers/drinking water
   flush toilets
   tables
   trailer dump station
70 picnic sites
1 group picnic reservation area
swim area/boat ramp/fishing
accessible campsites/restrooms for people with
   disabilities

Resources for Further Information

Oregon Tourism Information Centers

Oregon Tourism Division
775 Summer Street, N.E.
Salem, OR 97310
(800) 547-7842
(503) 373-7307

Central Oregon Recreation Association
P.O. Box 230
63085 N. Hwy. 97
Bend, OR 97009
(503) 382-8334
(800) 800-8334 (Outside Oregon)

Mt. Hood Recreation Association
P.O. Box 342
65000 E. Hwy. 26
Welches, OR 97067
(503) 622-3162

North Central Oregon Tourism Promotion
    Committee
901 E. 2nd St.
The Dalles, OR 97058
(503) 296-6616
(800) 255-3385

Eastern Oregon Visitors Association
490 Campbell St.
Baker City, OR 97814
(503) 523-3356
(800) 523-1235 (U.S. & Canada)

Northwest Oregon Visitors Association
26 S.W. Salmon
Portland, OR 97204
(800) 962-3700 (Outside Oregon)

Oregon Coast Association
P.O. Box 4
Lincoln City, OR 97367
(800) 858-8598

Southwestern Oregon Visitors Association
P.O. Box 1645
Medford, OR 97501
(503) 779-4691
(800) 448-4856 (U.S.)

Willamette Valley Visitors Association
300 S.W. 2nd Ave.
P.O. Box 965
Albany, OR 97321
(800) 526-2256 (U.S.)

U.S. Forest Service and National Parks Service

U.S. Forest Service
Pacific Northwest Regional Office
319 S.W. Pine St.
P.O. Box 3623
Portland, OR 97208
(502) 326-2877

National Parks Service
Pacific Northwest Regional Office
83 South King St., Suite 212
Seattle, WA 98104
(206) 553-5622
(206) 553-0170 (recreation information)

U.S. Bureau of Land Management

Bureau of Land Management
Oregon State Office
P.O. Box 2965
Portland, Oregon 97208
(503) 280-7001

U.S. Fish and Wildlife Service

U.S. Fish and Wildlife Service, Pacific Region
Eastside Federal Complex
911 N.E. 11th Avenue
Portland, OR 97232-4181
(503) 231-6828

Miscellaneous

American Youth Hostels
Oregon Council
311 East 11th
Eugene, OR 97401
(503) 683-3685

Nature of Oregon Information Center
800 N.E. Oregon Street #5, Suite 177
Portland, OR 97232
(503) 731-4444

Oregon Bicycle Program
Oregon Department of Transportation
Room 200, Transportation Building
Salem, Oregon 97310
(503) 373-3432

Oregon Coast Charter Boat Association, Inc.
P.O. Box 494
Newport, OR 97365

Oregon Department of Fish and Wildlife
P.O. Box 59
Portland, OR 97207
(403) 229-5403

Oregon Guides and Packers Association
P.O. Box 10841
Eugene, OR 97440
(503) 683-9552

Oregon State Marine Board
435 Commercial N.E.
Salem, OR 97310
(503) 378-8587

Rogue River Guide Association
P.O. Box 792
Medford, Or 97501

Index